Curveball

Curveball

The Remarkable Story of TONI STONE

The First Woman to Play Professional Baseball in the Negro League

Martha Ackmann

Lawrence Hill Books

Library of Congress Cataloging-in-Publication Data
Ackmann, Martha.
Curveball : the remarkable story of Toni Stone the first woman to play professional baseball in the negro league / Martha Ackmann.
p. cm.
Includes bibliographical references and index.
ISBN 978-1-55652-796-8 (hardcover)
1. Stone, Toni, 1921-1996. 2. Baseball players—United States—Biography. 3. African American baseball players—Biography. 4. Women baseball players—United States. I. Title.

GV865.S86A35 2010
796.357092—dc22
[B]

2010007019

Interior design: Scott Rattray

Published by Lawrence Hill Books
An imprint of Chicago Review Press, Incorporated
814 North Franklin Street
Chicago, Illinois 60610
ISBN 978-1-55652-796-8
Printed in the United States of America
5 4 3 2 1

In memory of N. Jean Fields
(1932–1998)

"It's noble to be good, and it's nobler to teach
others to be good, and less trouble."
—Mark Twain

Contents

Prologue

You're supposed to step into a curveball, not away from it.

—Thomas Burt, Indianapolis Clowns, Negro American League[1]

Toni Stone got suspicious when the occasional stranger called to ask about her remarkable baseball career. She had seen a lot of fools, and the seventy-two-year-old woman's guard went up immediately if she thought someone seemed interested in using her. Toni had learned the hard way that people could take advantage of her: someone once took some of her precious team photographs guaranteeing to "get Toni Stone the recognition she deserved" and then vanished with promises unmet and photos pocketed. Then there were the reporters who played fast and loose with the truth, trying to "improve" her story so that she would appear more sophisticated, better educated, or more feminine. She hated the inaccuracies, which she called "ad libs." It was like a jazz riff, she said, the ad lib. "I don't want no ad libbing. I want my real thing."[2]

In 1993, when baseball historian Kyle McNary called her on the phone, Toni wasn't sure she wanted to talk to him. The two had never met, and she warily suspected that McNary might be just another person wanting to "capitalize of me." She hated it when sportswriters claimed to rediscover her, then portrayed her as a sideshow oddity—a strange woman who long ago wanted to play baseball with the boys. It angered and hurt her when they turned her commitment to the game into a freak show. "I'm getting ready to go away," Toni told

McNary, leaving herself an opening to end the conversation if he turned out to be just another someone who wanted to make a buck. "I won't be back until the middle of the month." But when the earnest young man spoke to Toni about how much he loved baseball and only wanted to know more about her days in the Negro League, she warmed to him. Playing professional baseball had been the highlight of Toni's life, and, as painful as some of the memories were, she freely admitted she had more good recollections than bad. With each question McNary asked, a rush of images flooded her mind: a cast-off baseball glove bought at the Goodwill, junker automobiles in the 1930s full of hungry players touring the Dakotas, jazz clubs hot with music, crowds of reporters straining to get a look at the girl playing Negro League ball, a newspaper story proclaiming Toni Stone "the greatest attraction to hit the loop since Leroy 'Satchel' Paige."[3]

No other woman ever matched Toni Stone's accomplishments in baseball—during her nearly two decades of play or since. She was the first woman to play professional baseball on men's teams in the Negro League of the 1950s. When a young Henry Aaron moved from the Indianapolis Clowns to the majors, Stone replaced him on the team. "She was a very good baseball player," Aaron said.[4] Known as a tenacious athlete with quick hands, a competitive bat, and a ferocious spirit, Toni was a pro and "smooth," according to Ernie Banks.[5] Yet her story is about much more than baseball. It is also about confronting the ugly realities of Jim Crow America, in the days before Rosa Parks refused to give up her seat on the bus. Some of those stories Toni would share, and others were too difficult for her to admit—sometimes even to herself. There were memories of hurled epithets from the grandstands, "Whites Only" signs on railroad cars, and waitresses who would spit in glasses of Coke before serving them to black customers. During segregation, if you were a young African American woman and you wanted to play second base more than anything else in the world, you were in for a rough ride.

When Toni began to relax and talk less cautiously with him, McNary admitted to her that he was surprised by how young she sounded when she answered the phone. Everyone who met Toni for the first time was momentarily startled by her odd, breathless, high-pitched voice. It made her sound small and insistent, like a child struggling to be heard. Toni explained that once when she was young she mistakenly drank some Sloan's Liniment, an over-the-counter rub for stiff muscles. "It did me in, changed my voice," she said.[6] She joked about the way her voice sounded with a well-rehearsed line. "When I wanted to demand something, I had to use a whistle and a baseball bat," she said. "A whistle and a baseball bat." There was a tinge of weariness in her response, as if she had long ago grown tired of explaining herself.[7]

Stone eased herself into a chair by the phone to continue talking. Her knees ached, but she rarely complained, and she would not let the pain stop her. Toni was too full of pride. She could still climb a ladder and paint a ceiling if she needed to, and she was legendary in her family for doing her own repair work. Aunt Toni "could really put on a set of steps," her niece would say.[8] Stone's house—a small Victorian gem on Isabella Street in Oakland, California, had been her home for nearly fifty years after she left Saint Paul, Minnesota. "She needed to get away," relatives said. Saint Paul had grown too small for Toni, and she always had her eye on the next horizon.

When she was barely a teenager, people had already noticed that Toni Stone was far from ordinary. She was an astonishing athlete who seemed to excel at everything she attempted: swimming, golf, track, basketball, hockey, tennis, ice skating. She was even the most feared kid in the neighborhood when it came to playing red rover. She made a point of always breaking through the strongest link in the chain, just to prove she was tough.[9] But baseball won her heart. "Tomboy" Stone, as neighborhood kids called her, eventually became so well known in Saint Paul that when her younger sister announced her engagement the newspaper mistakenly ran a photograph of Toni instead of her sibling.[10] Editors, used to putting Toni in the paper, had hastily inserted the wrong photograph. But they got it right when the newspaper imagined a future for Tomboy that would extend well beyond Minnesota.

"We do not hesitate," the *Minneapolis Spokesman* declared in 1937, "to predict that she some day will acquire the fame of one Babe" Didrikson.[11] Years later Toni would state matter-of-factly, "I could outscore her and out hit her." Many agreed. Ball players who later faced both Didrikson and Stone on the baseball diamond confirmed, "Babe was a pretty good player, but Toni Stone was a *real* good player."[12]

After she left Saint Paul, Stone went to San Francisco, then New Orleans, and traveled with semi-pro teams throughout the South. "I love my San Francisco. I had my hardships there. But they treated me right. Old San Francisco folks taken me over," she said, her voice becoming softer. "I played ball. And I got a little job. I slept in the [bus] station. I have beautiful memories and very little bad ones. I guess it's a way of carrying myself."

Working hard was a virtue Stone learned from her parents. Boykin and Willa Stone moved to Saint Paul in the 1930s and started a business. Every day, Toni came home from school—or from skipping school—and knew her parents would not be home until late at night. Their drive to make something of themselves left an impression. "I watched my folks come home and scuffle. It was during the Depression and I watched them work hard. And I said, 'If I can't be among the best, then I'll just leave it alone.'"

"Scuffle" was an important word to Stone. She used it to underscore the grit needed to work against the odds: resolve, persistence, sacrifice. It was the price people were willing to pay to do what they loved. If anyone suggested that playing black baseball was an easy road, she bristled and her thin voice became pinched and direct. "They never was in it!" she argued. "Those old timers, they really had to scuffle and darn near get killed going down the highway, run onto some snakes that tore the bus up." During a time when a black person could be lynched for smiling the "wrong way," a busload of African American ballplayers looking for a place to stay overnight threatened bigots on either side of the Mason-Dixon line. She hinted briefly at an incident triggered by the double prejudice she faced as an African American woman, but she stopped short before fully describing what happened. "You see, I fought a lot," she admitted, "but they broke me of it. The fellas said they'd liable kill me." Keeping the degradation she experienced from imploding inside her was perhaps what Stone meant by finding "a way of carrying herself." A person had to listen carefully to Toni Stone.

Toni's hands ached with arthritis. Holding a phone had grown difficult for her. Even though he sensed she was tired and knew it was time to hang up, McNary had so many questions he wished he could ask: questions about playing with Willie Mays, cheering crowds at Yankee Stadium, Japanese trade rumors, the awful bus accident, Buck O'Neil, Joe DiMaggio, Babe Ruth, Louis Armstrong, Cooperstown. Did she play in the majors? Is that why people called her the female Jackie Robinson? "I'm just lucky to be alive," Stone told him, without a note of humor. She gazed across the dusky living room to an ornate family mirror that reflected her face. Years of scuffling had not diminished her determination. Her gray eyes shot the same stare her father had, the look that said, "Do not stand in my way." Fate had handed Toni Stone one imperfect chance to live her dream and she stepped into it.

A Question of Sin

From where she stood the air she craved
Smote with the smell of pine;
It was too much to bear; she braved
Her gods and crossed the line.

—COUNTEE CULLEN[1]

Tomboy Stone had a confession to make. The young girl knelt in the St. Peter Claver confession box and began to unburden her mind. "Bless me, Father, for I have sinned," she began, and admitted that she wanted to run away from home. Tomboy was having trouble with her parents, and their disapproval was more than the twelve-year-old could bear. She looked down at her hands, worn and dirty from all the hours she spent outdoors, and thought about how she had come to make such a difficult decision. For some time Tomboy had felt pulled between the love she felt for her family and her love for something else: baseball. "It was like a drug," she said. "Whenever summer would come around [and] the bats would start popping, I'd go crazy."[2] Boykin and Willa Stone did not understand their daughter's obsession. They thought it was wrong, that it was unnatural for a girl to be so consumed by a boy's game. Tomboy was well acquainted with their opinion. "My parents thought the idea of a little girl playing baseball was sinful," she said.[3] Her mother even sent a letter to teachers at school, informing them that her daughter's health might suffer if she played sports. She "told them I had a heart murmur, anything to discourage me."[4] Tomboy also knew her parents had appealed to Father Keefe, the family's parish priest, to dissuade her from playing baseball with neighborhood boys. But she could not give up the sport, and, after trying unsuccessfully to win her parents' approval to keep playing, Tomboy decided to run away. Her decision made her heartsick, but, torn between baseball and her family, her choice was clear.[5]

Father Charles Keefe listened as the young black girl recited the litany of her transgressions. Even out of sight in the confessional, children like Tomboy could not hide from Father Keefe. He recognized the children's voices, and sometimes he didn't bother to pretend that their disclosures were anonymous. He was like their mother or an alert teacher or the radio's fictional crime fighter the Green Hornet in his omniscient acuity. Once, after one of the neighborhood children confessed his sins, the boy was startled when Father's disembodied voice rang out from the opposite side. "By the way, Mel," he said, "could you get me a carton of cigarettes from the store?"[6]

Kids and adult parishioners alike trusted Father Keefe. As a white priest in a historically black congregation, he had gained the community's respect for his commitment to race relations.* Tomboy thought highly of him, too, and was drawn to his honesty. To her, he was clear and direct—straight across the plate. She also loved his pas-

---

*St. Peter Claver Catholic Church was named for the seventeenth-century Spanish Jesuit "slave of the slaves" who ministered for nearly half a century to men and women in the Caribbean. He was elevated to sainthood in 1888. Saint Paul Archbishop John Ireland worked with a black "congregation of converts" to establish St. Peter Claver in Minneapolis/Saint Paul. In 1910 Father Stephen Theobold, a native of British Guiana, began his ministry at the church. Theobold was legendary for his speeches on race relations and, along with other members of the Church, helped found the Minnesota NAACP. St. Peter Claver church members also played leading roles in working with W. E. B. DuBois in establishing the Niagara Movement—a campaign that called for a "mighty current" to end racial discrimination and disenfranchisement across the country. Theobold died of peritonitis in 1932 and was succeeded by Father Charles J. Keefe in 1933 (*St. Peter Claver Diamond Jubilee, 1892–1967,* 5–9).

sion for life. She called him a "big old Irishman" who had a "Joy to the World" enthusiasm about him.[7] He was a kind and creative man: the type to find a solution to a problem rather than issue a decree, she thought. A few years before, when the Stone family first started attending St. Peter Claver, Father Keefe had taken an interest in young Tomboy. He knew Mr. and Mrs. Stone were concerned about their daughter. The youngster was an outcast: she did not do well in school and was made fun of by some of her peers because she didn't look, act, or talk like other girls. Keefe even knew that Boykin and Willa Stone disliked their daughter's nickname, "Tomboy." They called their daughter by her given name, Marcenia Lyle Stone. But to children and everyone else around St. Peter Claver, she was Tomboy Stone—the best athlete in the Rondo neighborhood of Saint Paul, Minnesota, and the girl who got into fights for being different.

Tomboy completed her confession and agreed to recite several Hail Marys and Our Fathers. It was a light penance—what St. Peter Claver kids called "a slap on the wrist." [8] But Father Keefe knew he had to do more than require Tomboy to pray. He had to come up with a long-term plan for handling the girl's unconventional dreams while respecting her parents' concerns. Willa and Boykin Stone were strict parents, but Keefe believed their worry for Tomboy stemmed more from anxiety about her future than from a conviction that playing baseball was morally wrong. The Stones thought baseball was unladylike, that there was no future in it, and they were anxious that their daughter might get hurt, physically or emotionally. Boykin and Willa wanted all four of their children to amount to something. Willa especially was concerned about their three daughters' economic independence. She knew that for a young woman to truly have choices in life, she had to have money. Playing baseball would never give Marcenia that freedom, Willa thought. Boykin had additional concerns. He frequently lectured his children that even now—in 1933—black people in the United States faced unfair obstacles. Tomboy said her father explained "how rotten the whites were to us . . . and how he wanted us to get our education."[9] What could baseball possibly offer a twelve-year-old girl from a black neighborhood in Saint Paul, Minnesota, Willa and Boykin Stone asked their daughter? Everything, Tomboy thought.

After he finished hearing confessions from the line of youngsters standing in a neat row along the church wall, Father Keefe went to his office and considered how he could help Tomboy Stone. He did not believe Tomboy could be talked out of playing baseball: he had seen her play and knew she was a gifted athlete. He also wondered if sports might actually help the combative Tomboy more than hurt her. If she was proud of what she did on the diamond and gained some respect in the community, perhaps Tomboy wouldn't fight as much. Maybe she would forget about running away. Keefe thought about suggesting that the youngster become more involved with the Hallie Q. Brown Community Center—a lifesaver for kids with time on their hands and an inclination to temptation.* But Boykin and Willa Stone might feel more assured, Keefe wagered, if their daughter participated in something directly connected to the church. The diocese had a baseball league for boys, and he knew that Tomboy was acquainted with many of the players. "After Mass, I'd put my dungarees on and I'm out to find the fellas," she said. Keefe might be able to convince parish boys to let Tomboy play in the Catholic boys' baseball league if they realized how fast she could run and how far she could hit a ball. If he could channel her athletic ability into a Catholic activity, perhaps Mr. and Mrs. Stone would stop criticizing their daughter's interests. Father Keefe mentioned his idea to Tomboy. He "told me that since I wasn't going to stop playing," she said, "I might as well play for the church."[10]

Keefe's idea worked. After he spoke to the Stones and suggested their daughter try the Catholic boys' league, they relented. He calmed

---

*Hallie Q. Brown and its Minneapolis counterpart, the Phyllis Wheatley Center, were linchpins in the Twin Cities. "Hallie Q.," as it was affectionately called, opened after the black YWCA closed in 1928. It offered child care, athletics, senior activities, health care, and cultural, political, and social events. The center was named for Hallie Quinn Brown, an Ohio educator who spearheaded the black women's club movement in the nineteenth century. In Saint Paul, "Hallie Q" was led by the formidable I. Myrtle Carden from 1929 to 1949. Carden improved the lives of countless African American residents in and around Rondo. Children in the Rondo neighborhood, including Tomboy, also played at the Welcome Hall Center and took part in its activities sponsored by the Zion Presbyterian Church.

Willa and assured her he would look out for Marcenia. Tomboy was thrilled. The Stones' neighbor, Melvin—Father Keefe's cigarette runner—thought there was a more subversive reason the thoughtful priest wanted Tomboy involved with the parish baseball team. "She had the most talent," Melvin said.[11] Folks in the neighborhood didn't seem to mind that Tomboy Stone was an oddball girl playing baseball on a boys' team as long as she helped St. Peter Claver win the game. It was settled. "I got a chance," Tomboy said, and played outfield and infield.[12]

Tomboy was fortunate to have Father Keefe intercede with her parents. She also was fortunate to live where she did. The Rondo neighborhood in Saint Paul, named for the busy two-mile-long street that was its main artery, was heaven for a kid who loved baseball. Just blocks from Tomboy's home was Dunning Field, next to Central High School, where she could always find kids playing catch. Next to Dunning was Saint Paul's grand Lexington Park—the field Charlie Comiskey built before he took his name and his team to Chicago. The park was home to the Saint Paul Saints. Gabby Street, "the Old Sarge," managed the team after being fired from the World Champion St. Louis Cardinals a few years earlier. If he could manage the Cardinals' Gas House Gang with Dizzy Dean and Pepper Martin, "the wild horse of the Osage," surely he could handle a team of twenty-year-old kids who hoped to make it to the big leagues. Tomboy loved Lexington Park, not only for the stray baseballs that she found there but especially for the days when Babe Ruth came to town. The Babe came to town on customary trips, when the Saints were an informal farm team for the Yankees.* He'd sign baseballs, pose for pictures, and chat up the locals. But the Saints weren't the only game in town. A few miles to the west was Nicollet Park, home of the New York Giants' farm club the Minneapolis Millers. Kids like

*The Saint Paul Saints team was used as "development ground" by the New York Yankees from 1919 to the early 1930s. Bob Connery, a scout for the Yankees, bought the Saints in 1925. Among the players who moved from the Saints to the Yankees were Leo Durocher and Vernon "Lefty" Gomez (e-mail to author from Stew Thornley, November 13, 2008).

Tomboy waited all summer long for the big Fourth of July weekend doubleheader. The day would start with a game in Saint Paul, then fans would hop on streetcars and ride across the Mississippi River bridge for an evening nightcap in Minneapolis. Players enjoyed the Twin City doubleheaders as much as the fans did. They made a lot of money when crowds filled the bleachers. They called the Saints and Millers holiday doubleheaders "Pay Days."[13]

On days when the Millers or the Saints were playing away games, Negro League teams would schedule games and rent the vacant stadiums. The great Satchel Paige, barnstorming through the Dakotas, stopped in Saint Paul and dazzled crowds with his one-of-a-kind pitches, as impossible to hit as their names were to forget: the bat dodger, the midnight creeper, the bee ball, Long Tom, Little Tom, the trouble ball, the two-hump blooper. After the games, Paige would stroll the midway around Rondo, duck into a restaurant, and revel in the attention of starstruck fans. Tomboy swore she met Satchel on one of his walks around the midway. They talked about baseball, and Paige later sent a letter encouraging her to stay in school. She said that Satch had heard from Rondo folks about her extraordinary play in the Catholic boys' league and even spoke to her mother about the young girl's future in baseball. Years later, Stone's family said they never heard of the "Satchel story," although one could never be sure. Tomboy Stone loved the limelight and seemed to have a knack for finding celebrity. Rondo's vitality seemed to spark a child's imagination. "You could dream your dreams there," one resident said.[14] It never occurred to anyone that a girl might dream about baseball.

Tomboy's family had settled in Rondo and Saint Paul during the Great Migration, the movement of nearly two million African Americans from the South to the industrial cities in the North, West, and Midwest beginning in 1910. Families searched for better jobs, better schools, and better treatment as far from the grip of racism as they could manage. Growing up in South Carolina, Boykin Stone decided that scratching out a living as a farmer was not for him. The land was unforgiving. Instead he left his home in Log Town and entered the

Tuskegee Institute in Alabama in 1908 to learn a trade—barbering.[15] Booker T. Washington's philosophy at Tuskegee made a deep impression on him. Stone believed blacks should learn a trade that could support a family. Even if it meant sweeping out a store or washing windows, a person needed work, he said. Stone viewed any kind of labor as dignified and could not stand loafers or people who drifted without a realistic goal. Stone served in the U.S. Army in World War I and later married Willa Maynard. The couple had four children in rapid succession after the war: daughters Blanche, Marcenia, and Bernous and a son, Quinten. All the children were born in West Virginia; Marcenia was born in Bluefield, near the Kentucky border, on July 17, 1921. When other members of the family headed to Saint Paul, Boykin and Willa joined them in 1931.* They found a house two blocks from relatives and established a family compound of sorts, with multiple generations all living within walking distance. For a Stone child who occasionally misbehaved, as Tomboy did, punishment was difficult to escape. Grandparents looked out kitchen windows as they ate peach cobbler, aunts talked over laundry lines to inquisitive neighbors, cousins sat on front porches, putting rags on smoking smudge pots to ward off the summer mosquitoes. They heard and saw everything. "They were good people," a neighbor remembered, "hard working, strict with their children, friendly."[16] People passing by the family's homes often could hear music floating from open windows. Willa and her sister, Aunt Johnnie, would each play one of two pianos in their mother's living room. Tomboy's brother, Quinten, played saxophone. Another relative brought a trumpet. "They had it going on for hours," the family said.[17] Tomboy would sometimes join the group and bang on a drum set, but in order to carry on with the musical Stone clan, "you had to be good" and Marcenia couldn't keep up.

Saint Paul, in the early 1930s, when the Stones arrived from West Virginia, had a small, cohesive black community. They made up only

---

*I base the Stone family's arrival date in Minnesota on the fact that Boykin Stone and his family are listed in the West Virginia census for 1930, and Saint Paul school records indicate that Marcenia Stone enrolled in 1931.

1.5 percent of the city's population, centering mainly around Rondo. Residents in the Twin Cities referred to the Rondo neighborhood as "colored." Tomboy's friend Evelyn Edwards remembered that, in the 1930s, "colored" meant integrated: blacks and whites lived on the same block, and white women dated and married black men.[18] Even with a small population, blacks owned a significant percentage of homes in Saint Paul. Just after the turn of the twentieth century, Saint Paul had a larger percentage of black-owned homes than any other city in the country.[19] Generally speaking, families with jobs that paid lower wages lived in Cornmeal Valley to the east of Dale Avenue; those with more money settled up on Oatmeal Hill to the west.* The Stones lived in Cornmeal Valley. Further up Oatmeal Hill, adjacent to Rondo, were the mansions of Summit Avenue, where wealthy white people lived. F. Scott Fitzgerald rented a unit of one of the mansions while reworking *This Side of Paradise* before heading to Hollywood to try his hand as a screenwriter. The fathers of some of Tomboy's friends worked as waiters when the Summit families hired caterers. Status in Rondo was based more on who a person worked for than on what a worker did. To be employed by Summit Avenue families was a point of pride. To be one's own boss, however, was a mark of even higher status.[20]

Job opportunities brought most black families to Saint Paul. Some men moved from the South for "running on the road" jobs—porters and dining car waiters for the many railroads that crossed through the area. Others worked for tips as Redcaps out of Union Depot: hauling bags, cleaning toilets, and polishing endless sweeps of brass railings, a task many admitted was their least favorite.[21] Women worked primarily as cooks or did "day work" around town for white families who needed help with cleaning or ironing. In 1929, black families in Saint Paul owned twenty-seven barbershops, five pool halls, seven restaurants, three shoeshine parlors, seven tailor shops,

---

*Scholar Jennifer Delton in *Making Minnesota Liberal* noted "'Oatmeal Hill' reportedly referred to the lighter skin color of blacks in the solidly middle-class areas, as opposed to 'Cornmeal Valley,' the area west of Dale Street, where the southern migrants settled, the term referring to a southern food staple" (187).

one picture-framing store, and one piano-polishing business.[22] One of the barbershops was Boykin's Barber and Beauty Shop in the busy Seven Corners area, just east of the State Capitol. "My parents were survivors," Tomboy said, "and they opened a beauty shop in town."[23] Boykin and Willa opened the business together and served white clientele only. Many black-owned barbershops in Saint Paul and elsewhere exclusively cut white hair and, according to one resident, "strongly discouraged Black patrons."[24]

But by the 1930s the long tradition of black barbers who earned financial rewards, status, and upward mobility by catering to white customers was beginning to give way.* Italian and German immigrants set up shops and drew white customers away. In addition, some people within the community began to ask if black barbers contributed to segregation by cutting only white hair: "color line barbers," critics called them. Perhaps the community would do better, some argued, if segregation policies were challenged rather than maintained. While many black residents did not like the idea of segregated shops, they also could see other ways in which an individual barber contributed to the community. It was almost as if they said, "I hate what you're doing, but you're doing good things outside the shop."[25]

Although they did not outwardly speak of any conflict of conscience, Boykin and Willa may have felt ambivalent when the occasional black customer came into the shop looking for a haircut or a shave. How could they turn away a member of their own race? Many black barbers would silently escort a patron to the back of the shop

---

*Scholar Douglas Bristol Jr., in a study of black barbers, wrote that "from the 1820s to the Great Migration almost a century later, [black barbers] dominated the upscale market serving affluent white men even as other African American business people lost their white clientele. . . . A perceptive understanding of their customers, in the sense of W. E. B. DuBois's concept of double-consciousness, allowed black barbers to capitalize on racial stereotypes. Because they understood how whites saw them, they were able to create masks that white customers found appealing. . . . The willingness of black barbers to accept and exploit the racial stereotypes of their white customers represented an entrepreneurial innovation that secured their economic niche" (Douglas Bristol Jr., "From Outposts to Enclaves: A Social History of Black Barbers from 1750–1915," *Enterprise & Society* vol. 5, no. 4, The Business History Conference 2004, 596–597).

for a quick cut; others would shake their heads and show the customer the door. Some would only cut black people's hair at the customers' homes, in the back yard. Willa's sister said that her sibling couldn't do black hair if she tried. After years of cutting white hair, Willa simply did not know how to cut and style hair for a black customer.[26] Some barbers with a keen eye for the changing times took a cue from Madame C. J. Walker, who built a fortune creating grooming products for blacks. They opened new shops in segregated communities and expanded their business to a growing urban market. Whitney Young, who came to Saint Paul to work on a master's degree at the University of Minnesota, recognized that the older generation of blacks faced a changing world and represented a time when segregation was accepted as a condition of life.* Young did not fault the generation of barbers like Boykin and Willa Stone. It was difficult balancing the need for self-respect against the obligation to make money. "In dealing with the opposing forces, [the older generation] were skillful diplomats," Young wrote. "One might admit that at that time the strategic overtures of humility, servitude and inferiority were the best weapons for dealing with the powerful. Most of these Negro leaders' techniques have changed with the times and those who are living today are still courageous fighters for Negro rights."[27]

Of course, following the stock market crash of 1929, every worker in the United States felt the strain of trying to earn a living. Businesses closed, church revenues dipped, social programs were cut, grocery stores stopped giving credit, storefronts around Rondo began to sag from lack of maintenance, and vagrants came to the back door looking for food.[28] In 1930, unemployment among blacks stood at almost 50 percent in Saint Paul. Many hotels let go of black waiters and hired white waitresses instead.[29] Families became ingenious in devising ways to pay the bills. One Rondo specialty was the "house-rent party." A

---

*Whitney Young's 1947 master's thesis in the University of Minnesota School of Social Work addressed African American negotiation skills. Young (1921–1971) became executive director of the National Urban League in 1961, and he was one of the organizers of the 1963 March on Washington.

neighbor feeling the pinch would cook a big pot of food, buy a new deck of cards, and sell dinners and drinks by the shot to friends and family. "At the end of the night, we'd have the money for rent," a neighbor remembered. "It seemed that almost every month, someone was giving a house-rent party, and it was always well attended." [30] Tomboy's parents kept Boykin's Barber Shop and Beauty Salon running, and the family never lacked for the basics, although they did take in a German boarder to bring in additional money.[31] Around the neighborhood, every household felt the squeeze of hard times. As a friend of Tomboy's said, "Everything was taken in, let out, or made into quilts."[32]

Living in economically difficult times was one challenge, but living as blacks in Jim Crow America was quite another. To anyone who thought that the Upper Midwest was immune to racism, a person had to say just one word—"Duluth." The legacy of the Duluth lynching served as a chilling reminder to all African Americans that racism stretched beyond the South. On a warm summer night in June 1920, rumors began to spread that a white Duluth girl had been raped at a traveling circus. Three black workers for the John Robinson Circus were rounded up immediately and held in jail. An angry crowd of nearly ten thousand stormed the jail with bricks and timbers and seized the men. After a hasty and spurious trial, the men were found guilty and strung up by their necks on a town light pole. There was never any evidence to convict the men of the crime. While some people expressed outrage at the lynching, others thought justice had been served. The *Mankato Daily Free Press* declared "mad dogs are shot dead without ceremony. Beasts in human shape are entitled to but scant consideration. The law gives them by far too much of an advantage."[33] A ghastly postcard of the lynching circulated for years.* The tragedy sparked instant reaction in the black community. Many residents left Duluth, fearful that their families might be harmed. Others stayed and established a chapter of the NAACP (National Association for the

*Elias Clayton, Elmer Jackson, and Isaac McGhie were the victims of the lynching. In 2003, citizens of Duluth, in an effort to atone for and learn from the tragedy, dedicated a monument in their memory.

Advancement of Colored People). W. E. B. DuBois traveled to Duluth to speak at its initial meeting.* Nellie and W. T. Francis, prominent Saint Paul activists, pushed through the first anti-lynching legislation in the nation, signed into law a year after the Duluth lynching.

Tomboy and every kid in Rondo knew about the Duluth lynching, and they also had stories of their own encounters with Minnesota racism. They could describe slurs yelled from passing gangs of white boys when they gathered to play baseball, or tell how frightened they felt when a white kid hurled a cantaloupe that hit a black friend on the head.[34] The racist taunts were so commonplace that a black child developed a second sense about "which members of these groups could be insulted when I was alone and which ones required me to have a backup group." After being called a nigger one too many times, one of Tomboy's friends shot back with exasperation, "If your mother had married who she really wanted, you'd be a nigger too."[35]

Everyone knew that some stores would not serve black customers at lunch counters, and if they did—like the soda fountain at Walgreen's—waiters were aloof and sometimes hostile.[36] Even the sound of the organ music coming from the ice rink near Kent and Mackubin reminded Tomboy that she was not welcomed at the segregated rink.[37] When Tomboy's black friend Janabelle Murphy was invited to join her neighbor—a tall Norwegian named Clemy Hetznecker—and a group of white girls for lunch one day, service at the restaurant was noticeably slow. "Is there a problem?" Clemy asked a nervous waiter. A manager suddenly appeared and declared that as long as a Negro girl was in their party, the group would not be served. Clemy rose to her full height, looked the waiter in the eye, and announced to the

---

*W. E. B. DuBois (1868–1963) was one of the most prominent African American voices of the twentieth century. A prolific author, DuBois is most notable for his 1903 book *The Souls of Black Folk*. One of the founders of the Niagara Movement and the NAACP, DuBois was often at odds with other leaders such as Booker T. Washington concerning the best way for blacks to gain power and respect. While Washington believed blacks should assimilate into white culture, DuBois argued that white dominance should be challenged. DuBois was familiar with Minnesota politics: he worked at a resort on Lake Minnetonka near Minneapolis following his graduation from Fisk University in 1888.

girls, "I don't want a frown, not a tear, but because Jane cannot be served, none will be served." And out the door they went.[38] Meanness and hatred were bad enough, but pity was worse for the black children of Rondo. "I hated it when white people felt sorry for me," Tomboy's friend Evelyn said many years later. "As long as they were mean and belittling, my anger could protect me. But when they were sympathetic, my anger turned to shame and I was left defenseless."[39]

No one would ever call Tomboy defenseless. Her friends Janabelle Murphy and Evelyn Edwards would attest to that. To be fair, one really could not call Jane and Evelyn Tomboy's close friends. Tomboy spent a lot of time by herself and was more comfortable around boys than with girls her age. But Jane and Evelyn certainly knew Tomboy well, and represented two distinct choices for what a Rondo girl could be. Evelyn, who didn't enjoy sports, was always picked last for neighborhood games, preferring to play with paper dolls, listen to the black choir, "Wings Over Jordan," on the radio, or perform as the "little soloist" at the Sanctified Church. She loved the church dinners after Sunday services where women would be judged on the quality of dishes brought in picnic baskets covered with their best bib aprons. Evelyn believed that "hair is a woman's crown" and watched with fascination as the traveling corsetiere measured the women in her family for the latest girdles. She stood with Tomboy outside the chain-link fence watching white girls at the skating rink and once asked her mother about the Mason-Dixon line. "You mean somebody drew a line on the ground all around the world?" she asked.[40]

"Tomboy reminded me of me," Janabelle Murphy declared. As the shortest and slightest kid on the block, Jane did not look like a fighter. But when neighborhood girls needed help with mean boys, they went looking for Jane. She'd stare down the bully, yell at him with her loud, deep voice, then run between his wide-spread legs, landing a powerful bare-knuckle punch right against his knees until he collapsed to the ground. She was by her own admission a "phys ed girl"—a girl who fell in love with physical education classes taught at the Hallie Q. Brown Community Center. Jane proudly accepted the description of herself as a "roughneck." Roughnecks could take care of themselves, she said. She and Tomboy were confident, knew when to stand their ground, and did not take guff. "'Don't get caught' was my 11th commandment," Tomboy said.[41] Jane's mother begged her daughter to be more ladylike. "It's OK for you to scare the boys," her mother said. "But don't BE a boy! You're a girl!"[42] Perhaps hoping that Jane's "feistiness" could be transformed into something more productive, her mother also enrolled her in sports programs across the river at the Minneapolis Phyllis Wheatley Negro Community Center. [43] Jane went from being a neighborhood bully's worst nightmare to organizing girls' sports programs at Hallie Q. She even adopted the Q's philosophy about goal-oriented activity: "you were either going someplace or going home."[44]

While she did not go looking for fights, Tomboy protected herself and could take someone down if she felt threatened. "Worst drubbing I ever got was from Tomboy Stone," one of the neighborhood football players said. "It was right down here on a playground on Western Avenue. Field had rocks all over it and I come around with the ball and . . . man, I can still feel that spot where she hit me.[45] When Willa Stone recommended a sport her daughter might try, her suggestion was more about transforming Tomboy into a feminine Marcenia than proposing a new activity. "Try figure skating," her mother said, perhaps thinking of the "toast of Saint Paul"—a young white competitive skater who captivated crowds with her spins and twirls and her satin outfits trimmed in fur.[46] Willa bought Tomboy a pair of skates, and her daughter promptly beat all competition to win the citywide competition at Como Park. "I took [the trophy] home, and gave it to my mother and picked up my glove and bat," Tomboy said.[47]

Then there was the matter of Tomboy's name. Everyone in Rondo had a nickname. There was "Rock Bottom" and "Flat Head" and "Turkey Breast" and "Puddin'." The names stuck, and sometimes kids couldn't even remember how they got the names or what they stood for. Tomboy's neighbor Norman "Speed" Rollins could not recall if "Speed" came from the fact that he always ran home as fast as lightning or that he liked to dance fast. "Hey, Speed. You're speeding. Slow down," friends used to tell Rollins on the dance floor.[48] Ask anyone at Dunning Field who "Marcenia Lyle Stone" was and you were apt to get a blank stare. Tomboy knew the nickname embarrassed her parents.[49] The Stones were formal people. Willa was so proper that she would not go anywhere without her hair done up in rosettes and her fingernails polished, and Boykin was a member of the elite Sterling Club of serious, civic-minded black professionals. The Stones aspired to the likes of Thomas and Eva Neal, the elite black family of Rondo who entertained prominent educator Mary McLeod Bethune and later welcomed first lady Eleanor Roosevelt to the city. The Neals supported "worthy Negro causes" and took a special interest in neighborhood girls, showing them the correct way to make conversation, use a dessert fork, and avoid wearing the color red. "Red is the color for street women," Mrs. Neal once told Evelyn.[50] Tomboy knew her place was not with women like Mrs. Neal. "I wasn't high on the elite side," she said. "That's why they called me Tomboy."[51]

Feeling unrefined and not understood by family and friends—like an outcast, Tomboy said—made Father Keefe's help with playing baseball all the more welcome.[52] Not only did she finally receive neighborhood recognition for the victories she brought the St. Peter Claver team, but she also attracted citywide attention as the one of Saint Paul's outstanding girl athletes. For the time being, Tomboy decided to stay put in Rondo. She shelved her plan to run away from home, like the forgotten ice skating trophy in her upstairs bedroom. Although her parents had yet to watch her play and still wished Tomboy would turn more attention to her schoolwork, Boykin and Willa were grateful to see their daughter's confidence grow. They even were willing to admit that Father Keefe's decision had been right. In playing baseball, Tomboy Stone had crossed a line. But it wasn't sin that she was embracing. It was salvation.

Miracle in Saint Paul

> I do feel, in my dreamings and yearnings, so undiscovered by those who are able to help me.
>
> —Mary McLeod Bethune[1]

Tomboy Stone loved her baseball glove. It was smooth and dark and worn in all the right places. Although she sometimes envied the new gloves that other kids had, this old beauty she had bought for twenty-five cents at the Saint Paul Goodwill would have to do. To earn the money for the glove, Tomboy had worked around the neighborhood for small change.[2] Her parents would not offer money for equipment that might lend her encouragement to play even more baseball. "They wanted me to do anything but wear old tennis shoes and spend all day hitting baseballs," Tomboy said. The baseball shoes that she admired in store windows were expensive, and she realized she shouldn't pine about them to her mother and father. Even though she knew the shoes were out of reach, she couldn't get them out of her head; they looked so professional with their rows of shiny, teethlike spikes. "Professional"—that's the word Tomboy used to confer her highest praise on anyone or anything associated with baseball. When she let her aspirations run unchecked, she admitted that she hoped one day to be a professional baseball player. After playing in Saint Paul's Catholic boys' baseball league for almost four years, Tomboy said, "I knew I wanted to be an athlete," adding, "I didn't concern myself that there weren't any women in the game."[3]

Boykin and Willa Stone resigned themselves to Tomboy playing baseball during the summers with the Catholic boys' league and, later, the Saint Paul's HighLex girls' softball team. Given her strong arm, Tomboy played the outfield and occasionally pitched. But she did not stay with the girls' team for long; she quit a little after a year. "Not [for] me," Tomboy said. "It wasn't fast enough," and the girls' play failed to challenge her the way the Catholic boys' did.[4] When Tomboy decided to quit softball, her parents were relieved; at least it meant one less team she would be playing on.

What the Stones didn't know was that Tomboy had another opportunity in mind. She started to hang out at the meatpacking plants in South Saint Paul. She'd ride her Silver King bike, the one her father bought for her for eleven dollars, or grab a streetcar and head down to the Armour or Swift plants, situated side by side next to the groaning stockyards and the Mississippi River.[5] The workers, many of whom were black men, organized company baseball teams—some integrated—that played on the weekends. The Armour squad was so good they won the Minnesota Municipal League State Championship for several years in the 1920s.[6] Tomboy hoped there might be a way for her to join the workingmen's league or at least get the men used to the idea.[7] She also liked hearing the men talk. They had an easy way about them, and—years before—a few had played in the Negro Leagues. She felt more comfortable listening to old men discussing balls and strikes than she did hearing girls her own age chattering about who had won the Jitterbug contest the previous weekend. "I wasn't popular with the girls because I loved to play with the boys," she said. When girls around Rondo called her "Tomboy" in their derogatory way, the sneer fueled her determination, and she vowed to keep playing baseball until she could earn a living at it. "One day this is going to be my game," Tomboy said.[8]

Father Keefe's gamble of encouraging Tomboy to play Catholic baseball did affect her in positive ways. She was consistently attending school, and she was reading more. But not her textbooks, necessarily. History classes disappointed her the most. It wasn't that she wasn't interested in history; it was that the books did not offer any record for understanding who she was. She didn't have the words to describe how she felt about that absence, but she knew that a significant part of history was missing from the books her junior high teachers asked her to read. All the women and black people in her textbooks led subservient lives, it seemed to her. They were either assisting a white man in an invention or traipsing along after some clear-eyed blond who "discovered" a territory that Indians had been living in all along. Tomboy's friend Evelyn Edwards agreed. School history books, she said, presented blacks only as slaves or victims, and there was little mention of any black achievements. Evelyn knew for certain that blacks had contributed greatly to music; she had learned that at her prayer meetings.[9] For Tomboy, blacks in her textbooks "were all cotton pickers."[10] Her neighbor Speed Rollins knew what she meant. One of his most humiliating days at school occurred when his teacher insisted that—as a black child—he read the Little Black Sambo part during story hour. The experience felt degrading to him.[11] Tomboy knew there were many distinguished black Americans. She'd heard her father talk about his time at Tuskegee and the indelible marks Booker T. Washington and Dr. George Washington Carver made on the country. W. E. B. DuBois's trips to Saint Paul made clear that he too was an accomplished man. Textbook history always boiled down to "Captain-John-Smith-and-Pocahontas," Tomboy said. Even fifty years later, that phrase remained her shorthand for describing the intellectual impoverishment she experienced at school.[12]

Hungry for inspiration, Tomboy turned to the local library for sports books. She searched for stories about athletes who made names for themselves. When she found books that inspired her, like biographies of Babe Ruth, she read them twice, sometimes three times.[13] The Babe had recently made one of his visits to the Twin Cities, playing exhibition games after his retirement from baseball. "I wanted to be Babe Ruth," she said. "He was everybody's hero."[14] Tomboy especially looked for books about women athletes, but she found few trailblazers. The absence of women role models seemed to underscore the sentence she had heard many times. Tomboy could recite the line by heart: "a girl going to play ball was a disgrace to society."[15]

Tomboy also read books to help improve her athletic skills and learn game strategy. While she was grateful for Father Keefe's help in finding her a baseball team, she often felt frustrated when the Catholic team's coaches ignored her. Coaches pulled the boys aside to teach them how to turn the double play or hit to the opposite field, but they always assumed Tomboy would not be interested in the finer points of play or couldn't execute them. "The coach would tell the boys stuff but not me," she said. Rather than stewing about being excluded, Tomboy immersed herself in the science of the game. "I got a rule book and studied it," she said. "I knew it more than the boys." [16]

Tomboy also discovered newspapers. The local papers interested her, especially when they ran stories about athletes, local baseball teams, or neighborhood kids who broke into professional sports. Gordon Parks, a few years older than Tomboy, was already receiving coverage. "Gordon Parks Returns Home," the *Minneapolis Spokesman* proudly declared. It described the "young Twin City photographer's" three-month tour with a traveling semi-pro basketball team.* More than anything, however, Tomboy loved reading the *Chicago Defender*. She would ride her bike to the train depot and wait for stacks of the *Defender* to be dropped off by the Great Northern line out of Chicago.[17] The newspaper opened up a world of possibilities and was "the best book," she said. "I used to call it my Bible, when Mama wasn't listening."[18] *Defender* readers scanned the newspaper for political, social, and sports news affecting the country's black citizens—news that the white newspapers either did not care to cover or didn't know existed. Founded in

---

*Gordon Parks (1912–2006) gained national attention as a photographer, musician, writer, and film director. He is best known for his *Life* magazine photographs and for directing the 1971 motion picture *Shaft*.

1905 by Robert Sengstacke Abbott, the *Defender* reportedly began with a twenty-five-cent investment, a three-hundred-copy print run, and "offices" located on the kitchen table of Abbott's landlord. Long a champion for racial equality, the *Defender* called for blacks to migrate to the North and was credited with helping to triple the black population of Chicago in the 1930s. It rallied against lynching, condemned racist voting barriers, and put pressure on the military to integrate. "That *Chicago Defender* Abbott, he told it like it was," Tomboy said.[19] "It was like my book, and I studied that. It told me what the Negro was doing, what we were contributing."[20] Pullman porters, cooks, and waiters took copies of the *Defender* to relatives and other readers down South. Barbers in black neighborhoods sold the newspaper in their shops. By the early 1920s, the newspaper was the largest and most influential black publication in America.[21]

Once as a birthday present Tomboy received a "deadheadin'" ticket—a free pass to ride the train. She went down to Chicago, stayed overnight, and happened to meet *Defender* editor Robert Abbot. "I was a young kid," she said, "but I knew he was somebody."[22] The chance meeting stayed with her. Tomboy continued devouring the paper, especially the inspirational essays by Reverend Benjamin Mays of Morehouse College, columns by Mary McLeod Bethune and Langston Hughes, and, of course, sports coverage of black athletes. "You had so few role models," she said. She read news of track star Jesse Owens, the Negro Leagues' Oscar Charleston and Satchel Paige, and her greatest hero, the man she called "the champion's champion," boxer Joe Louis.[23] As a good storyteller herself, Tomboy appreciated the *Defender's* sportswriting style: a mix of staccato flash and unabashed enthusiasm that delighted her. A reader could almost hear the pop of a baseball bat in the paper's sports stories. "More than 20,000 baseball enthusiasts came to the 'House that Ruth built,' here Sunday to witness four teams battle for top honors," one story began. "The nightcap gave the fans a chance to do some old fashioned back-lot yelling for the Pittsburgh Crawfords went on a wild rampage knocking down the poles, busting the bleachers seats with long—and equally hard—line drives and causing the utter embarrassment of one 'Slim Jones,' ace hurler for the Philly Stars, by sending him to the showers in the first inning."[24]

But Tomboy did not need a newspaper to tell her when the Saint Paul Saints were in town. The Saints were a minor league affiliate of the Chicago White Sox and played at nearby Lexington Park, not far from her home. Tomboy was so used to spending summer days on the playing fields around the ballpark that she called the area her "second home." When the Saints were in town and she heard the game day commotion begin, she made a point of stopping by the park on routine bike rides through the neighborhood.[25] Although they were a white team and were never affiliated with the Negro Leagues teams she admired, the Saints were a team she could learn something from, Tomboy believed. Attending games, like reading books, had become as much a part of her sports education as playing ball. The Saints had their ups and downs in the standings, but under new manager Gabby Street the 1936 squad won more games than they lost and were in second place in the white minor leagues' American Association. Early one morning before a Saints game, Tomboy rode her bike over to Lexington Park and watched Street coax young men through a strict regimen of drills. Street did more than coax: he also yelled and shouted when athletes didn't try hard enough. The shouting didn't bother Tomboy. Since she was always looking for a coach who would take the time to instruct her, she thought even a loud old man was better than someone who ignored her. After studying the practice from the perch of her bike, Tomboy pushed down the kickstand of her Silver King and walked through the open gates of the still-empty Lexington Park. She wanted to get a closer look at what was going on. Street barely looked up at the young interloper coming into the park. But when Tomboy kept walking closer and they finally did eye each other, neither the fifty-three-year-old white manager nor the fourteen-year-old black girl ever could have imagined how their separate worlds would collide during that 1936 summer.*

---

*Later in her life, Toni Stone could not remember the exact year she met Gabby Street in Saint Paul. My research into the years Street managed the Saints indicates that he most likely met Stone during the summer of 1936.

Tomboy didn't know a thing about Gabby Street. She certainly didn't know what a gift he later would give her.

There were few major league ball players who had seen more good and bad luck than Charles Evard "Gabby" Street. He had managed a World Series winner, and he had witnessed the minor league team he played on vanish in an earthquake. Street was born in Huntsville, Alabama, in 1882 and began his baseball career as a twenty-year-old in a Kentucky semi-pro league playing for sixty dollars a month. Coaches thought of Street as a scrappy catcher with a good arm and a less-than-impressive bat. By the time he was twenty-four years old, he was playing with the San Francisco Seals baseball team and living at the Golden Gate Hotel in the Bay Area. During the early hours of April 18, 1906, a sudden and violent jolt threw Street out of bed. He picked himself up, rushed to the window, and saw people running out of buildings, yelling "Fire!" and "Earthquake!" Street later told reporters, "If I live to be a hundred, I shall always remember that scene" of the great San Francisco earthquake. The cast members of *Beauty and the Beast* and *Babes in Toyland* also lived in the hotel. "What the female members of those troupes wore as they hiked for the exits is nobody's business," he said. The rear of the hotel began to shudder as the groups scrabbled down swaying staircases to the pavement below. Just as they reached the ground, a second shock split a water tank atop the hotel in half, sending water cascading over those lucky enough to escape the building's complete collapse. Street worked his way through the bricks and flames until he reached Golden Gate Park, where he spent the night with the weary and numb masses. After three days, he started for Oakland until a policeman stopped him. "You're going to take off your coat and begin pitching bricks out of the street," the guard ordered him. Everyone was needed to help out, and Street complied until two days later, when he happened upon one of his team's pitchers. The teammate knew how they could get out. "Don't hurry," he said, "but start for the ferry at the end of Market Street and pitch brick all the way." It took Street nine hours, but he made it to the wharf and crossed to Oakland, where the Elks Lodge gave him money to get as far as Denver. In Denver, the Red Cross bought him a ticket to Chicago. In

Chicago, the Refugee Committee handed him fare to Pittsburgh. In Pittsburgh, a local baseball pal lent him money to go as far as he could. The loan took him to Williamsport, Pennsylvania, where Street finally stopped. Pennsylvania seemed far enough away from earthquakes and fires. Later that summer, he convinced the town's Tri-State club, the Millionaires, to let him join the team. Being called a "Millionaire" was a name the indebted catcher would have been far too exhausted to find ironic.[26]

Street stumbled around a few more years before he made it to the big leagues in 1908 as the battery mate for Walter "Big Train" Johnson of the Washington Senators.* Big Train was at the beginning of his celebrated twenty-year career, perfecting a fastball that some hitters said was so invisible, it was like hitting a watermelon seed. "The first time I faced him, I watched him take that easy windup," Ty Cobb said. "And then something went past me that made me flinch. I hardly saw the pitch, but I heard it. . . . Every one of us knew we'd met the most powerful arm ever turned loose in a ballpark. "[27] While Street proved to be a good catcher for Johnson, his weak bat and problems with drinking—he was reportedly "lost" for five days during the 1909 season—forced a trade to the New York Highlanders in 1912.† After several more years roaming the minors, Street joined the army at the outbreak of World

---

*In his career, Johnson won 417 games, lost 270, and had a 2.36 ERA. Other achievements include striking out 3,508 batters, a record that held until 1983, when it was surpassed by Nolan Ryan. He was the only pitcher to win twenty games and hit .400 in a season. He also ranks third of all time in innings pitched with 5,923, and fifth of all time in complete games with 531. In 1936, Johnson was among the first five players inducted into baseball's Hall of Fame (www.cmgww.com/baseball/Johnson).

†Street was considered by many to be Johnson's most effective catcher. He recalled a time when he was out of catching action with an infected foot; a new pair of shoes had given him a serious blister. The foot had become infected, so "the doctor had to stick a knife into it . . . and I was laid up for eleven days," he said. The day Street returned to the bench, he watched as a young substitute catcher was unable to handle Johnson's fastballs. "Walter was just about blowing the little fellow down," Street remembered. "The ball would handcuff him and go all the way back to the grandstand and all the hitters were doing was striking out and running the bases." Finally manager Jim McAleer turned to Street and asked, "Can you stand up?" When Street replied that he could hop on one leg, the manager barked back, "Well, then, for God's sake, get in there and stop that" (Frank Graham, "Setting the Pace," n.p., n.d. Baseball Hall of Fame, Gabby Street file). During Street's career in the major leagues he hit .208, with one home run; his field percentage was .974, according to statistics in baseball-almanac.com.

War I and served two years with the First Gas Regiment—Chemical Warfare division in Argonne, France. He distinguished himself during the war as a sergeant, won a Purple Heart, and returned home where he "toured the bushes" as both a player and a manager.

The "Old Sarge" had few illusions about where his baseball career had ended up. While managing a Class C club in Muskogee, Oklahoma, Street was dejected and direct. "You can't go much lower than that in organized baseball," he said. "Not much of a job; not getting anywhere."[28] But the low period did not last for long. In 1929, he became a coach for the St. Louis Cardinals. Team vice president Branch Rickey helped him beat his drinking habit, and a year later Street was named manager of the Red Birds. He led the rough-and-tumble Gas House Gang to two consecutive pennants and one World Championship. By 1932, though, the Cards had slipped to sixth place, and the next year, the Cardinals' front office fired him. Some said a young upstart sensation, Dizzy Dean, had an argument with the older, easygoing Street. Cardinal executives thought they needed a firmer hand at the helm. Street's firing was followed by another dismal round of minor league clubs. He thought he was finished with baseball forever and would return to his family's home in Joplin, Missouri, but his love for the game would not let him go. "I'm going to put on a uniform just for the smell of the dust again," he said. "I've got baseball in my blood, I guess. I can't leave it alone."[29] In 1936 he moved his wife and two children to Saint Paul, where he became manager of the Saints.

When Tomboy stood observing Street that morning at Lexington Park, he was directing a baseball school for Twin City white boys.* There was not a single black child among the boys inside the ballpark, and there were certainly no girls, white or black. But Tomboy was used to being the exception and she began plotting ways to get Street's attention. She hoped he would let her into the school, even though it was

---

*Previous accounts of Tomboy's life described Gabby Street's baseball school as sponsored by Wheaties breakfast cereal. After consulting numerous Saint Paul historical sources and corporate archives at General Mills, I have been unable to confirm or deny that the school was associated with any Wheaties promotion (e-mail to author from Suzy Goodsell, manager, Internal Communications and Archives, General Mills, December 19, 2007).

obvious she would be bending a policy—formal or unspoken—about who could attend. Even as a young teenager, Tomboy already had learned how to get around the rules. She had been playing as the only girl in the Catholic boys' league for nearly four years, and she was used to boys' initial resistance, even hostility. Sometimes when she took a turn playing second base, boys would slide into her on double plays, hoping to rattle what they assumed was an inexperienced infielder. But Tomboy had been playing the game long enough to know how to take care of herself, as she said. Even more important, she also had learned that apprehension rather than anger fueled some of the resistance she met from boys. "It took a few years," she said, "but I realized some [male teammates] felt threatened by my presence."[30] Some of the young men attending Gabby Street's baseball school might have felt threatened by her presence at Lexington Park as well, but Tomboy continued to move closer to the clutch of players circled around Gabby. She strained to hear what the old coach was saying.

Street loved nothing better than a group of young players who were eager to learn more about baseball. He had just about had it with players in the major leagues who seemed to have only a passing interest in the game. "Today's players don't live and breathe baseball," he complained. "After a game they're more likely to head for a golf course or a country inn or a talking picture."[31] In the old days, he said, "we lived out baseball over a glass of beer and a ham sandwich. We played baseball around the hotel at night. Boys nowadays have too many automobiles. They drive up to the park two hours before the game, get in their suits, have a meeting, dress quickly after the game, jump in their cars and are 50 miles from each other in two hours. You can't learn baseball on a blackboard. You have to live the game, breathe it 24 hours with fellows who talk your language, know your problems. All the kids think of now is hit, hit, hit—no teamwork."[32] Street wanted to reach kids who loved the game the way he did. Perhaps that's why he felt Tomboy staring at him from outside his circle of students.

Dressed as she nearly always was, outside of school, in dungarees and a clean shirt, Tomboy stood waiting for the right moment to approach

Gabby. Street had no idea who she was, what she wanted, or why she kept studying him so intently. She had a beat-up old baseball glove in one hand and held her other arm cautiously against her side. Two months earlier, Tomboy had fractured her arm while riding her bike around Arundel and Washington in Saint Paul. She hit something in the road, tumbled into traffic, and instinctively stretched out her arms to break the fall. As she landed, a car hit her. "Miss Marcenia Stone," the newspaper reported, "was struck by a hit and run driver Tuesday night."[33] The injury had taken nearly six weeks to heal, but Tomboy prided herself on being tough and had rejoined her team. Not giving in to pain was another way Tomboy proved she was "one of the boys." Once when she took a turn as catcher in the league, she was hit by a ball and knocked unconscious. She decided to give up catching—"I left that alone"—but the injury never once made her swear off baseball.[34]

Gabby Street looked at this girl with curiosity; he knew nothing about what her arms could do—injured or otherwise. As a white man who never read black newspapers and barely knew they existed, he would not have known that local reporters called the young woman observing him "one of the best young girl athletes in St. Paul."[35]

A teammate once described Gabby Street as being built like a sergeant, "rather dour of countenance and with a real vocabulary in the two languages required in the army—English and profane."[36] Without thinking, Street gruffly shooed Tomboy away and turned his attention back to the boys in the baseball school. Undaunted by his rough demeanor, she returned to the school a while later, stood in the same place outside the group of white teenagers, and waited to ask Street if she could join them. Tomboy had no illusions and understood that a girl playing baseball was not only unwelcome but was also considered reprehensible to some. "[My parents] would have stopped me if they could, but there was nothing they could do about it," she said. Neighborhood boys "told me to go home and be a girl and others asked why I insisted in playing baseball." She was called a "bull dagger" and "was did everything but spit on," Tomboy later said, but she continued to play.[37] In the past her persistence had paid off, so she continued to wait until Gabby Street, annoyed that she had returned to his school once more, told her to get out and go home. Girls didn't play baseball, he thought, and he wasn't going to waste his time on some black girl who no doubt couldn't keep up. Baseball required discipline and a dedication to strategy. Why include a girl when a boy might really get something out of the instruction? Baseball is "a good thing for boys," he always told reporters, and that's why his teams always invited white boys out to the park before games "to try their baseball wings," as he put it. Baseball brought out the best qualities in a boy, he said, and helped young men become professional. "Professional," the word Gabby Street used to motivate his young charges, was the same word that signaled excellence to Tomboy Stone.[38]

Of course, Street being Street, he couldn't simply teach baseball strategy to the white boys; he also had to pepper his lessons with stories about the old days. He had a storehouse of anecdotes that he was happy to share with anyone who loved baseball. Before spring training that year, Street talked baseball to civic and professional groups in Saint Paul—sometimes appearing before as many as two luncheons and two dinners a day. He accompanied his talks with lantern slides depicting the lighter side of baseball and generated so much good will in the community that a newspaper said he was as good as a "March thaw."[39] Sitting now with his baseball school boys at the Lexington ballpark, Street would put aside a strategy session for a while and spin a tale. It was almost as if he were back with the St. Louis Cardinals after a game, sitting around the hotel with a clutch of young teammates gathered to hear the old man sit up late, smoke his pipe, and talk of playing with Ruth and Cobb and Big Train. While hearing Street's tales of baseball's great players was thrilling, everyone always wanted to hear the same story. It wasn't about playing baseball but about the ball—the one Street caught in Washington, D.C. If he tired of telling the legendary story, he didn't let on. Street would lean back, rewind his memory nearly thirty years, and begin.

It was like this, he said. It was 1908. He was twenty-six. It was the year Ty Cobb and Honus Wagner won the batting championship.

One night a group of writers drinking at the National Press Club in Washington were talking baseball and arguing about who was the best catcher who ever lived. "Street," Preston Gibson, the society editor of the *Washington Post*, said. Gibson claimed Street had such a deft touch, he could pick daisies with a catcher's mitt. I bet he could catch anything, he wagered. How about catching a ball tossed from the top of the Washington Monument, one of the writers suggested. After pestering Street with the dare for weeks, Gibson finally cornered the catcher and asked if they could try to accomplish the feat the next day. Street agreed, and on the morning of August 21, 1908, he accompanied Gibson and few onlookers to the Washington Monument. Street looked up—555 feet up—into the blinding sun to the top of the obelisk. Gibson had called ahead and received permission from the superintendent of grounds to try the stunt. Street looked up again. He was bareheaded, in plain clothes, and had not brought his chest protector or any of the other regulation equipment he usually wore when catching for the Washington Senators. Gibson headed to the top of the Monument with a basket of baseballs and a twenty-foot wooden chute he had cobbled together to send the balls hurtling through the air. Gibson carefully set the first ball on the chute and sent it rolling. On the ground below, Street lost the ball in the sun, and it landed with a heavy thud on the grass. A second, third, and fourth ball fell out of the sky. Again, Street could not find them against the sun. Let's move to the shady side, someone suggested, and Street walked around to where he hoped he could get a better look at the balls. He positioned himself to make a waist-high catch rather than one over his head. That way, I may only break a wrist or an arm, he thought. Gibson rolled a few more balls down the chute. Street missed them all. Toss them out a bit further away from the Monument, he called to Gibson. Street could see Gibson's arm as it stretched out the window, but the ball was invisible. The strain of looking up into the sky for so long had grown too much for Street, so he asked his friend George McBride—the Senators shortstop and his old pal who lent him money after the San Francisco earthquake—

to spot the balls for him as they came hurtling down. Street figured he would only look up when McBride told him to, when the ball was about two hundred feet over his head. A tenth, eleventh, twelfth ball rushed past Street. One ball remained: the thirteenth. Gibson let the ball fly. McBride yelled out. Street looked up and instinctively raised his glove above his head as though he were snagging a pop foul for the Senators.

He caught it.*

Gibson later told Street that when he caught the ball, the pop sounded like a .38 revolver going off. The next day, fans at the Senators game, who had read about the feat, gave Street a wild ovation. Newspaper headlines proclaimed "Fans Get the Willies Figuring on Street's Feat."[40] The ballistics department of the army estimated the ball fell at 290 miles an hour, with an equivalent weight of nearly three hundred pounds. "Sure they were heavy," Street later said, "but not too heavy. I just used my regular mitt—no sponge or anything."[41]

Tomboy loved old baseball stories as much as the Saint Paul boys at Street's baseball school. It would have surprised Gabby Street to know the young black girl who kept pestering him knew baseball history better than most and had read nearly every baseball book published.[42] She would have liked to hear about the old catcher's mitt that he rigged to make balls sound extra loud when they slammed into the leather, or tales about how he had broken nine out of ten fingers in thirty years of catching, or about the time Pepper Martin put an alligator in the St. Louis Cardinals' team car.[43] Tomboy certainly was not what Street expected. And when Tomboy showed up one more time at his baseball school after being told to go away, the old white man began to smile at her determination. Of course, Tomboy did not realize that Gabby Street was not what she expected, either. Street was a member of the Ku Klux Klan.

---

*The ball that Gabby Street caught is enshrined in baseball's Hall of Fame in Cooperstown. The ball, a scuffed Spaulding, is commemorated with a plaque: "Attempts to catch a ball dropped from the top of the Washington Monument failed since its 1888 dedication, until Gabby Street succeeded by snaring this ball on August 21, 1908."

Street once told New York sportswriter Fred Lieb that he was a member of the Klan. "Gabby Street, Rogers Hornsby, and Tris Speaker, fellow stars from the old Confederate states, told me they were members of the Ku Klux Klan. I don't know whether Cobb was a Klansman, but I suspect he was," Lieb wrote.[44] Lieb's hunch about Cobb was well founded. Lieb said Cobb "had a contempt for black people" and, in Cobb's own language, "never would take their lip." When Cobb was with the Detroit Tigers, he stayed out of Ohio for a year and a half to avoid arrest in Cleveland for knifing a black waiter. Lieb reported that the Tigers settled the case out of court by paying the victim.[45]

Street's racism, while not as violent as Cobb's hatred, nevertheless revealed itself in the way he reduced black people to stock characters, erasing their individuality and even their names. While most people assumed Charles Street's nickname, "Gabby," came from his constant chatter behind the plate, the name actually had roots in his racism. "We used to call the colored boys 'Gabby' down in Alabama, and when I wanted a new baseball thrown into the game I used to call, 'Hey Gabby, where's the baseball?' . . . If you see a black boy and want him, and you don't know his name, you yell, 'Hey, Gabby.' It works in St. Louis, too, and if you don't believe it, try it. To me all black boys have been 'Gabby,' and I got my nickname from the use of that word and not, as is commonly believed, because I am a chatterbox."[46]

Tomboy was not immune to the reach of the Klan, even in Saint Paul. In 1923, several universities in the Big Ten had student Klan groups, and units of the Ku Klux Klan existed in Saint Paul and Minneapolis. The 1923 University of Minnesota yearbook featured a photograph of a KKK homecoming float rolling down the streets of the Twin Cities.[47] At one time in the 1920s the Minnesota KKK published three newspapers and bought twenty acres of land in Owatonna in hopes of creating a "Klan Park"—a development that never materialized, though the Klan owned the land for years.[48] Minnesota Klan activities primarily focused on Catholics, Jews, immigrants, and socialists, although the Klan's reach would have intimidated anyone who was not a white Protestant. Nationally, the Klan's influence peaked in the early 1920s, when it claimed nearly three million members. By the 1930s, membership had fallen to several thousand men. The 1925 murder conviction of Indiana Grand Dragon D. C. Stephenson virtually ended national Klan activities. When Street came to Saint Paul in the 1930s, the Klan's public demonstrations were almost over: the last Minnesota meeting had been held in 1927. Public displays of racism, however, took other forms. The same year that Street ran his baseball school, Saint Paul's celebrated International Festival of Nations admitted "confusion" over how blacks would be depicted in a parade. Black residents were represented by a "procession featuring Booker T. Washington, George Washington Carver, James Weldon Johnson, Marion Anderson, and a group of tap dancers—as indigenous Americans."[49]

By the 1930s, some men like Gabby Street who had been members of the Klan in its early days expressed their beliefs less in violent action and more in personal philosophy. They would not let their racist principles stand in the way of practical or economic pursuits. At times, they even could treat an individual black person or a Catholic with kindness and respect while at the same time denouncing the racial and religious groups the person represented. When the Alabama native Street saw Tomboy Stone return to his baseball school time and time again, he may have seen her passion for the game more than her race, her gender, or her religion. He could make an exception for one black girl who seemed obsessed with baseball without re-evaluating his own racist attitudes toward all black citizens. After watching Tomboy return to his baseball camp so many times with her request to be included, Street finally relented. He temporarily put aside his racist assumptions and told the persistent girl to go out on the field and "show those boys up."[50]

Street later recalled, "I just couldn't get rid of her until I gave her a chance. Every time I chased her away, she would go around the corner and come back to plague me again." When Tomboy took to the field at Gabby Street's baseball school, her ability astonished the old manager. He was impressed with the way she fielded: her neat handling of hard-hit grounders, the way she snuck up on slow rollers and stretched to "spear line drives." Her batting caught his eye as well. She had discerning judgment and knew when to be patient. Her hitting was a repertoire of long flies, line drives, and "grass cutters." Street took a liking to Tomboy, and she enjoyed the old catcher as well. As they talked, Tomboy confessed that she wished she had more professional equipment, especially professional baseball shoes like some of the white boys had. My mother couldn't afford to buy any, she said, neglecting to add that her parents wanted to keep her appetite for baseball under control. "I haven't anything to do with the color line that keeps your people out of baseball," Tomboy remembered Street telling her. "And I haven't got anything with that other unwritten law that keeps women out of the game," he said. "But if I did . . ."[51] Several days later, on July 17, Tomboy celebrated her fifteenth birthday. The Old Sarge gave her baseball shoes.

"It was just like a miracle," Tomboy said.[52]

By July of the following year, Gabby Street was gone. He resigned his position with the Saints and joined the hapless St. Louis Browns in the major leagues, first as a coach and later as manager. But after a year and a half with the Browns, Street retired from baseball entirely. Reporters caught up with him at his home in Joplin, Missouri, where Gabby tried to convince them that his life in baseball was happily finished. "Ah," he said, as he lit his pipe and patted his dog. "This, ladies and gentlemen, is the life. No ball club to worry about and no bad front office to be [scared] of. This, I repeat, is the well-known life."[53] When the summer of 1936 came to a close for Tomboy, she had behind her four years of Catholic boys' league play, over a year of HighLex girls' softball, a couple of years hanging around the Saint Paul Men's Meat Packing League, and a hard-earned stint at baseball school with a former World Series manager. The cleats Gabby Street gave her were more than equipment. They were a gift of validation to her—a stranger's belief that someday she might be able to go forward in baseball. With the shoes neatly placed in their original box and ready to be laced up, Tomboy Stone felt her life in professional baseball was just beginning.

Barnstorming with the Colored Giants

I've stayed in the front yard all my life.
I want a peek at the back
Where it's rough and untended and
hungry weed grows.
A girl gets sick of a rose.

—Gwendolyn Brooks[1]

Gabby Street's baseball camp ended with the close of summer, and fifteen-year-old Tomboy reluctantly returned to classes. "I wasn't happy going to school," she said. "I don't know if I was slow to start or what, but it was rough." Tomboy entered the Saint Paul public schools when she was ten, after her family moved from West Virginia. When she turned twelve and was ready for junior high, local teachers recommended Hammond, the district's school for special education students. Teachers realized that Tomboy had difficulty keeping up with the other youngsters in class, did not appear interested in academic work, and often grew frustrated. She may have had an undetected learning disability, but schools during the Depression rarely had resources for evaluating students' specific learning problems. Without knowing exactly what her learning difficulty was, Tomboy entered Hammond—a school that emphasized vocational subjects to prepare pupils for work in the trades. Members of the Stone family and others who knew her said Tomboy did have trouble discerning subtleties—academically and socially. As one relative later put it, Tomboy "couldn't read between the lines." Her literal mind often caused her to miss nuances. She saw simple explanations where others found complexity. A short attention span and an inability to keep still also contributed to her problems in the classroom. Being labeled a "special child" by educators and her family because she went to Hammond Junior High humiliated Tomboy. She realized the word "special" was a euphemism for intellectually slow, and the label felt patronizing and demeaning to her. "I was in a category of my own," she said sarcastically. She often would dredge up the phrase "special child" when describing how others viewed her. Tomboy Stone, she said, was the "special child," an odd, even aberrant girl. That perception eroded her confidence and stole her self-respect at times. Years later, describing herself as a teenager, Tomboy said that "a 'special child' [was the] kind of youngster who didn't have too much love for themselves."[2]

As much as Tomboy felt stigmatized for attending Hammond Junior High, the school did have teachers who found a way to build on the talents they saw in her. "A teacher told me I could use my hands," Tomboy said, and "Mrs. Covern, Mrs. Van Heusen, Mrs. Egan knew that I loved sports." Teachers realized, as Father Keefe initially suspected, that if Tomboy could excel in one area, her self-esteem might rise. Florence Egan, Hammond's physical education teacher, invited her along to watch competitive skaters at the city's Hippodrome rink. Another teacher spoke to Boykin and Willa Stone about their daughter's extraordinary reflexes and hand-eye coordination and encouraged them to allow her to join the school's girls' sports teams. By Tomboy's final year at Hammond, in the spring of 1937, she had so distinguished herself as the school's top athlete that she was the honored guest at Saint Paul's Emblem Dinner for junior high school athletes. The *Minneapolis Spokesman* noted that Miss Stone "is always taking away honors." Tomboy became the first girl in eighteen years to letter in three sports in a single year: track, high jump, and diamond ball (a Minnesota version of softball). When Tomboy accepted her award at the evening banquet, she acknowledged that Hammond had made a difference in her life, and she thanked Mrs. Egan as well as her principal and her music and social studies teachers for encouraging her athletic abilities.[3]

Tomboy's parents were pleased with her Emblem Dinner recognition since they had long preached the importance of personal accomplishment. "I just want you to be somebody," Tomboy's mother told her.[4] Willa and Boykin believed there were two ways to get ahead: know the right people and get an education. By the "right people" they meant doctors or lawyers, people who had money or notable achievements. Willa took pride in frequently entertaining the "right people" from Saint Paul's black community. She would call the local bakery and order special bread for luncheon sandwiches. Tomboy would be put on cleaning detail in order to make the family's large Victorian home proper and inviting. "Mrs. Boykin Stone," the newspaper reported, "entertained her mother, Mrs. J. B. Smith of Bluefield, W. Va., with a birthday party . . . at her home. Several classical selections were given by Miss Johnnie Mae Smith, sister of Mrs. Stone."[5] Tomboy knew her mother could be demanding and called her "the sergeant" when she couldn't hear. Willa was just as firm as her husband about the importance of personal distinction and independence, and she socialized as a way of "getting ahead" in business. She even went so far as to join different churches from time to time in order to participate in a variety of social activities. At one point, Willa attended the Methodist church, her daughters went to the Catholic church, and her sister Johnnie sang in the Lutheran church choir. Unlike Tomboy, who looked to the Catholic church for moral guidance, Willa viewed her religious involvement as a way of establishing herself in the community. But as much as Willa was concerned about propriety and what the "right people" thought, she eventually did give her daughter permission, of sorts, to follow her heart. She knew Marcenia would never feel at home in a world of ladies' luncheons and music recitals. As unconventional as playing baseball was for a girl, Willa Stone knew the sport gave her daughter confidence. "If people are going to talk," she told Tomboy, "then give them something to talk about."[6]

When Tomboy approached her mother with an idea about an even more serious baseball possibility than Catholic league baseball and junior high sports, Willa Stone may have regretted her earlier words. After the interest Gabby Street had shown in her, Tomboy felt emboldened and her baseball aspirations grew. She asked her mother if she could start traveling on weekends with a barnstorming baseball team of black men. The idea developed after one of the teenager's routine circles around Saint Paul playgrounds looking for pickup baseball games. Tomboy had noticed a group of men taking batting practice at a local park. She may have been hesitant in the classroom, but she rarely was shy on the baseball diamond. She asked the man who seemed to be in charge if she could shag balls for them, and George White said yes. White had once played center field for a semi-pro team and now spent his free time organizing games for area youngsters and managing the local Twin City Colored Giants. "I stayed around them," Tomboy said, and earned a few bucks for shagging balls. White always had his eye on the lookout for talented young people who could add youth to the traveling Giants team. Most of the players White managed were former semi-pro athletes who had baseball smarts but who were not as fast on the base paths as they once had been. George White had found thirteen-year-old John Cotton playing against a local fast-pitch softball team at Rondo's Welcome Hall fields. The young second baseman was surprised when Mr. White asked if he would be interested in a Colored Giants tryout over at Como Park. Cotton showed up, did well, and White opened a spot for him on the team. "My mother and uncle knew everyone" on the Giants, Cotton said, and they did not worry about him spending weekends playing in nearby towns. Mrs. Cotton may have thought twice, however, when the team started one-month summer road trips to Canada. John was too young to have any official identification and once was detained at the border when the squad tried to re-enter the United States. Only when the team scrambled to the back of the bus and found a game handbill featuring the young boy's photograph were border guards convinced that the boy was a ballplayer barnstorming through Ontario and Manitoba.

When George White discovered that Tomboy could do more on the baseball field than shag balls, he asked if she'd like to join John Cotton and the other Colored Giants and barnstorm on the weekends. "Mother wanted me [close] to her," Tomboy said, "but I told her it was a way to make a little extra money." Mrs. Stone gave her daughter permission, and George White gave Tomboy her first professional uniform—a ragtag, used one but a uniform nonetheless. No one on the team made much money, Tomboy admitted. The team would "travel back and forth to Wisconsin," she said, and "go out of town on the weekend, because [older players] had to hold jobs during the week." On a typical Sunday, Tomboy would attend St. Peter Claver mass, then get in old cars with the team and drive someplace such as Kenosha, Wisconsin, for a game. She was sixteen and the only girl on the team. "She was a ballplayer," John Cotton said, plain and simple, and "could throw just like a man." Tomboy made two or three dollars a game: the team played percentage or "PC" ball, with the winners earning 60 percent of the gate and the losers 40 percent. Tomboy enjoyed playing with the men, even though some were former semipro baseball players and far more experienced athletes than she. Tomboy did not mind being occasionally overmatched on the diamond; it helped improve her game, she thought. Playing for the Colored Giants also gave her a taste for traveling, getting out of her Rondo neighborhood, and meeting new people. "That was good," she said. "Traveling was the greatest education I could have."[7]

When Tomboy joined the Colored Giants, she became part of a long line of traveling Midwest baseball teams. Black baseball players in Minnesota went as far back as the nineteenth century when Prince Honeycutt, a former Union Army "mess boy," played for the white Fergus Falls North Stars in 1873. During one game that year, Honeycutt scored eight runs as the North Stars defeated the Big Fellers with the unbelievable high score of 60–54. Two years later, the Fergus Falls team—then named the Musculars—traveled a day and a half by wagon for a game in Perham. This time they were on the receiving end of a defeat, 43–64. Organized black baseball teams first made their appearance in Minnesota in 1876 and achieved prominence in the early part of the twentieth century with the great University of Minnesota first baseman Bobby Marshall. Marshall played for the Saint Paul Colored Gophers against Midwest regional teams including the well-known Chicago Leland Giants. The Colored Gophers and other teams such as the Minneapolis Colored Keystones were so successful that they gave rise to other traveling teams, including the Colored Giants in Duluth, the Hub City Browns in Aberdeen, South Dakota, and the Wonders in Buxton, Iowa. Frequently black ball clubs played white touring teams from Chicago and beyond. When traveling black players came into towns for a game, the residents viewed them as a novelty. Black families in prairie towns were few, and curious white fans packed the stands. But the matchups at times moved beyond novelty and sparked more than a flicker of racial competitiveness as white fans cheered for white teams to beat black ball clubs.[8]

The Twin City Colored Giants already had achieved distinction and some local fame—for their gumption, if nothing else. If there were no black teams available to play, the Colored Giants played semipro white teams in towns across Minnesota and Wisconsin—and they usually won. Occasionally they played integrated teams that included Negro League stars and whites from minor league teams. Integrated baseball teams in the Upper Midwest were not uncommon. With fewer blacks in the region, white residents were less concerned by the larger ramifications of integration. They felt less threatened, for example, than the white population in larger cities by the prospect of an integrated job force.[9] In August 1935, the Colored Giants squared off in one series against an integrated team, the Bismark Churchills, that boasted an extraordinary lineup including black pitchers Ted "Double Duty" Radcliffe, Hilton Smith, Barney Morris, and Leroy "Satchel" Paige. During the year, the Bismark pitching quartet combined for fifty-five wins and six losses; the team's offense was equally impressive, outscoring opponents by nearly three hundred runs. Nearly a decade after he played with them, Paige said that the 1935 Bismark team was the "best team I ever saw; the best players I ever played with."[10] Given that the team played across the desolate Dakotas and their games were rarely mentioned by metropolitan newspapers, few baseball fans recognized the team's brilliance. "Who ever heard of them?" Paige said.[11]

The Colored Giants from Saint Paul had. Many of the players such as right fielder and power hitter Maceo Breedlove knew about the exceptional team and were eager for the challenge. A few teammates, however, were nervous. When the Colored Giants pulled up to the Bismarck, North Dakota, ballpark, they were astonished by the big-city look of the field. Club owners had pumped five thousand dollars into the field for improvements, adding three thousand new seats, bleachers for children, and a five-hundred-slot car park for fans who wanted to watch the game along the outfield fence. An elevated train track stood over right field for standing-room-only crowds. Fans said the field was the best in the Upper Midwest and larger than any major league park outside of Shibe Field in Philadelphia. It was 332 feet down each line and 460 feet to center. Paige said the Bismarck farmers loved the team and relished betting on games. They came to the field, he said, "with hats full of money."[12] No wonder some Colored Giant players felt wary.

The Colored Giants held their own in the first two games, even though they lost 8–5 and 9–5. Breedlove went two for four in the opener and two for four in the second game, including a home run against Smith. For the closing game, the Colored Giants knew they would be facing Satchel Paige. One Colored Giants player left word he was sick that day and couldn't suit up. "He didn't want to play against [Paige]," Breedlove said. Bismarck exploded out of the gate with five runs. Saint Paul answered with two. In the second, Bismarck added another four and then nine more in the fourth. Only Breedlove could figure out how to hit Paige. He homered early in the game and later added two doubles. As a team, however, the Colored Giants were completely overpowered. By the bottom of the eighth, Bismarck and Paige were ahead a whopping 21–5. When Bismarck came to bat, the players swung around to the opposite side of the plate to give their opponents a break—or perhaps additional humiliation. In the top of the ninth, Satchel took control of the game and made an announcement. "A catcher and a first baseman," he declared. "That's all I want." The grandiose gesture was a favorite of Paige's—a way to stir up crowds that might have been dozing during a lopsided slugfest. On command, all fielders trotted into the Bismarck dugout. In short order, Paige struck out the first two batters. Breedlove came to the plate. "Looked like everybody in North Dakota at that ball game," he remembered. Satchel threw; Breedlove fouled it off. The Colored Giants in their motley uniforms looked up to the stands and saw crowds of people now yelling and screaming, urging Satchel on. It didn't make them feel any better to know that they were the center of attention for thousands. *Why don't you let Satchel strike you out and get it over with?* one Giants teammate thought. Breedlove dug in, fouled off another, and another. "I bet I hit fifteen foul balls," he said. A Bismarck player who knew Breedlove from Saint Paul yelled from the opposing dugout, "Satchel done picked the baddest boy on the ball club to show up." Paige was throwing the ball so fast, Breedlove couldn't get around in time to make contact and fouled off a few more. Tired of throwing his heater, Paige served up a curveball. Breedlove was waiting for it, connected, and whacked the ball into an empty left field. With no one there to catch the long fly, Breedlove trotted around the bases with his second home run of the game. When a teammate later asked where he found the grit to keep up with Paige's endless blaze of fastballs, Breedlove was definitive. "I wouldn't let nobody make a fool out of me in front of all these people."[13]

Perhaps it was the determination, self-respect, and perseverance that Breedlove and other Colored Giants represented that appealed to Tomboy. Their local renown impressed Boykin Stone as well. While Willa would never sit in the stands and watch her daughter play ball, she had learned that baseball offered Tomboy more than recreation. "When I found out I could throw a baseball that was it. I knew then what I wanted to do," Tomboy said.[14] Unlike her friend Janabelle, who turned to coaching and teaching as a way to maintain her involvement with sports, Tomboy only wanted to be in the game. Coaching was too far from the action, and she liked being part of a team. The Colored Giants needed her, not just as a novelty to bring in crowds but as a legitimate player who could help win games. "They took her seriously," John Cotton said, "because she produced [runs]."[15] If fans came to their games because they wanted a look at Tomboy and more money came into players' pockets as a result, everyone on the Colored Giants was happy. By the end of July, the team had played eight games and won five. A Minneapolis newspaper reported that the Colored Giants had "the distinction of having a girl pitcher on its roster. No other team in the Northwest can boast the same. Miss Marcenia Stone, 16-year-old girl athlete, has been doing much to amuse the fans with her great catcher and wonder hitting power."[16] Tomboy was eager to play any position she could. During the season, she took a turn at the infield, played center field, and occasionally pitched. From the multiple playing positions to the bouncing from town to town to the mismatched uniforms—all the improvisations appealed to Tomboy. There was an inventive, extemporaneous, fuguelike quality to the games that she loved. Playing baseball felt as if the rules she lived by—at home, in school, at church—no longer applied and she was making up her own on the fly. "Shag ball," she called it.[17]

Playing was only part of the incentive of joining the Twin City Colored Giants. Traveling with the team to games was another. When Tomboy took a seat in one of the team's two beat-up cars, she enrolled in an on-the-road seminar in black history and the science of baseball. The Colored Giants' stories became the textbook her public school classes ignored. Breedlove talked of being recruited ten years before to play for the original Negro House of David barnstorming team.* He had to keep his hair long and grow a beard in order to look like the other House of David players. He also had to master the art of entertaining the crowds. House of David teams knew that crowds came to barnstorming games to watch baseball and be entertained. Between innings, players quickly tossed the ball around to fans' delight. Soon the rapid ball-handling transformed itself into the House of David's signature play. At nearly every game, in the middle of the fifth inning, four players would line up and play an acrobatic game of catch, complete with balls thrown behind their backs, fake tosses, and wobbly baseballs sliding down their arms. Young John Cotton loved it. The performance wasn't demeaning, he said. "It was fun. Everybody knew we could play ball."[18] Chinx Worley, the Colored Giants' third baseman, told of playing for the New York Cubans—a team where African American players posed as Cubans in order to bring crowds through the gate. Then there were all the team nicknames, those imaginative concoctions that were a fixture of Rondo. There was "Rubber Man" Johnson, a right fielder, Tom "Rotation" English—so called for his slick pool cue maneuvers—and Bobby "Grand Old Man" Marshall, of University of Minnesota fame, the team captain. While riding around in the cars, talk would turn to strategy, as older players explained a few tricks to the youngsters. Tomboy listened carefully. Their conversation was the instruction she had craved. Take, for example, the "swing bunt." To lay down a swing bunt, an older player said, a batter winds up, takes a full swing, and drops the ball lightly right between the catcher and the pitcher. Every-

*The Israelite House of David was a Christian commune in Benton Harbor, Michigan, known for its devotion to vegetarianism and celibacy. Founded in 1903 by Benjamin and Mary Purnell, the colony reached its peak in the 1920s when it had as many as nine hundred members. In 1914, men who played baseball in the colony began playing outside teams around the country, and by the 1930s there were multiple House of David teams consisting of hired players. House of David teams often traveled with accompanying black teams and made a condition of play that the hosts also take on the black team. Many baseball historians credit the House of David teams with helping move major league baseball toward integration.

body is fooled. Or the "delayed steal"—a combination of pretense and nonchalance that gave the infield jitters.

Just the process of getting to the games was a lesson in spontaneity. The Colored Giants traveled in two old cars with a handmade wooden trailer rattling behind. Breedlove's nephew, Smokey—the team's all-round driver-cook-mechanic-and-sometimes-player—occasionally slept in the rickety enclosure. The trailer held bats and balls, bases, benches when necessary, even one ambidextrous pitcher's six-fingered glove. When one of the cars broke down, Smokey lassoed one automobile to the other with the trailer bringing up the rear. The team limped into the next town like an old dog trailing a bum leg. Money for gasoline was always a problem. The split of gate receipts did not always pay much money when divided among all the players. Sometimes payment came in the form of a ham sandwich and a glass of lemonade. On one occasion, after a couple of rainouts left no gate receipts to divide, Breedlove had to hock his watch in order to buy gas for the trip back to Saint Paul. Not every road trip could be completed in an afternoon. There were times when the team brought tents, found campsites, slept in the cars or in the dugout. Like the other male teams she had played with so far, teammates looked upon Tomboy as a baseball player, not a girl. "She was thin, kind of built like a boy," a teammate said.[19] "We never thought of her as a date, she was such a good player." If Tomboy or her parents had any concerns about impropriety on the road, those worries were not sufficient to keep her from playing.[20] The Stones were too strict to place their teenage daughter in a risky situation.

Not all that Tomboy learned from the Colored Giants was about baseball. She also witnessed subtle signs of racism that older teammates tried to shield from her. There were whispers about which restaurants would serve black people or questions about why opposing white players—so seemingly friendly during the game—would turn their backs once the game was over. Even John Cotton and Tomboy, the youngest players on the team, could sense the cold treatment. Rarely were they invited to join white teams for food or drink after a game—rarely did conversation between the two teams even continue after the last out. Their opponents made it clear that they wanted the Colored Giants to pick up their equipment and get out of town. Manager George White had seen more flagrant expressions of bigotry, of racism so deeply rooted that the offender was unable to recognize it. On a road trip to Bloomer, Wisconsin, a field announcer presented the Bloomer lineup, then turned to the Colored Giants. "And now, the starting lineup for the niggers," the announcer said. White was so stunned and angry that he ran out of the dugout. "We will not play unless that man [the announcer] is gone," he forcefully said. Unaware of how he had triggered the confrontation, the announcer asked, repeatedly, "What did I do wrong? What did I do wrong?" Tears were in his eyes. "He really didn't know," a player said.[21]

Playing on the Twin City Colored Giants showed Tomboy a world outside Saint Paul. Of course, that world was only a few hundred miles away from her Rondo neighborhood, but it did help her sense the future. It suggested a way to make a living that did not involve being a nurse or a teacher or a secretary—careers her family and school envisioned for young women. When her brother, Quinten, began to show talent in sports, Tomboy told him to stay out of her world. "You get your own dreams," she told him, "because I've got mine."[22] She also continued hanging around the meatpacking plants down by the stockyards until she finally persuaded workers to add her to a local team in the men's Meat Packing League.[23] More times than not after the barnstorming summer of 1937, Tomboy skipped classes at school. After Hammond Junior High, she moved up to Mechanic Arts High School in Saint Paul. Perhaps she did not find attentive teachers like the ones who encouraged her at Hammond, or perhaps she simply decided that school would always be too much of a personal struggle. "I was a dropout," she said. "I'd come in and come out."[24] To remove her from distractions and show their daughter more conventional possibilities than baseball, the Stones sent her to New York to spend the Christmas season with her aunt Byntha Smith, a registered nurse at Sea View Hospital on Staten Island.[25] Later the family tried another trip, a much longer stay with her grandparents in West Virginia. Tomboy enjoyed rural life. Her grandmother taught her to cook beans and ham hocks. She was especially fond of her grandfather, who trained horses. "I love riding bareback," she said. Tomboy also enjoyed the currents of country life: gardening in the sun, eating the hearty chicken patties and handmade biscuits that her grandmother prepared early in the morning before the family went out to the field.[26]

What she did not like was the journey to and from West Virginia. Riding a train through the Jim Crow South was a new experience for Tomboy—an encounter with a more aggressive racism than she had ever known. Her friend Evelyn Edwards worried for weeks before she traveled with her mother to Georgia. Evelyn had heard so much about "the conditions" that going south terrified her. "I knew what slavery and lynching and tarring and feathering were," she said, "but I didn't know what 'conditions' were." She expected "conditions" to be worse than anything she could imagine.[27] To travel to West Virginia, Tomboy boarded the train in Saint Paul and rode through Wisconsin, Illinois, Indiana, Ohio, and on over the Ohio River into Kentucky. While she could sit anywhere she wanted to as the train passed through the Midwestern states, the minute it crossed into Kentucky, she had to move. Porters would nudge colored riders who were in the "wrong" car and point to the signs at the door. "Whites Only." Tomboy's friend Jimmy Griffin traveled the same route when he went from Rondo to West Virginia for college. A porter came up to him and said that if he didn't move to the Jim Crow car, the conductor would put him off the train. Griffin moved. As he walked with his bulky luggage into the black car, he noticed the train seats had not been cleaned. He had only one suit and he was wearing it. Wanting to keep his clothes presentable for college, he took pages from a newspaper and spread them over the seat. A black woman noticed and approached the nineteen-year-old. "Son, where are you from?" she asked sympathetically. "You must be from up North somewhere. I've been watching you." After an hour or so, the porter came back to the car and tapped Griffin on the shoulder, informing the young man that he could return to his previous car. "We just passed into Kenova, West Virginia," he said. "In West Virginia there's no Jim Crow laws on the railroad." It was lucky for young adults from Saint Paul that the porters were helpful. "I don't know how far you're going," a porter told Griffin, "but if you're gonna eat in the diner, you've gotta eat before you get to White Sulphur Springs, West Virginia, 'cause then you cross into Virginia and then the Jim Crow goes back into effect."[28] For Tomboy, Evelyn, and Jimmy, riding Jim Crow trains was not an education they wanted.

After the summer of 1940, when she turned nineteen, Tomboy officially dropped out of high school. She did not earn her diploma. She spent her days working small jobs and playing baseball as often as she could.[29] There were so many teams that played for only a half season and then disbanded that Tomboy could not keep track of all the teams she had been on. "I think I played for the House of David," she said.[30]

Tomboy was not the only one who could not keep straight all the many black baseball teams. Black ball was a lively jumble of subdivisions, playing levels, and schedules. There were local recreational teams that played on Sundays and statewide barnstorming teams that traveled on weekends. There also were semi-pro teams that played throughout the week for meager money and across a regional area, California, Oregon, and Washington state, for example. In addition, there were independent national and regional barnstorming teams, such as the Negro House of David. Some geographic areas also had semi-pro leagues, such as the Negro Southern League, with organized schedules, promotion, and league championships. Athletes, many of whom played baseball without a contract, were apt to "jump" from team to team when they were offered better pay, a longer season, or greater visibility for moving up. Playing schedules also were idiosyncratic and hastily organized, with semi-pro teams occasionally playing regional barnstorming teams or any other black team that was passing through the area. Team owners were more concerned about filling up a ballpark with paying fans than they were playing another team in their specific league or region. As varied and at times disorganized as local, semi-pro, regional, and independent black baseball was, all ambitious black ballplayers during the Jim Crow era aspired to one goal: the Negro League. The Negro League offered black players the highest level of play, equivalent to the white major leagues.

Even though baseball players had moved from playing for regional teams such as the Twin City Colored Giants to the Negro League, Boykin Stone was not pleased with what he saw as his daughter's floundering in baseball. A person has to "have a purpose," he declared. In his eyes, the spare change that Tomboy earned barnstorming did not amount to anything. He could see no future for her in the sport. By 1943, as she moved into her twenties, Tomboy continued to drift. With the drifting came some problems. One problem was William Gillespie, an acquaintance and forty-five-year-old troublemaker who saw himself as Tomboy's suitor. For several months, Gillespie harassed her with telephone calls and telegrams, even after Tomboy said she had no romantic interest in him. One night in March, Gillespie attacked Tomboy. He jumped her, knocked her to the pavement, and kicked her in the face. He was arrested, and when the judge asked why he had attacked Tomboy Stone, Gillespie replied, "Because there were no witnesses." He was sentenced to sixty days in the workhouse, and Tomboy got to thinking.[31] Everyone was moving on. Her older sister, Blanche, was a student at St. Catherine's College studying music. Her younger sister, Bernous, or "Bunny" as the family called her, had joined the army and was engaged to be married. Brother Quinten helped out at his parents' barber and beauty shops and showed an interest in going into business with them. Even Tomboy's friends had plans. Janabelle Murphy attended "the U," hoping to graduate from the University of Minnesota with a degree in physical education. Evelyn Edwards enrolled in Globe Business College to study accounting. Even Father Keefe had accepted a new challenge. He became the new priest at the Church of St. Anne in Le Sueur, Minnesota, an hour away.

"When you finish high school, they tell a boy to go out and see the world," Tomboy later said. "What do they tell a girl? They tell her to go next door and marry the boy that their family's picked out." It wasn't right, she thought. "A woman has her dreams, too," she said.[32] The army shipped Bunny to San Francisco, and before too long she sent letters home saying she could use some company. Willa gave Tomboy the money, and with little more than a plan to meet her sister "somewhere" in San Francisco—she didn't even know exactly where Bunny was stationed—Tomboy boarded a bus for California. "I had to see what was over there," she said, "on the other side of the fence."[33]

Golden Gate

Suitcase packed, truck's already gone
Goin' to San Francisco, gonna make it my home
Yeah, San Francisco please make room for me
Well, I'm goin' to San Francisco
If I could crawl on my knees.

—LOWELL FULSON[1]

Tomboy's first sight of San Francisco took her breath away. About the same time she reached the city, author John Dos Passos arrived to write a profile of San Francisco in wartime for *Harper's* magazine. Whoever designed the city's streets didn't have the "slightest regard for the laws of gravity," he wrote. The city was a jumble of steep slopes and precipitous curves, and the result was thrilling. "Whenever you step out on the street there's a hilltop in one direction or other. From the top of each hill you get a view and the sight of more hills to the right and left and ahead that offer the prospect of still broader views. The process goes on indefinitely. You can't help making your way painfully to the top of each hill just to see what you can see."[2]

As captivating as the view was, Tomboy was on a mission and wasted little time. She needed to find her sister. In May 1943, Bunny

Stone married Steward Louis Bell. The couple shipped out to separate military assignments. The army sent Bunny to the Bay Area and the navy returned Bell to his Pearl Harbor fleet.[3] The marriage was rocky. For many years Bunny and Louis quarreled and made up and began the cycle again. Bunny needed some comfort from home, and Tomboy was happy to supply it.[4] As she disembarked at the San Francisco Transit Depot on Mission Street, Tomboy was immediately engulfed in a big city wartime crush of humanity. Soldiers with duffle bags dashed toward idling buses; women with a child on each hip kicked heavy suitcases through a maze of moving legs; young people like Tomboy stepped off buses from Arkansas and Texas and wondered where they'd find one of the good defense jobs everyone was talking about.

In 1941 President Franklin Roosevelt had signed Executive Order 8802, which required federal industries to end discriminatory hiring practices based on race, color, or national origin. Hopeful workers read leaflets tacked on post office bulletin boards around the country exhorting the wonders of California: good jobs, beautiful weather, palm trees! The Kaiser and Moore Dry Dock shipyards in Richmond and Oakland were hiring tens of thousands of workers to build nearly fifteen hundred vessels to support the war effort.* "A ship a day" was being produced by men and women, blacks and whites, Mexicans, Portuguese, and Italian workers laboring side by side in integrated divisions. Within the span of three years, the population of Richmond, California, swelled from 23,000 to nearly 125,000. The docks needed painters, welders, riveters, forklift drivers, and crane operators for their six-days-a-week, round-the-clock schedule.[5] If you stood still in the bus terminal for just a moment as Tomboy did, it seemed that everyone in the country was rushing to San Francisco to find a future.

---

*While African Americans were hired for many jobs in the World War II shipyards, some unions created separate "auxiliary units" for blacks. Auxiliary units had no union votes or representation. The Boilermakers Union and Teamsters Steamfitters' Union were completely off-limits to blacks (Katherine Archibald, *Wartime Shipyard: A Study in Social Disunity*, with a new introduction by Eric Arnesen and Alex Lichtenstein, Chicago: University of Illinois Press, 2006, 81).

Tomboy's first few days in the Bay Area were so bizarre and improbable that her odyssey later became the stuff of Stone family legend. From the money her mother gave her, Tomboy ended up in California with fifty-three cents—no, sixty-seven cents—no, seven dollars—she said at other times. Surely it wasn't much. She did not have an exact address for Bunny, didn't know the area, and had no prospects for employment. She didn't even have much luggage, just some dungarees, pressed slacks, and clean shirts. She also carried her old baseball glove from the Goodwill and the baseball shoes Gabby Street had given her. Tomboy had eaten all the food her mother had packed for the trip and was hungry and tired, but she knew she had to fend for herself. Although she noticed prostitutes walking around the area, making what seemed like easy money, Tomboy never for a moment considered such a desperate idea. "It was easy to go into street walking," she said. But she believed no woman needed to prostitute herself if she was willing to work. "That was out. I couldn't see that. That was like . . . doing dirty dishes."[6] Within a matter of days, the ever-resourceful Tomboy found a place to live and a job. Even more incredible, Tomboy was walking down a street when Bunny just happened to look out a nearby window. The two Stone sisters found each other. Whether it was luck, coincidence, divine providence, or foolishness—everything Tomboy needed, she said, fell right into her lap.[7]

In truth, Tomboy's beginnings in San Francisco were more intentional. When she arrived at the terminal, Toni approached an attendant in the Travelers' Aid station for help. The station supervisor told her to return later for an official appointment regarding job possibilities and lodging. Tomboy spent the first few nights alone in the bus station, but by the time came for Tomboy's appointment with the Travelers' Aid, she already had found a job and a room. The day she first arrived at the terminal, she spotted a black man in the station and asked for help. "Where would you find our kind of folks?" she asked. The stranger laughed and directed her to the Fillmore. As she passed Foster's Cafeteria on the corner of Sutter, she noticed a help wanted sign in the window. Foster's was a bustling warren of mirror-top tables where drifters and neighborhood residents converged over lumps of warm meatloaf and bowls of chili.* The cafeteria was looking for all kinds of help—waitresses, salad makers, dishwashers. "I knew something about salads," Tomboy said. She got the job: fourteen dollars a week and one eat-in meal a day. "That boosted me," she said.[8]

The next order of business was finding a place to stay. Tomboy knew that she would have trouble finding a room as a single woman. "A single girl? People don't want you in their house," she said. Some landlords might think she was a sporting girl or a hustler. As she usually did when she was in a pinch, Tomboy sought help from the church. She went over to St. Benedict's in nearby Oakland and asked the priest for assistance. The priest initially thought she was a runaway. Tomboy sensed his unease, and before he could jump to more conclusions, she produced some papers. She had a letter from her father addressed "To Whom It May Concern," asking Catholics, Masons, and other organizations to which he belonged to assist his daughter. The priest softened—"the redness went out of his face," Toni said—and he called women in the parish's Altar Society for suggestions. With the women's help, Tomboy located a room in a Polish woman's home; Mrs. Kardeski's two sons were off to war and her house felt vacant.[9]

The job at Foster's did not provide Tomboy with as much work as she wanted, and soon she was looking for a way to earn more money. She secured a job as a welder in the South San Francisco docks, working alongside longshoremen for the Matson shipping lines. She failed, however, to pass along one piece of information to her boss: she didn't know anything about welding. "I was burning up that steel," she said. When her boss realized she had no experience, he had already been won over by Tomboy's eagerness and sincerity. He offered her another chance and teasingly asked, "What the hell can you do?" At that moment, Tomboy looked around the docks and saw an army truck

---

*Foster's Cafeteria had several locations in San Francisco. The Montgomery Street cafeteria later became famous as the site where many Beat poets, including Allen Ginsberg, gathered to talk and write.

pulling up. "I can drive that," she said. Toni hopped into the driver's seat. When she heard the gears start to grind, she knew she could do the job. "I'm home!" she said to herself.[10] The physical work at the docks suited her, and, dressed as she usually was in men's work shirts and pants, she fit right in with the Rosie-the-Riveter coverall set on the dock.

Tomboy was one of nearly twelve million women across the country who worked alongside men in the defense industries, from shipyards to steel mills to foundries. As higher paying local shipyard jobs opened up, many black women found recently vacated positions in canneries, railroads, or military supply facilities. Women were able to forge a path out of traditional domestic work. Drivers pulling up for gas at the Richfield station on the corner of Lombard and Broderick in San Francisco temporarily gasped when female service station attendants asked, "Check your oil, sir? National emergency shortage on men, y'know." In the Bay Area, women took over as streetcar conductors, street sweepers, hospital orderlies, and playground directors. Up in Santa Rosa, the DeTurk Winery started employing women to harvest grapes and drive delivery trucks. Also invaded was "man's last sacred domain," what one soldier called his barbershop. At Camp Roberts in San Miguel, women were allowed to apply for jobs cutting men's hair. "Hitler was the one that got us out of the kitchen," one woman said.[11]

Not everyone was happy with the invasion of what had been exclusively white men's territory. "It's too bad every skirt in Moore Dry Dock can't be given her quit slip right now," one angry foreman stated. When women in the shipyards, like Toni, began to be hired as shipwrights, painters, and welders—jobs that usually were off-limits to them—some men protested or looked for faults in the women's work. "You ask any man, and he'll tell you that a woman in the shipyards is in the way. They don't none of them belong here." Some women would not back down and fought for their right to jobs. They organized, met with local priests and ministers, and secured the support of male allies. While the close quarters of the shipyards and the inevitable daily interactions between men and women moved the workforce toward more equality, proximity only brought the transition part way, an observer said.* Women's inclusion continued to be "conditional," and their status never became equal to men's. Many men believed women took away work that was rightly theirs and scrambled to keep the shipyards white and male. Some critics said men who complained were really afraid of competition. They said aggrieved men revealed an "obvious, persistent and perhaps more basic fear" than many males were willing to admit.[12]

Concern about blacks "invading" San Francisco reflected the same fear, many believed. When Mayor Roger Lapham addressed a 1944 press conference, for example, his question betrayed his anxiety. "How long do you think these colored people are going to be here?" he asked the only black reporter in the group, Thomas Fleming. "Mr. Mayor, do you know the Golden Gate?" Fleming responded. "It's permanent. They are here to stay and the city better find jobs and housing for them, because they are not going back down South." Fleming might have thought the mayor's comment only slightly less disquieting than the note he had found a decade earlier pasted to the typewriter in his newspaper office: "You niggers go back to Africa," it read. [13] Vandals had stolen into the offices of the *San Francisco Spokesman* and smashed plate glass windows and the Linotype after Fleming wrote an editorial saying blacks deserved to be hired for waterfront jobs.†

---

*Beginning in 1942, a graduate student at the University of California—Berkeley, Katherine Archibald, spent two years working at Moore Dry Dock. Her examination of the integration of women and minorities in the workplace formed the basis of her remarkable 1947 study, *Wartime Shipyard: A Study in Social Disunity.* Many of Archibald's conclusions about the difficulties women and minorities faced in the shipyard workplace mirrored Toni Stone's experience as the lone woman on men's baseball teams.

†Fleming had witnessed California's racism as a young man growing up in Chico around 1926. The Ku Klux Klan gathered near his home where Fleming and his grandfather, Moses Moseley, sat on the front steps. Moseley "was so mad that he sat out on the porch with a loaded .30-caliber rifle and I sat beside him with a loaded .25-.20, plus we had loaded shotguns," Fleming said. "I don't know until today whether either of us would have fired if the Klansmen had decided to march on the street where our house was located" (Thomas Fleming, "Reflections on Black History: The Klan Marches in California," *Sun-Reporter*, December 31, 1997).

In Saint Paul, Tomboy had used her baseball skills to break down prejudice she faced as a girl on the local diamonds. In San Francisco, Tomboy used the same technique in confronting discrimination—joining pickup games on Sundays after mass with black boys and even some whites. But not all blacks arriving in San Francisco were welcomed by white residents as Tomboy was on the Post Street playground; Jim Crow attitudes were alive in the city, though communicated less directly than in the South. One area where blacks were warmly accepted was the Fillmore in the city's integrated Western Addition—the area to which the black man in the bus station had directed Tomboy. She loved the diversity of the area and found it "filled with world-wide views."[14]

As early as the 1890s, Japanese immigrants joined Jewish residents in the Fillmore and built a thriving community. After Pearl Harbor and the sudden removal of Japanese and Japanese Americans to relocation camps, the area became a center for the burgeoning black population. Willie Brown, a young Bay Area immigrant from Texas, said the Fillmore "had to be the closest thing to Harlem outside of New York."[15] He loved the Victorian gingerbread houses, the black barbershops, barbecue joints, pool halls, restaurants, and vibrant shopping district. Brown found work at Kaufman's Shoe Store on Fillmore Avenue, and the neighborhood became his playground.* Like everyone else, though, Willie Brown came to the Fillmore mainly for the music. Marguerite Johnson, who moved there from rural Arkansas, worked at the busy Melrose Record Shop in the heart of the district. She said that "[b]lasts from [the store's] loudspeakers poured out into the street with all the insistence of a false mourner at a graveside."[16] Jazz, the blues, bebop—the Fillmore was hot.

Nightclubs stretched for twenty blocks. There was the Club Alabam on Post, Town Club on Sutter, the Long Bar and Minne's Can Do on Fillmore, Jimbo's Bop City, the New Orleans Swing Club, Elsie's Breakfast Nook, the Texas Playhouse, Leola King's Blue Mirror. The most well known was Jack's Tavern, which opened in 1933 and was the first

---

*Willie Brown served as mayor of San Francisco from 1996 to 2003.

club to be managed by black people. Alroyd Love and Lena Murrell* ran the "hottest colored nite spot in town," which exploded in popularity during the war years when immigrants like Brown, Johnson, and Tomboy came looking for work and a good time.[17] Among the Fillmore nightclub set, Jack's was considered an elite establishment. Men wore satin ties with diamond stickpins; women wore fur coats, fancy hats, and lots of jewelry. "You saw great peacocks," Brown said. "People would get dressed to kill. . . . Stacy Adams shoes with the white [stitches on the soles] showing they had been cleaned up with Clorox."[18] In the evenings, patrons formed lines outside Jack's door, eager to hear the music, dance, and taste the dinner specials the tavern's famous cook dished up. Dinner began at seven and was served until two in the morning. The dining room in the back had a small dance floor and a bandstand where Saunders King's rhythm and blues alternated weeks with Johnny Ingram's five-piece band. King said a person went into Jack's "at one o'clock [in the morning] and the music was just beginning to feel good."[19] Bandleader Frank Jackson observed that although the dance floor was small, it enticed a few dancers eager to show their moves. Jack's was a feast for the eyes, the ears, and the stomach.

Jazz musicians like Frank Jackson knew that other clubs often were rough—places where women were apt to be harassed, where drugs could be found, and where gangsters hung out. Jack's Tavern was nothing like that, Jackson said. If a woman came to the club alone and a man tried to make a move on her, a gentleman would "take that up right away. 'Are you being bothered?'" someone would ask and the offender would apologize and walk away.[20] Men would sometimes buy a woman drinks, but they would rarely give her a problem. Some said the first place a black person would go in San Francisco was Jack's Tavern. Tomboy was no exception.

The music drew her in, but the people inside kept her returning. Conversation at Jack's Tavern was urbane and sophisticated, and Tomboy felt pleasantly "taken in," as she put it.[21] She had found in

---

*Lena Murrell's last name has been variously spelled as Murell and Morrell. I have taken the spelling of her last name from a business card for Jack's Tavern circa the 1940s.

San Francisco a place to transform herself. As one migrant to the city put it, "there was a reshuffling of everybody . . . a whole new set of criteria set down for who was insiders and who was outsiders."[22] You could make a fresh start, reinvent yourself, even change your name. Marguerite Johnson, a record clerk, became a singer and a dancer and changed her name to Maya Angelou. Tomboy Stone decided her name no longer fit. It sounded too much like the special child from Saint Paul. "Tomboy" became "Toni"—a sassy, confident metamorphosis more in line with the kind of people she met at Jack's, people like Aurelious Pescia Alberga—a man whose dress and demeanor matched the lyricism of his name. Toni loved listening to the trim, dapper gentleman everyone seemed to know. The son of a Jamaican seafarer, Alberga was active in political circles, ran a bootblack stand at the Ferry Building, operated a bail bond business, and assisted a blind millionaire in managing real estate throughout the city. As Toni got to know him better, she realized Alberga's current entrepreneurial occupations were sedate compared to the high adventures of his youth. In his sixty years, he had worked aboard a ship in the Arctic, survived the 1906 earthquake, won prominence as a boxer, and served as one of the first black army officers in World War I.[23]

Alberga could talk for hours, and he loved the limelight. Like Toni, he enjoyed celebrity and took pride in knowing local politicians, business owners, musicians, and sportsmen. And, like Toni, he was good at telling stories. One of his favorites was about skullduggery at the Need More, a saloon his uncle owned on the Barbary Coast, just below Montgomery Street in San Francisco. The Need More sat on pilings right on the estuary and was a favorite of weary crews just back from long voyages to China. Sea captains often found they needed two or three more men to make up a crew for the return trip to the Far East. So the captain hired hoodlums or "footpads" at the saloon. Sailors would get drunk, Alberga said, and footpads would drop them out the back door into a waiting boat where they'd be transported back to the ship bound for China.[24] Alberga liked stories of people who broke rules, were unconventional, and charted their own course.

Once Tomboy told her stories about barnstorming through Canada with the Twin City Colored Giants, Alberga was hooked. He and Jack's owner, Al Love, began thinking about how they could help Toni become part of a local team.[25] Love was known for his generosity. When Saunders King's electric guitar did not have adequate amplification, Love "saw what I was drivin' at," King said, and bought the musician a better instrument.[26] He also was not the type of man to let barriers stop him. During the war, Jack's Tavern was famous for keeping the music playing even during blackouts. Heavy drapes bordered the front door, and when the air raid sirens went off, the curtains were closed. "No one could see the lights," musicians said, and the partying continued.[27]

Love and Alberga called upon their connections with the local American Legion to ask if Toni could join one of their sponsored teams. Toni had played a little American Legion ball back in Saint Paul, but team officials had denied her a uniform and she, naturally, felt left out in her own shirt and dungarees.[28] But she was open to trying a new Legion team in order to get the chance to play ball. The A. H. Wall Post 435 met at the War Memorial Building on Van Ness, just around the corner from Jack's. The post included many in the Fillmore music world and in fact was named in honor of Archie H. Wall, principal musician for the 24th Infantry in the Spanish-American War. Alberga knew the black veterans of Post 435 well. During World War I, he'd served as a first lieutenant and acting captain in Company A of the 365th Infantry. Some people around Jack's Tavern still called him "Captain." In the army, Alberga was responsible for recreation—organizing his regiment's boxing matches, cross country runs, and baseball games. His commander praised his skill, observing that Alberga demonstrated "exceptional aptness for this line of work."[29] Apparently the Captain's talent for sports promotion paid off. Toni became a member of the American Legion A. H. Wall Post 435 baseball team.* "I was the only woman," she said. "We played twi-

*A. H. Wall Post No. 435 was chartered in 1933 and deactivated in 1955 (Bill Silar interview with the author, December 8, 2008). *The Oakland Tribune* of August 12, 1934, described the post as "San Francisco's colored veterans' unit."

light games and I met many, many friends."[30] Like other Junior Legion teams, players were required to be seventeen years old or under.[31] As long as Toni was in the act of reinvention, the time seemed right for another modification. "I put my age back," Toni said, lopping off a decade.[32]

Fudging her age was hardly the only policy Toni violated in joining the American League team. Breaking the "girl rule" was disobeying a regulation that had been on the books since 1928 when a young woman from Brazil, Indiana, tried to play with an American Legion team. Officials balked with the same old response that Toni had heard before: girls shouldn't play baseball because they might get hurt. But some Legion coaches did not view female baseball players as fragile, especially if a girl could help a team win, with or without a uniform. "Not everybody followed the rules," an American Legion spokesman admitted, and unless an opposing coach protested (or even knew) about Toni playing, most teams looked the other way.[33] If an opposing coach did not realize Toni was a girl, it wouldn't be the first time. Back in Saint Paul, a young man from the neighborhood spent years watching a team before realizing that the talented infielder was Marcenia Stone.[34] Some American Legion fans even reveled in the "oddities and amusing stories" of eager players out to prove themselves—they took it as a mark of a player's grit. Since Legion players were "kids" presumably, some adults were more apt to excuse a few irregularities—perhaps even one as "irregular" as a twenty-six-year-old woman playing a boys' game. Toni took her position in center field for the Wall post team and reported that Al Love kept his eye on her and made sure she was not patronized with easy drills. He "worked me to death," Toni said.[35]

Toni's decision to play on the American Legion team was an informed move for someone who wanted to be taken seriously in baseball. Major league scouts looked closely at Legion players. Representatives from the St. Louis Cardinals, New York Yankees, Pittsburgh Pirates, and Brooklyn Dodgers trolled the national Legion tournament in Los Angeles at the end of August. They estimated the level of play was up 40 percent from the previous year and kept in mind those big league players such as Bob Feller and Bobby Doerr who once played junior Legion ball. That summer the great Babe Ruth, with only a year to live and looking ill, also made a swing through California's Legion circuit observing new talent. By the end of the season, San Francisco's Rincon Hill Legion club won the 1947 Northern California playoffs and went on to the state tourney. Toni's A. H. Wall Post 435 did not advance, but playing Legion ball did bring her to the attention of other area teams. The next summer, hoping to raise the level of her play, she joined a local semi-pro team in the Peninsula Baseball League, becoming the only young woman to play Bay Area baseball with men."* "Miss Stone performed for the A. H. post American Legion Juniors last year and she is an accomplished player," a San Mateo sportswriter noted.[36]

Restless and searching for a way to make baseball more than a pastime for evenings and weekends, Toni talked with the manager of her Legion team—a man Toni had won over with her persistence, as usual. He encouraged Toni to consider the possibility of West Coast professional baseball. The San Francisco Seals, a white team, just might take a chance on her, he said. Toni liked what she heard, as farfetched as the proposition was. "It's in my mind to get to be wondering," she later said.[37]

San Francisco Seals Stadium stood on Potrero Hill at 16th and Bryant Streets, not far from Jack's Tavern. The Seals squad was a member of the Pacific Coast League (PCL), a white league that was considered the top baseball organization on the West Coast. Because

---

*American Legion records indicate that a San Francisco team won the 1943 and 1947 California state championships. At that time, there were fifty-five American Legion posts in the Bay Area. While some accounts of Stone's activity indicate her American Legion team was a "championship" one, newspaper records confirm that the Rincon Hill team was the Northern California representative to the state championships.

The Peninsula Baseball League operated from the World War II years until 1975. High school, college, and semi-pro players participated. Several players moved from the PBL to the majors including Dick Stuart (Pirates), Don Giles (Red Sox), and Charlie Silvera (Yankees). (www.smdailyjournal.com/article_preview.php?id=57282)

major league baseball had not yet come to California, the PCL offered the best baseball west of St. Louis. Many observers believed the players were as good as those in the major leagues. Beautiful weather, a longer playing season, and a schedule that didn't involve much traveling added to the league's allure. Some players called the PCL an older players' league because some athletes could last longer in the better climate and with less travel.[38] But the PCL boasted many young players as well. Eighteen-year-old Joe DiMaggio got his start playing with the Seals in 1932, while down in San Diego another Pacific Coast League team signed seventeen-year-old Ted Williams. Williams's mother did not want him traveling far from home, so young Teddy pitched for the Padres in 1936 and 1937. Future major leaguers Bobby Doerr played second base for the Padres, and Vince DiMaggio played left field.[39]

During the wartime migration to California, sports promoters pressured the PCL to begin signing black players. Many promoters believed baseball's color barrier could be broken on the West Coast long before discrimination ended in the major leagues. The West, they argued, had always been the destination of pioneers and was less set in custom and convention than many other areas. Chet Brewer, a former Monarchs pitcher, thought he had a chance to integrate the league in 1943, but his shot never materialized.[40]

Professional opportunities for black baseball players on the West Coast were few. There were no Negro League franchises in the West since the number of black residents in cities like San Francisco did not compare to Detroit and Birmingham. But the war changed that demographic. With thousands of blacks flocking to the West Coast for defense jobs in the shipyards, the time seemed right for integration—or, if not yet, for enterprising business owners to think about bringing some black baseball to the Pacific. If the Pacific Coast League would not change its segregationist policies, then perhaps a professional black league could be formed. In the fall of 1945, two Berkeley firefighters, Eddie Harris and David Portlock, called a summit of like-minded entrepreneurs interested in organizing black baseball on the

West Coast. The group met at the Elks clubhouse in West Oakland and drew up impressive plans. They organized six teams with a one-hundred-game schedule: the San Diego Tigers, Los Angeles White Sox, Oakland Larks, Seattle Steel Heads, Portland Rose Buds, and San Francisco Sea Lions. Abe Saperstein, the white owner of the Harlem Globetrotters basketball and baseball teams, became president; Olympic champion Jesse Owens assumed the vice presidency; Portlock and Harris served as secretary and business manager. The organization called itself the West Coast Negro Baseball Association (WCNBA) and sought players from Negro League teams in the East as well as local talent such as Lionel "Lefty" Wilson, a young standout from the Oakland area.* Salaries ranged from $175 to $300 a month, enough to draw some pitchers from the Negro Leagues such as Marion "Sugar" Cain. On May 12, 1946, a cloudy, cold day, California Governor Earl Warren threw out the first ball at Seals Stadium for the inaugural season of the WCNBA. Like Negro League teams, the WCNBA rented stadiums owned by white teams when those teams were on the road. That same day, across the Bay, the Oakland Larks hammered the visiting San Diego Tigers 16–1 in a game that ended in a concession after eight innings.[41]

The concession should have been an omen. Several weeks later, Abe Saperstein complained that money wasn't coming in as expected. The league was in trouble. "If anyone would have a definite complaint I would say the Portland club would have," he wrote. "They arrived in the San Francisco area on May 18 and remained in the area through May 30 . . . a span of approximately two weeks which certainly cost them better than $3,000.00 in salaries, lodging, meals and whatnot . . . and the sum of their receipts in three dates played was approximately $170.00." The problem, he said, was in "through-the-week" baseball. Towns other than the league cities had not been secured. There was lit-

---

*Wilson became the first African American mayor of Oakland in 1977. He served three terms during a particularly turbulent time in Oakland's history.

tle publicity. The Seattle team made two trips to Sacramento, played two games against San Francisco, and didn't even recoup gas money, Saperstein complained.[42] The Steelies had even more bad luck during a home series against San Diego. The Seattle team was in Salem, Oregon, when the bus broke down and they had to hitch rides to the game.[43] By July, business manager Harris reported that the West Coast Negro Baseball Association was at the financial breaking point. By the middle of the month—just eight weeks after its hopeful beginning—the league ran out of gas.

The WCNBA's San Francisco Sea Lions and Oakland Larks were not willing to give up. If the West Coast couldn't sustain a black league, then perhaps the two teams could make it barnstorming through the West and Canada. Hal King, a San Francisco sportsman, and Harold "Yellowhorse" Morris owned the Sea Lions. Morris had won fame as a pitcher for the Negro League's Kansas City Monarchs, the Chicago American Giants, and the Detroit Stars and held the League record for complete games and most innings pitched. He earned his nickname for his light complexion and Native American lineage.[44] After the WCNBA league folded, the men signed Cleo "Baldy" Benson, a former catcher for the American Giants, as the Sea Lions' manager. The crew painted a red bus with the team's name across the side and began booking barnstorming dates from North Dakota to Louisiana. While the road was grueling, players earned more money barnstorming than they had playing in the ill-fated league.

Morris had another idea for making money. He hired the Oakland Larks' featured attraction, Little Sammy Workman. Workman was a dwarf whose hands and feet had been amputated after he contracted a rare disease as a child. A man of remarkable resilience and skill, Workman astonished crowds with his ability to hit, throw, and catch, running the bases in shoes that he wore on his knees—turned backward in order to give him better balance. Morris brought Workman on the team to perform a show after the third inning. San Francisco Sea Lions pitcher Herald "BeeBop" Gordon heard Morris's standard introduction of Workman so often that he could recite the script from memory.* "Ladies and gentleman, I would like to bring to you our featured attraction, Little Sammy Workman, the Wonder Boy, the boy without hands or feet catchin' the ball, throwin' the ball, hittin' the ball, and runnin' around the bases doin' his death slide from third base. Incidentally, Ladies and Gentleman, Little Sammy travels with this ball club entirely on his own and any kind of donation that you might give will be highly appreciated inasmuch as he's workin' his way through college. Incidentally, Ladies and Gentleman, Little Sammy's hands and feet fell off at the age of two. Without further ado, I will now present to you, Little Sammy Workman."[45] Workman would then go into his routine, tossing a ball back and forth to the pitcher, hitting a ball to the outfield, and rounding the bases. Workman and the Sea Lions outfielder had his hit timed so that by the time he ran toward third, the ball would be on its way and Sammy would "go into his death slide." The fans went wild, Gordon said. "That guy was something else. He could play pool, he could play the piano, he could play drums, he could play cards with those nubs. He was strictly a miracle type of guy."[46] The funds for Workman's college education that Yellowhorse asked for never funded Workman's college career. Workman didn't go to college. A Sea Lions pitcher who wasn't on the mound that day would take the steel box into the stands and fans would stuff dollars into the slot. Then he'd return the box to Yellowhorse. "He's the only one had the key to it," Gordon said.[47]

The Sea Lions proved to be a profitable team with high visibility. In December 1948 they traveled to the Philippines for a month, going 13–3 against university, U.S. military, and Filipino teams.[48] That same year, the Sea Lions toured twenty-two states, winning 150 games and losing 20. They also took second place in the *Denver Post*'s Invitational

*Herald Gordon pitched for the Sea Lions in 1949. He also played for the Detroit Stars and Chicago American Giants from 1950 to 1954. Gordon earned his nickname, "BeeBop," for the large round glasses he wore that resembled those of Dizzy Gillespie. Gordon didn't need the glasses; he "just liked the style" (Gordon interview with the author, July 18, 2008).

Baseball Tournament.* Besides captain Baldy Benson, the Sea Lions included other former Negro League players including John Scroggins, a pitcher for the Monarchs; David "Speed" Whatley, an outfielder for the Homestead Grays; and the legendary Biz Mackey, a catcher who had made the rounds in Negro League ball for almost thirty years. Yellowhorse was working on bookings in Mexico and across Canada when Toni approached him. As she always did when asked about her experience, Toni stressed the fundamentals. "I work as hard as any of the fellows. I know what hit-and-run is, and I can steal bases, if necessary." Years of playing as the only woman on male teams also had taught Toni that the odds against her were always formidable and skill alone would not persuade a manager to take a chance. She needed to sell herself. She told Yellowhorse a woman on a team could bring in crowds.[49]

Everyone in baseball realized a lot had changed in the few short years since the West Coast Negro Baseball Association had gone belly up. During the 1948 season, John Ritchey, a catcher with the Negro League's Chicago American Giants, finally broke the PCL color line and signed with the San Diego Padres. A rumor circulated that Luke Easter of the Homestead Grays might be next. The time was right for daring moves, and "I was a daredevil," Toni said.[50] As much as she peppered her argument to Yellowhorse with examples of change, Toni—or anyone else—had to only say two words to make her case: Jackie Robinson.

On April 15, 1947, Jack Roosevelt Robinson broke the color barrier in baseball's major leagues when he trotted out to first base at Ebbet's Field in Brooklyn, New York. Toni followed Robinson's every move in the pages of her beloved *Chicago Defender*. She knew Robinson was the only black man among 399 players in the major leagues

*The *Denver Post* tournament was introduced in the 1920s and proved to be a highly successful semi-pro invitational. The integrated tournament ran for ten days in the summer with ten teams selected by the *Post*'s sports department (Harold Seymour, Dorothy Z. Seymour, and Jane Mills, *Baseball: The People's Game*, New York: Oxford University Press, 1991, 271).

and that he was twenty-eight years old, two years older than she was. She also knew Robinson went hitless that historic day and hitless for the next sixteen at bats that followed before his average began to rise. The pressure on Robinson must have been nearly unbearable. Satchel Paige had warned that being a pioneer would be difficult for Robinson or anyone. Maybe too difficult. "You keep blowing off about getting us players in the league without thinking about our end of it," Paige told a group of black reporters. No one really thought about "how tough it's going to be for a colored ballplayer to come out of the clubhouse and have all the white guys calling him nigger and black so-and-so," he said. "What I want to know is what the hell's gonna happen to good will when one of those colored players, goaded out of his senses by repeated insults, takes a bat and busts fellowship in his damned head?"[51]

As a woman player in a man's game, Toni had experienced some of the prejudice Paige and Robinson described. She heard classmates call her "crazy" for playing baseball; she heard the jokes about her being far from ladylike. She even received occasional rebuffs from teammates when her play outmatched theirs. Like Robinson, she felt what it was like to be the odd one out: to sit alone in the dugout, to be excluded from the game's camaraderie, to be regarded as a barely tolerable experiment.[52] When Brooklyn Dodger general manager Branch Rickey told Robinson that he wanted "a ball player with guts enough not to fight back," Toni knew what he meant.[53] Jackie took the taunts and the strained hostility from some of his teammates, because he believed fans and other players would have "a change of mind when they realized I was a good ball player who could be helpful in their earning a few thousand more dollars."[54] Toni took the jeers because she wanted to play.

Maybe it was the rhyme going around at the time about Jackie's drawing power that convinced Yellowhorse to hire Toni. "Jackie's nimble / Jackie's quick / Jackie's making / The turnstile click."[55] Just as she had done with the St. Peter Claver team, the Twin City Colored Giants, Wall Post 435, and the Peninsula Baseball League, Toni became the first woman on a men's team. She started earning a couple hundred dollars every month and was able to send a little money home to her mother in Saint Paul. "Things turned out for me at the Lions," she said.[56] By the spring of 1949, Toni was headed to Missouri, Arkansas, and Texas as the female second baseman for the San Francisco Sea Lions. Life again had the improvisational rhythms she enjoyed—traveling around on a bus, seeing different towns every day, grabbing meals on the fly. She batted lead off and took advantage of any chance to get on base, including getting hit by a pitch. "Pitches come in now at ninety miles an hour," she later said. "It'll tear your brains out. You've got to know what you want and you've got to know where you're going."[57] One reporter covering a game in Maryville, Missouri, was so impressed with Stone's tenacity that he remembered her for years. "Let me tell you," he wrote, "she'll make your eyes pop out with the way she handles herself."[58] Gentry Jackson, the Sea Lions shortstop, argued that Toni was more than a curiosity. "A lot of people were looking at her as a woman ball player, but when she was on the field, the ball was hit to her as sharp as it was hit to me and she would pick it up and throw it. She wasn't just a lady in uniform."[59] The Sea Lions shortstop was also impressed by the way she could take rough dugout language. "There were occasions," Jackson said, "where someone would say things a lady wouldn't want to hear. But she was able in most cases to join in the dialogue without getting embarrassed."[60] Like all barnstorming teams, the Sea Lions expected players to pull their weight in every aspect of the game, from pushing meandering cows off a field to serving as groundskeepers. On the swing through Texas, days of rain made the local field too wet for play. The Sea Lions poured kerosene over wet grass and set fire to it, in hopes the blaze would burn the diamond dry. It worked well enough to get the game started, but Toni slid on a wet patch during the game and injured her ankle. She was out of commission for weeks, but returned to the lineup when the team rolled toward the Deep South.

Back in California, Yellowhorse's old friend from the short-lived West Coast Negro Baseball Association was feeling hopeful. As impossible as it seemed just three years earlier, Eddie Harris, the former business manager of the association, was now working for the formerly all-white Pacific Coast League, scouting black talent for teams like the newly integrated Seals and the San Diego Padres. "I believe this is the greatest chance for Negro talent here on the Coast," he wrote. "If they make good here there is a great chance of making the big League." Harris asked his friends to let him know of "any good players that you think could make the grade." All their expenses would be paid in California. "They'll get the best of everything while in spring training . . . act quickly," he said.[61] The letter's eager tone was like the post office flyers that lured defense workers to Oakland with the promise of good jobs, beautiful weather, and palm trees. Toni also thought the future looked encouraging. Her play with the barnstorming Sea Lions was making her into something of a Bay Area celebrity. One local reporter hunted her down to ask if she thought a woman would ever play professional baseball on the West Coast. Toni let her optimism spill over. Everything was changing, she said, and predicted a woman would sign with the Pacific Coast League by the 1950s.[62] As the Sea Lions bus rumbled toward New Orleans, Toni, Little Sammy Workman, and the rest of the team tried to catch some sleep before another round of back-to-back games. The sun felt good and Yellowhorse's steel money box glinted in the light. It was bright as a penny.

Finding the Heart of the Game

> We all do "do, re mi," but you have to find the other notes yourself.
>
> —Louis Armstrong[1]

When Toni stepped off the Sea Lions bus in New Orleans, she was grateful for the breeze. Summer was still a few weeks away from wrapping the Mississippi River delta in heat and humidity, but the gusty wind made the warm air a degree or two cooler.[2] The Sea Lions were scheduled to play a tripleheader with the local New Orleans Creoles and the visiting Fort Worth Tigers. Like nearly everyone else in New Orleans on a hot May day, Toni would have enjoyed a shady walk or maybe a swim. But here, deep in the Jim Crow South, walking and swimming were restricted for blacks—whether by law or by custom. Toni would have been either brave or foolish to walk through New Orleans' beautiful Audubon Park, where she was not welcome. There was no specific ordinance that banned her, but, as the city park superintendent explained in bureaucratic contortions, "There is the possibility of racial conflict where the two races gather together in large numbers on public property wherein it has not been the practice before."[3] The only public pool for New Orleans' two hundred thousand black residents was so small and crowded a swimmer could barely get wet. Even the five-mile shoreline of Lake Pontchartrain was off-limits to her. Years before, when the lakefront was still undeveloped, a small stretch of shoreline called Seabrook became an unofficial black beach. However, when whites began building suburban homes along the shore and complained about black people using one-sixtieth of the beach, the Parish Levee Board banned blacks from Seabrook and redirected them to an alternative spot. Lincoln Beach was a miserable spit of land. Fifteen miles out of town, inaccessible by public bus or streetcar, Lincoln had facilities controlled by a white racketeer and was polluted with raw sewage.[4]

Everybody in New Orleans knew where blacks were welcome and where they were not. Toni was quick to note the boundaries, even if others did not explicitly warn her about where she could walk without harassment. To many in New Orleans, Jim Crow was so unexamined and buried so deeply that racial separations seemed natural, or at least unremarkable. Accommodating whites was not only customary, it was also an act of survival for many Crescent City blacks. As one man put it, "As long as blacks accepted their place in the racial order, whites could be remarkably friendly."[5]

Toni remembered what her Saint Paul friend Evelyn Edwards had told her about "conditions" below the Mason-Dixon line. She also knew how segregation had become a way of life in New Orleans. Thanks to her parents, Toni learned of Homer Plessy's long-ago defiance of New Orleans's streetcar laws. In 1892, Plessy challenged a law that separated black passengers from whites traveling on streetcars and trains in Louisiana. His action led to the landmark 1896 U.S. Supreme Court decision of *Plessy v. Ferguson*, which upheld the "separate but equal" statute. The federal decision was used to legalize segregation in education, public accommodations, and transportation. Toni saw the legacy of *Plessy v. Ferguson* everywhere in Louisiana:

buses, taxicabs, hotels, restaurants, nightclubs, museums, even religious institutions.

When Toni first arrived in New Orleans, she might have considered for a moment a visit to stately St. Louis Cathedral on Jackson Square. She always made a point of learning as much as she could about a new town. If nothing else, the cavernous stone sanctuary offered relief from the sun, and the sweet, thick smell of incense would remind her of Father Keefe and St. Peter Claver back home. But the Cathedral, like Seabrook beach or the front seats of the streetcars rumbling down Canal Street, was like the rest of New Orleans: separate and unequal.

Toni dropped her belongings at the Page Hotel on Dryades Street in the city's black section of town. "Everybody liked to come to New Orleans," the Kansas City Monarchs' Buck O'Neil said. "You could have a good time after the game."[6] There were other appeals to playing in New Orleans besides the nightlife. For most visiting players, rooms in black boarding houses were a treat compared to restless nights on the bus.[7] But in New Orleans, Toni and the Creoles had the uncommon luxury of the Page Hotel. If their two-dollars-per-day meal money didn't stretch far enough in the hotel dining room, they could always buy a good meal at the bus station. "They had black cooks and black waitresses and they got to know us and gave us special treatment when we hit town," a Birmingham Black Barons player said.

People came and went at the Page Hotel all morning, as it also served as black baseball's ticket office. Alan Page, who owned three hotels in the city, seemed to be at the center of everything in New Orleans: business, sporting events, even soft drinks. He also owned the Creoles baseball team, and watched the price of Coca-Cola like other business owners watched the stock market. When Cokes went from five cents to ten cents all over the country, Page raised the price of Creoles baseball tickets. Men were charged one dollar, women seventy-five cents, soldiers sixty cents, and children thirty-five cents.[8]

Toni knew the upcoming day would be a long one. She wouldn't play all three games for the Sea Lions, but she would take all the innings that Yellowhorse offered her the chance to play. Toni's goal was always to get more playing time. More time in the game meant a better chance to study pitchers, perfect her curveball hitting, and practice the quick pivot of double plays. She would be lucky if Yellowhorse gave her four innings, though.

But Alan Page predicted that Toni would bring in a good crowd at Pelican Stadium. Sunday, May 1, was Opening Day for the New Orleans team, and Page and his crew had been busy propping up baseball advertisements in store windows and taping handbills to street lamps. When a gust of wind blew, loose posters turned cartwheels down streets until fans stooped down and picked one up. More than one person did a double take of the player whose photograph was prominently featured on the broadside. Smiling confidently for the camera—hands on hips, legs wide apart, Toni Stone looked like any other ballplayer except for the bold headline beneath her name: "Sensational Girl Player."[9]

Since the tripleheader was the official start of the Creoles' Negro Southern League season, Toni joined other players in a motorcade parade from Shakespeare Park, a city recreation area for black players where the New Orleans team held spring training.* Neighborhood kids made a practice of gathering at Shakespeare to watch the ballplayers. "What we felt for those players was almost worship," one fan said.[10] The previous year's parade had been memorable for featuring "300 future Jackie Robinsons"—young boys who whooped and hollered, many sporting new Brooklyn Dodgers baseball caps. Advertisements for Jackie Robinson caps were everywhere: "Kids, Men, Women! Get in on this Great Three for One Offer. Plus 8 × 10 of your hero suitable for framing and his life story—all for only $1.69

*The Negro Southern League, not to be confused with the Negro League, began in 1920 and reached its peak in 1932. By the late 1940s, when Toni Stone played against the Creoles, the Negro Southern League was less organized and generally considered a level below such Negro League teams as the Kansas City Monarchs. Negro Southern League teams expanded their season by playing other black teams such as the barnstorming San Francisco Sea Lions and occasionally Negro League squads including the Monarchs and the Indianapolis Clowns.

from Sports Novelty Company of Joliet Illinois."[11] Toni knew that fans couldn't get enough of Jackie Robinson; back in California she even heard talk of a motion picture about Jackie's life. But players in the parade hoped that fans would remember other black baseball players too. Everyone's pay for the day depended on good gate receipts, and a parade down Dryades Street was the best way to generate excitement and money. Over two hundred businesses stretched from one end of the street to the other, reminding Toni of the Fillmore in San Francisco with its music and swarm of activity. There were Dizzy Gillespie, Lollypop Jones, Dinah Washington, Ethel Waters, and Chubby "Hip Shakin' Mama" Newson all appearing in New Orleans clubs within a span of a few weeks. Dr. Daddy O, the city's first black DJ, played all the new LPs on his "Jivin' with Jax" radio show and then promoted them the next week in his newspaper column.* If you liked what you heard on the radio, Jiles Records on Rampart Street was only too happy to send a boy with records for purchase to your home.[12] It was as though the whole city agreed that music was as essential to life as a quart of milk or a loaf of bread, and that sustenance could be delivered right to your doorstep.

Toni enjoyed the parade. While she earned less than two hundred dollars a month playing for the Sea Lions, the money was secondary to doing what she loved. "Salaries [in Negro baseball] don't compare to Williams or DiMaggio," Buck O'Neil acknowledged. "But it beats the hell out of loafing on Central Ave or Beale Street or Eighteen and Vine."[13] Fans along the parade route cheering and shaking Toni's hand more than made up for modest wages. Barnstormers rarely enjoyed such notoriety, and Toni relished the attention. After winding their way through the black sections of the city and stopping at a few sponsoring taverns, Toni and the other players ended at Pelican Stadium. "Pel," as the locals called it, was home to the New Orleans Pelicans, a white minor league affiliate of the Pittsburgh Pirates. The stadium stood on the corner of Tulane and South Carrollton, next to the rail

---

*Dr. Daddy O was Vernon Winslow, a music reporter for the *Louisiana Weekly*.

line, and was available to the Creoles when the Pelicans were out of town, just like Seals Stadium in San Francisco. Back in 1914 when the stadium was built, mule teams brought over wooden bleachers from the old Sportsmen's Park, in hopes of maintaining a tie to New Orleans sports past—its white past.[14] Toni entered the park, as all black players did, from the "colored" entrance in center field, not the "whites only" gate in front. Once inside the dugout, she parted company with the rest of the Sea Lions. While her teammates headed to the visitors' locker room, Toni looked around for the umpires. She had no issue to discuss with the officials; she was looking for their good will. Toni knew better than to dress in the players' locker room: it was too small to offer any privacy from thirty men who were throwing off shirts or rubbing each others' arms with medicinal-smelling liniment. She knocked on the umpires' door and asked if they would mind vacating for a moment while she changed into her uniform. Toni wasn't sure why, but umpires were sensitive to her situation and rarely denied her request. Perhaps they felt a kinship with Toni—they were outnumbered in the game, too. She changed quickly and made sure to fold her street clothes meticulously for the return to the hotel. Then she walked down the dark hall and onto the bright field for infield practice. "You don't look like no ball player," her teammates teased her. Toni was used to their ribbing and welcomed it. Joking made her feel part of the squad. Other players always thought her uniforms looked too clean, and they would playfully toss a handful of dirt at her as she took her position at second. "Most of the players didn't know what a clean uniform was," Toni said. They equated grime with good luck and had an irrational fear of freshly laundered clothing. To Toni, ballplayers "were the most superstitious people in the world."[15]

Pel was a large stadium. Some players thought its horseshoe shape resembled the Polo Grounds in New York where the Brooklyn Dodgers played. The field had short foul lines, huge power alleys in right and left center, and a deep area behind home plate. It was a space so vast that a fast runner like Toni could advance from first to third on a wild pitch.[16] Toni thought it strange that a 260-foot fly ball would be a "Chinese home run"—a foul ball into the stands—and a four-hundred-foot wallop to one of the deep alleys was an easy out.[17] Pel was built for a new brand of sluggers—players who didn't depend on bulk and power but who were trim and fast and had strong wrists.[18] A hitter didn't need strength for Pel as much as precision. Just ask Sam Lacy about using finesse—every kind of finesse—in that ballpark. Lacy, a black sportswriter for the Baltimore *Afro-American*, once staged a protest at Pel when some white writers wouldn't let him in the press box to cover Jackie Robinson. Undeterred by the discrimination, Lacy took a chair and went up to the roof. "The next thing I know, several of them [white writers] came up to sit with me. I asked Dick Young, 'What are you guys doing up here?'* He said, 'Well, we decided we need some sun, Sam.'"[19] Young's knowing comment was rare: most white people didn't go out of their way to stand with blacks against Jim Crow. Most ballplayers, sportswriters, and fans gathering in the park obeyed Jim Crow restrictions. Negroes headed to black seating in the bleachers under the big Jax beer sign; whites filed into the box seats and grandstands along the third base line. Toni no longer was surprised to see whites at a black baseball game; sometimes as many as five hundred would show up on a Sunday. She never could be sure, however, if whites came to support black teams or make catcalls. "Left-handed compliments," players called some of the remarks heard from the whites only stands. Take the fan in Shreveport who yelled that his city's white team needed a few "niggers so we can win some ball games." Veteran players advised newcomers to ignore the comments, even the offensive taunts of "watermelon," "dice shooter," and "cotton picker"—a phrase that always sent Toni reeling. "As long as

---

*Sam Lacy (1903–2003) began his career selling peanuts in the Jim Crow section of Griffith Stadium in Washington, D.C. He was one of the most outspoken critics of segregation in baseball. After writing for the *Chicago Defender*, he later exclusively covered Jackie Robinson for three years for the Baltimore *Afro-American*. He was elected to the baseball writers' wing of the Hall of Fame in 1998. Dick Young (1918–1987) was a sportswriter for the *New York Daily News*. Known for his abrasive prose style, Young was a president of the Baseball Writers of America and was elected in 1978 to the writers' wing of the Baseball Hall of Fame. He also was an early advocate of women sportswriters.

they don't touch you or put their hands on you, then you have no recourse."[20] At Pel there were other signs of racism that were more difficult to ignore—signs like the chicken wire in the stands.

In the Pelican Stadium grandstands, chicken wire separated white fans, who sat under a roof, from blacks, who sat in the sun. The same was true in Kansas City for black fans attending Blues games, the city's white ball club.[21] The sight of chicken wire caging the fans was an assault to every black athlete who played in those stadiums. Some players were able to push the infuriating image out of their minds. Others could not. Pitcher Wilmer Fields could never forget the chicken wire at Pel. Later, during the 1953 season, while Fields was on the mound warming up for the Homestead Grays, he scanned the crowd, trying to locate his wife in the stands.* "I looked out there and saw my wife, smiling back at me and waving, penned in with chicken wire, like she and all the other blacks were just farm animals." Seeing his wife behind the chicken wire made it difficult to summon control. "I got this sick feeling in my stomach, really sick. It was the only time the racism and segregation and all that really got to me. I took the ball and I slammed it into my glove as hard as I could, hurting my hand, and said, 'Wilmer, just forget about it and pitch. Just pitch.'"[22]

Swallowing anger on the diamond was a learned response for black players. "You just went about your daily duty whether it was baseball or anything else," Paul Lewis of the New Orleans Black Pelicans said.† "It was just another thing you had to live with."[23] Players followed an unspoken motto: keep your head down, play well, and ride it out.

---

*Fields pitched for the Homestead Grays in the Negro League during the 1949 Colored World Series held at Pelican Stadium. The Grays won the series 4–1 against the Birmingham Black Barons.

†The Black Pelicans were part of a long history of African American teams in New Orleans that went back to the 1860s with the Aetnas, the Fischers, the Dumonts, the Unions, and the Pinchbacks, named for the first nonwhite Louisiana governor. The Black Pelicans played in the early 1900s and claimed with pride that they were "the first professional lineup to be mowed down" by Satchel Paige. "'We're gonna beat ya this time, Herman,'" the manager of the Chattanooga Black Lookouts said to Herman Roth, who managed and caught for the Black Pelicans in 1926. "'See that l-o-n-g boy out there?' said the Chat manager pointing to a string bean pitcher loosening up." Roth remembered that

Jackie Robinson knew he could not challenge an umpire's call for fear he would be unfairly tagged as a hothead.[24] Black players understood that if they lashed out at racist fans, owners would confront the players, not the fans. "I knew I had to keep my composure, never using profanity to respond to critics," Toni said.[25] But bottled-up anger could not be corked forever, as Satchel Paige had warned. Some players who did not explode found ways to use taunts to their advantage. Bill White remembered his difficult postwar summer in Danville, Virginia.* "I was only 18 and immature," he said. At times he yelled back at prejudiced fans, but then found a more effective target for his anger. He took it out on the ball. "The more fans gave it to me, the harder I hit the ball. They eventually decided to leave me alone." It was a "victory over bigotry," White said.[26] Finding a way to beat racism was like staring down a knuckleball, one player said. "If a guy's got a good knuckleball and you know he's going to throw you knuckleballs, you learn to hit it. You know it's hard, but you still have to do it because he's not going to throw you anything else."[27] Hitting the ball was more than a batting average statistic to many black players.

With batting practice over at Pel, BeeBop Gordon of the Sea Lions went through his pregame ritual and tried to count heads. "There were college guys on our team," he said, who could estimate the number of fans in the stands and quickly do the math to calculate how much money each player would earn from the day's gate receipts. Sometimes it seemed to BeeBop that dollars were more on the minds of players than playing, but he understood their concern. Many play-

---

"Baby-faced Satch" beat the New Orleans team 1–0. By the end of the year, Paige jumped to the Black Pels. New Orleans also had the Caulfield Ads and the Crescent Stars in the Negro Southern League in the 1920s, the Zulus, who played in the 1930s, and a host of local teams such as Dr. Nut's Algier Tigers in the 1940s. Later, in the 1950s, New Orleans inherited the Eagles, who moved to Houston when Effa Manley shut down the Newark-based team (Old Timers Baseball Club Collection, Amistad Research Center, Tulane University, New Orleans, LA).

*Bill White hit .298 for the Danville Giants and went on to play thirteen seasons for the New York and San Francisco Giants, the St. Louis Cardinals, and the Philadelphia Phillies. White served as president of the National League from 1989 to 1994, the first African American to do so.

ers had families to support and were always debating whether playing baseball paid as much as factory work back home. In a few years, BeeBop would decide the pay and the time on the road were not worth it, and he moved to Detroit for a job at the Ford Motor Company.[28] But looking out at the crowd on the 1949 Opening Day in New Orleans, BeeBop was happy. Alan Page had accurately predicted a good turnout. Nearly five thousand fans came through the gates at Pel. The Creoles smashed the Fort Worth Tigers 20–7 in the opener and fought a closely matched contest with the San Francisco Sea Lions until darkness forced the game to be called at 7–7.

The *Louisiana Weekly*, the city's black newspaper, had a new editor covering the game. Jim Hall worked as a maintenance man at the newspaper before he started writing sports. He had no sports reporting experience, although he had played basketball at Dillard University.[29] Hall wrote, "The highlight of the afternoon was the exhibition put on by San Francisco handless and footless wonder Little Sammie Workman, which was worth the price of admission alone. The little fellow performed feats that were truly amazing and kept the crowd . . . mystified and almost unbelieving. The applause which followed his act was deafening and fully justified."[30] No doubt Toni was disappointed that Hall did not give more attention to the game. There were no statistics in the article, not even a box score. She received one mention with her nickname, middle, and last name scrambled almost beyond recognition. "Lyle Stone Tony," Hall wrote, was in the lineup.

Inaccurate, incomplete, or inadequate newspaper coverage was a constant source of frustration for Toni and the other black players. Most black newspapers like the *Louisiana Weekly* were published once a week, and events that happened four or five days before the paper went to press would not be included in the paper. "Why cover a game Sunday if the paper didn't publish until the following Thursday?" some editors asked.[31] The sports department had one or perhaps two employees who covered multiple baseball venues: from Jackie Robinson and the major leagues to Negro League ball; semi-pro and barnstorming teams, local squads, and public school and college teams;

and other summer sports such as tennis, boxing, and track. Some sports editors had to divide their time among additional responsibilities as city editors or entertainment reporters. Rarely did Jim Hall have the resources or the space on the *Louisiana Weekly* sports page to include an interview with a player or in-depth coverage of a game. Hall never had the luxury of attending an away game. Edward Harris of the *Philadelphia Tribune* said baseball was the toughest black sport to cover because teams were always traveling. "You'd see [players] occasionally, sit in the bullpen to chat, and the next thing you know, they were off on a bus going somewhere."[32] Most of the time editors relied on club owners to send in their teams' final scores and highlights. When the scores did come in, they usually were too late for weekly newspapers. Many times an announcement of a game would appear in the *Louisiana Weekly* and no follow-up could be found. Readers who tried to follow the Creoles or the Sea Lions could not be sure of final scores or if games had even been played. To add to the problem, teams frequently forgot, were too busy driving to the next town, or were too strapped for money to mail, phone, or telegraph scores to area newspapers. For barnstorming teams such as Toni's Sea Lions, the situation was even worse. Games with other traveling squads or local teams were often scheduled at the last moment. Local reporters may not have even noticed that a team was in town if they missed handbills distributed around barbershops or promoters' phone calls hastily made from corner phone booths. Some players even swore that scores were printed in local newspapers only when club owners paid editors to print them.[33]

Even teams in the Negro League often failed to keep the press informed. Wendell Smith of the *Pittsburgh Courier* pleaded with Negro League club owners to stay on top of scores. "They must inform [the public] what is happening, where their teams play, supply the papers with the proper standings and weekly results and keep their version of the game on a level of dignity."[34] While many newspapers relied on the Elias Howe News Bureau for statistics, Howe also depended on receiving statistics from club owners. Occasionally the bureau posted incorrect results. Tom Baird, owner of the Kansas City Monarchs, pointed out that "some owners don't send 'em in only when their teams wins, some just sends 'em in now and then and a lot of times when we pay a sports writer, they don't send them in."[35] Baird had little recourse since the league did not have any procedures to ensure scores were collected or a way to penalize teams that did not accurately and promptly assemble data. At least one time, Howe's final standings for the complete Negro League season were inaccurate.*

Statistics were another problem because box scores and players' batting averages were sent in even less frequently. Often players' names were misspelled, abbreviated, or otherwise barely recognizable. Occasionally owners asked a relief pitcher to keep the scorebook, but if a starting pitcher got in trouble and a reliever went in, the scorebook sat on the bench unattended.[36] Some players became so frustrated that their individual statistics were not kept that they began keeping their own records, including data on strengths and weaknesses of opposing players.[37] The problem was compounded, of course, by a white press that rarely covered black baseball teams. Scanning the New Orleans *Times-Picayune*, a newspaper to which white residents subscribed, a reader would hardly know that blacks made up a third of the state's population. They were all but invisible.[38] In addition, many small towns were not large enough to support a black newspaper. Lack of press coverage exasperated Toni, who would play a great game and find no written record of it. The flawed record keeping made it difficult to offer a quantitative argument that she played as well as the men, or that black players were as good as whites. Louisiana sportswriter Russell Stockard realized that the accomplishments of many extraordinary black players were simply lost. "I feel a weakness in my heart for every day they didn't keep stats," he said.[39] The great Negro League center fielder James "Cool Papa" Bell knew firsthand what

*In 1954, Howe listed the Kansas City Monarchs in last place for both halves of the season—a record Baird disputed. Baird emphasized that poor record keeping could have disastrous results for a team if fans perceived the team as a losing enterprise and not worth supporting.

Stockard meant. "I remember one game I got five hits and stole five bases," he recalled, "but none of it was written down because they forgot to bring the scorebook to the game that day."[40]

While Jim Hall was not an experienced sportswriter, he was resourceful and learned reporting quickly. Soon he began writing on the political significance of sports, using his column in the *Louisiana Weekly* to lobby on behalf of black athletes. In one column he called on the major leagues to consider squads such as the Sea Lions and Creoles as minor league feeders. A "mixed farm system could materialize in democratic sections of the country. (Remember Truman won the South)," Hall wrote.[41] Earlier that month, the Pacific Coast League's San Francisco Seals added another black player to the league in signing pitcher Percy Fischer. Paul I. Fagan, president of the PCL, was a new and unequivocal voice in support of integration. "Baseball is an American game. Every American should have an opportunity on the basis of his ability alone," he wrote. "That is our policy and I personally guarantee that this policy will be obeyed. If anybody in my employ does not like this American ideal, he can turn in his contract."[42] Jim Hall chided New Orleans sports promoters—black and white—for being too accepting of the racial divide. "Frankly in New Orleans, the promoters of baseball, basketball, football, along with track, lack the drive to break down the barriers of Jim Crow in sports," he wrote. "With the exception of boxing (the Louisiana law states there shall be no fistic combat match between any person of the Caucasian 'white race' and one of the African or 'negro' race and, further, it will not be allowed for them to appear on the same card), there is no reason nor law that calls for segregation in sports except it is the usual custom and practice." Maintaining the status quo of segregation and relying on the hope that the race might achieve equality "someday" infuriated Hall. "New Orleans as a city should never stand up and proclaim democracy in our way of life as long as 'custom and practice' serves as its foundation for everyday living. For New Orleans, 'Jim Crow sports situation' is regarded today as one of the South's worst. This writer asks, 'New Orleans, what is your next move?"[43]

Toni might have asked the same question of herself. After leaving New Orleans, the Sea Lions headed north for games in the Midwest. On the bus ride through Arkansas and Missouri, Toni thought about the Creoles and how their team owner, Alan Page, carefully watched her play. Page was responsible for the good will many supporters felt toward the Creoles. "Genial Alan Page," Jim Hall wrote time and again, as if "genial" were the promoter's first name. Few baseball owners across the South were more innovative, more successful, or more of a risk taker than Alan Page. He was always "pull[ing] one from his bag of tricks," observers said, including adding women to the game.

Lucille Bland remembered Alan Page saying, "If I could just find a girl." Bland was a cashier at the Page Hotel, and her father was a close friend of the promoter's. Page thought that if he could hire a young woman who knew baseball and was willing to travel with the team as a coach, the novelty would bring curious fans to the game. "He thought that would be the come-on," Bland said. Page placed an advertisement in the newspaper, stipulating interested candidates had to know baseball and be "full of pep."[44] He couldn't find a girl who met his criteria until he turned around one day and took a look at Lucille behind the cash register.

Lucille Bland loved sports, played basketball and baseball at Dillard, and read everything she could about her hero, Babe Didrikson Zaharias. Bland joined the Creoles as a third-base coach and sat in the front seat of the bus with her "dresser," Inez, who made sure Lucille was attired in fashionable wear after the game. Mr. Page insisted she look stylish, Bland said. For two years, Bland traveled from New York to Texas and enjoyed the game's showmanship. Lucille Bland knew how to entertain. "I'd get right in an umpire's face and let him have it," she said. Coaching the players, however, took a while to perfect. "At first they resented it immensely," she said, but after they saw she understood the game, the men became more open to her suggestions. "I was a sister to them," she said. An automobile accident in 1948 sidelined Bland, and she resigned her position with the Creoles.[45]

To fill her spot as the girl attraction, Page found Fabiola Wilson—"comely and dimpled," his press release said—and "attractive" Gloria Dymond, both recent graduates of a local New Orleans high school. They were billed as "extra outfielders." Wilson wasn't an athlete, Bland said. She was the girlfriend of one of the Creole players.[46] In Bland's mind, Page did not regard the women as serious athletes, and Wilson and Dymond were gone in a year. If fans expected entertainment from Toni Stone when she played against the Creoles at Pelican Stadium, they were surprised. She was an exceptional athlete and a woman player Alan Page began to take seriously.

After their games in New Orleans, the Sea Lions headed north for a long and uncomfortable ride to Arkansas. Luggage rattled on top of the bus, and players hoped that a sudden downpour wouldn't drench their somewhat clean clothes. Players talked, read the sports pages, got on each other's nerves, or tried to wall off themselves from sensory intrusion, including the stench of sweat-drenched uniforms hanging in the back of the bus. Sometimes players broke up the numbing travel by throwing empty bottles at telephone poles as they passed at fifty-five miles an hour.[47] A few players, like Toni, grew restless and searched for a little activity to break the monotony. "Playing the dozens" was a Sea Lions favorite. The dozens was a trash-talking game that tested the participants' limits. Each player took turns insulting the other, the jabs increasing in flash and barb until one player couldn't offer a response. Some people called the back-and-forth arguments "yo mamma fights," and occasionally the game ended with a tussle of fists as tempers flared when the insults cut too close. Somewhere around Kansas City, BeeBop Gordon remembered, Toni and another Creole player, John Scroggins, got into it playing the dozens. Scroggins and Stone went back and forth, back and forth. Toni held her own, quickly slinging insults with more and more flair and wild word play until Scroggins sputtered and stammered and staggered into silence. "She got the better in that 'discussion,'" BeeBop said. [48]

Shortly afterward, Stone left the team.[49] BeeBop thought Scroggins couldn't stand losing face to a woman. Tensions on the bus became uncomfortable for Toni. But, more important, she found out that she was being paid less than the men on the Sea Lions. When Alan Page offered her a better deal, Toni knew it was time to go. In a matter of weeks, she was back at Pel Stadium in a hand-me-down uniform with CREOLES spelled in blue letters across her chest.* Toni quit the Sea Lions at the right moment. By the time the San Francisco team wrapped up games in Kansas City and headed to Canada, so many players had jumped to other squads that Yellowhorse Morris was left with only Sammy Workman to entertain fans. Even the white press noted Morris's headaches. "Harold Morris, owner of the San Francisco Sea Lions, touring Negro baseball team, was a troubled man when he arrived in Regina Saskatchewan today—minus his team," the *New York Times* reported. "He said his players jumped the club and signed to play with the Buchanan, Sask, All-Stars for the remainder of the season. The only 'player' Morris has left is Sammy Workman, an armless and legless performer who has been traveling with the team." Morris reported that what was left of the Sea Lions team would stay in Canada until the end of August to drum up barnstorming games. He also indicated that former players could be deported to the United States "for jumping their bond."[50] The Sea Lions bus, minus any players to fill it, sat on the Canadian prairie until Morris hired a local to drive it back to California. No player felt too bad for Yellowhorse, though. The Chicago Cubs hired Morris to scout black players on the West Coast.[51]

Toni knew she would be in for a period of adjustment with the Creoles. She had enough experience being both a newcomer and the only woman on a team to understand that the other players would be testing her athletic skills. But the Creoles also would wonder about her spine. Playing on a Southern team was quite different from playing against a Southern team, they said. There would be the chicken wire, the jeers, the Jim Crow buckets of drinking water in the dugouts

*Other accounts of Toni's life state that she also played with the New Orleans Black Pelicans, a fact I have been unable to confirm.

labeled "whites" and "colored." Now that Toni was a Creole and playing most of her games in the South, she had to steel herself against daily humiliations. She quickly learned what her teammates meant during a game in Florence, Alabama. An old white man "who practically owned the town," Toni said, was sitting near her and the players' bench. "Come on, nigger gal, hit that ball," he yelled, thinking he was offering encouragement. After the game, the man's mortified son searched for Toni to apologize. When he found her, Toni listened and accepted his apology, but lied about being within earshot of the insult. "I told him I didn't hear the remark," Toni said.[52] Sometimes deception—even lying to herself—served as an anesthetic against pain.

Toni had good reasons to be cautious in her response. That spring the Klan promised trouble when Jackie Robinson and the Brooklyn Dodgers toured the South. Branch Rickey signed deals for the Dodgers to play a series of preseason games with local white teams as Robinson and his teammates traveled from their spring training site in Florida to New York. Record-setting crowds in Miami, Florida, and Macon, Georgia, warmly greeted the Dodgers, but the Klan protested a game against a white team, the Atlanta Crackers.* The owner of the Crackers knew integrated games were against local law and sought a municipal "approbation" that allowed Robinson, Roy "Campy" Campanella, and Don Newcombe to play on the same field with whites.† Dr. Samuel Green, Grand Dragon of the Ku Klux Klan, was incensed and implied that Robinson and other black players might be at risk on the field. "You can bet your life I'll look up segregation law and investigate thoroughly," Green said. "In my opinion, it's illegal." Robinson confronted Green's attack during his Friday night radio program on WMCA in

---

*The Atlanta Crackers were known as the Yankees of the minors. An independent team, the Crackers played in the Class AA Southern Association. From 1950 to 1958 they were affiliated with the Boston and then Milwaukee Braves organization. The Atlanta Black Crackers were an independent team in the Negro Southern League. The ABCs folded in 1952.

†After Jackie Robinson integrated major league baseball, he was followed in July 1947 by center fielder Larry Doby of the Cleveland Indians, catcher Roy Campanella of the Brooklyn Dodgers in 1948, and pitcher Don Newcombe of the Brooklyn Dodgers in 1949.

New York. "I will play baseball where my employer, the Brooklyn Dodgers, wants me to play," he stated. Rickey's ire was piqued. "Nobody anywhere and at any time can tell me what players we can use," he said. "This is a decision I leave entirely to my manager, Burt Shotton." The Klan vowed to petition the Fulton County solicitor general and hoped that Governor Herman Talmadge, "busy pushing through anti-Negro legislation," would support them.[53]

Robinson's wit also helped ease the tension. "We expect that we'll run into a lot of name calling down there. I hope that's all—but you never can tell. I know one thing; there'll be plenty of colored people at those games. If anything starts to happen, Campy and I are going to make a bee-line for the middle of them and stay there."[54] When the day finally arrived for the game, nearly eighteen thousand fans crowded the stands at Ponce de Leon Park. Writing in the *Sporting News*, Joe B. King observed that so many black fans filled the "colored" sections that they pushed against "restraining ropes" around the outfield. Seeing the overflow crowds in Jim Crow seating, the Crackers' president turned on the stadium public address system and announced that black fans would be permitted to sit in previously restricted areas. King described the rush for seats as a "mob action which even [filmmaker] Cecil B. DeMille could only dream." Black fans ran from right field to open seats along the third base side. "There must have been a half-dozen unknown sprinters of Jesse Owens caliber leading the charge," King wrote. "Many went down . . . from overeagerness [sic] to gain a position in the bleachers where no Negro had ever been permitted to sit." Violence might have erupted at the moment black fans broke through the Jim Crow barrier, but King observed there was only laughter at what many white fans viewed as spectacle. Before the game began, the team president "thanked all the white fans as they fled from the bleachers to the grandstand." He later acknowledged receiving only one complaint.[55] King did not record the comments of black fans.

In 1949, even the name of Toni's new team—the Creoles—sparked racial argument. Black citizens frequently quoted a line attributed to the late Governor Huey Long about the state's distinct racial mixture.

"You could feed all the 'pure whites' in Louisiana," he was credited with saying, "with a nickel's worth of red beans and a dime's worth of rice."[56] Some residents believed that Creoles were "pure-blooded whites" who descended from French and Spanish settlers. Descendants of African slaves disagreed and said Creoles were mixed-race blacks who had French characteristics in name or culture. Still others said any resident who paid taxes in the state of Louisiana was Creole. "Honey, we's all Creoles as far as I can see," one anonymous black woman said. "We don't ask what it is, we just be's it. . . . Everything down here is Creole."[57] But even as part of the region's distinctive mixture, blacks still faced threats. Just weeks before Toni joined the team in 1949, an attempted lynching and a case of police brutality rocked the region. In St. Landry Parish, west of Baton Rouge, a black rape suspect being held for trial was kidnapped by whites and almost lynched before he escaped into the Atchafalaya River.* In Gretna, a town on the outskirts of New Orleans, a white policeman shot and killed a black man. The shooting was unwarranted and unprovoked, black residents said. At a meeting to demand an official police department response, a Dillard

---

*Edward Honeycutt was jailed on a rape charge after he was found walking alone on a road outside town. Deputies alleged that after making a lumber delivery in town, Honeycutt got drunk and raped a white housewife. Honeycutt reported that deputies beat a false confession out of him. Later, three white kidnappers scaled the courthouse, dropped through a roof, grabbed Honeycutt, and drove out to the Atchafalaya River where they tossed coins to see who would lynch him. Honeycutt broke away and jumped into the river as bullets shot over his head. The next morning, a fisherman found him on the opposite side of the river, hiding in a tree. An all-white jury found Honeycutt guilty and sentenced him to death. The NAACP stepped in and the case went to appeal. Even though some of Honeycutt's defense team expressed doubts about his innocence, his lawyers argued that the case was also about a black citizen's right to a fair trial. African American jurors were rare in Louisiana, and so were lawyers defending blacks. Fearful that defense attorneys would be assaulted as they drove to the courthouse, a group of blacks appealed to Governor Earl Long to provide protection. State troopers stood at every intersection for sixty miles between Baton Rouge and the courthouse in Opelousas where African Americans crammed the gallery and the courthouse lawn. When the defense objected to one potential juror described as "one of the best niggers in Opelousas," the judge overruled. "I don't think it is meant to be derogatory in any way," he said. "On the contrary, he was referring to the laudable characteristics of the person." Honeycutt lost his appeal, and on June 8, 1951, he died in the electric chair. Advocates of fair trials for African Americans said that legal lynching were as deadly as literal ones (Adam Fairclough, *Race and Democracy: The Civil Rights Struggle in Louisiana, 1915–1972*, 124–129).

University professor stepped forward and warned the community that a government dominated by whites was not likely to change.* The professor urged the assembled to put their faith in their own ability to organize and protest. "Such contempt will touch all persons who have no recourse in the body politic," he warned.[58] To blacks in the area, the two cases both demonstrated that racism went beyond how whites treated blacks. Racism also was built into the foundations of social structures all around them—government, law, education, and economics. The time had come to shift attention from individuals to institutions that disadvantaged blacks. While agreeing with the need to protest white domination, some black residents of New Orleans also argued that blacks sometimes contributed to their own subjugation. Nowhere was the talk about black complicity more heated than in arguments about Louis Armstrong and the uproar over the recent Mardi Gras parade. To many, the actions of Armstrong and the Zulu Social Aid and Pleasure Club were silly, stupid, and demeaning. "Self-respect first," one critic declared.[59]

For years, New Orleans native Louis "Satchmo" Armstrong dreamed of leading the Mardi Gras Zulu parade, but he never imagined his moment in the local spotlight would end in such controversy. Most blacks in the city were thrilled in 1949 when Armstrong finally was chosen to lead the city's largest black parade. "For the first time in their thirty-three-year history, they had an internationally known famous person as their King," observers said. "We like to think of Louis as a Babe Ruth of jazz!" On the day before the Zulu parade the New Orleans mayor, DeLesseps S. Morrison, presented Armstrong with a key to the city and teased the musician about saying his life's dream had been fulfilled and he was ready to die. "Well, I just hope that the Lord won't take me literally on that," Armstrong joked back.[60]

The next morning at dawn, a barge carrying Armstrong as King of the Zulus slipped into the New Basin Canal. By 9:00 A.M. Armstrong

---

*The *Louisiana Weekly* (April 3, 1949) reported that Roy C. Brooks Sr. was killed by Gretna policeman Alvin Bladsacker. Dr. Oakley Johnson of Dillard spoke about white control of government.

was ready, decked out in his King of the Zulus regalia. Armstrong stood in a grass skirt over long black underwear. A red velvet cape draped his shoulders and a gold cardboard crown sat cockeyed on his head. His face was blackened, and large, white circles rimmed his eyes and lips, exaggerating his features into a stark racial caricature. Then the parade began, weaving its way down a twenty-mile route through the black neighborhoods of New Orleans. "Man, this is rich," Armstrong said. "This king stuff is fine, real fine. It's knocking me out." Every few miles, Satchmo would stop the parade at a sponsoring tavern—"Zulus Will Stop Here!" signs said. While Armstrong entertained the crowds, his subjects drank beer and ate turkey and ham sandwiches, olives, and potato salad. Each tavern stop grew longer and each renewed start more boisterous and unsteady. As Armstrong's float turned the final corner toward the main viewing stand, the crowd erupted into cheers. There was Louis Armstrong, King of the Zulus, swaying in blackface atop the wobbly confection of glitter, gaudiness, and palmetto leaves. Someone helped Satchmo down, and he entered the Gertrude Geddes Willis Funeral Home, where he offered a toast to his queen, Bernice Oxley, a ticket taker at the Ace Theatre. The rest of the parade bucked to an exhausted and dissipated end when—as was tradition—participants smashed and tore apart the King's float, reducing Armstrong's throne to a trash heap for souvenir hunters. At night, the celebration continued with parties all over the city.[61]

But Louis Armstrong and the Zulu blackface were not "hilarious" to everyone. Black intellectuals called them "offensive vestiges of the minstrel-show, Sambo-type Negro." In fact, many of the city's black residents believed the Zulu parade escalated racial prejudice and should be abolished. Days after Mardi Gras, the People's Defense League denounced Armstrong for "contributing to one of the most disgraceful spectacles on Carnival Day." The *Louisiana Weekly* condemned the Zulus, suggesting that Armstrong should not have used his fame for such a degrading and debased display. "The Zulu parade of 1949 was normal," the newspaper wrote, "and that is awful by any standard. Louis Armstrong did nothing for it and it did less for him."

Time magazine noted that some supporters of the parade thought critics missed the point and failed to see the Zulu celebration as a "broad dark satire on the expensive white going-on in another part of town."* Nellie B. Lewis, who worked as a cashier in New Orleans, was typical of many blacks who thought that embracing racial caricatures in any form led to reinforced prejudice. "As whole, I enjoy Mardi Gras . . . [but] I dislike seeing the race participate in certain types of masking, imitating characters that they have never seen."[62]

The protest over Louis Armstrong's Zulu parade appearance sounded familiar to Toni. For years she had heard criticism about clowning performed by some black teams. Her old friend John Cotton from the Saint Paul Colored Giants thought it was fun to perform acrobatic ball tosses between innings, and fans laughed when players sitting in rocking chairs at the plate took wild, comical swings at the ball. Clowning in baseball went back even further than blackface at the Zulu parade. James Weldon Johnson, one of the writers the Saint Paul Hallie Q. staff members always praised, wrote about black "baseball comedies" that took place in the late nineteenth century. "Generally after a good play," Johnson wrote in *Black Manhattan*, "the whole team would for a moment cut monkey shines that would make the grand stand and bleachers roar." But when the Negro League was established in the 1920s, team owners wanted nothing to do with clowning. It was unprofessional, they said. Clowning teams were not taken seriously. But barnstormers and semi-pro teams such as the Florida Colored Hobos or Zulu Cannibal Giants thought clowning brought in crowds, and pointed out that their teams often made more money than con-

---

*Journalist A. S. "Doc" Young believed criticism of Louis Armstrong was shortsighted. In a 1971 oral history, Young said, "It's easy to be pointed [to] as an Uncle Tom. It was Louie Armstrong, as little as anybody knows, who was responsible for President Eisenhower sending the troops to Little Rock [in 1957–1958 to protect black students at Central High School]. A lot of young black people didn't know. . . . Just because he had that white handkerchief and was smiling all the time didn't mean he was an Uncle Tom. He refused to play New Orleans as long as he couldn't play for an integrated audience. . . . They didn't appreciate him because they didn't take the time to find out" (Jim Reisler, *Black Writers/Black Baseball: An Anthology of Articles from Black Sportswriters Who Covered the Negro Leagues*, Jefferson, NC: McFarland & Company, 2007, 177).

ventional league squads. After white promoter Syd Pollock took over the Ethiopian Clowns in 1937, fans lined up to see Pollock's brand of clowning. His players dressed in grass skirts or clown outfits; they wore whiteface and performed outlandish comedy routines. Player Dave Barnhill said, "We'd come to the park with paint on our faces like a clown. Even the bat boy had his face painted, too. We wore clowning wigs and the big old clown uniforms with ruffled collars. My clowning name was Impo." The crowds loved it, Barnhill said, and the money was good. "They'd pay us extra money to do it over again, that's how good it was." Bob Bissant, who spent four years with the Zulu Cannibal Giants, remembered, "We'd have a dice game, steal bases the wrong way and cut up with the crowd. My specialty was to turn my butt to the pitcher and then jump out of the way and hit the ball." Bissant, who later captained the New Orleans Black Pelicans in 1945, noted that clowning paid off in both money and better uniforms. "The uniforms were cooler than anything anybody else wore, and it was all a lot of fun to me. I was making $12 to $15 a day when back home I might be making $6 or $7 a week."[63] Comedy was at the center of black culture, proponents said. To forbid clowning on the baseball diamond would stifle an expression of the race.

But Cumberland Posey was sick of clowning and Syd Pollock. Posey owned the Negro League's Homestead Grays and now penned an influential sports column for the *Pittsburgh Courier*. Clowning debased blacks and played into dangerous stereotypes, he argued. If that weren't bad enough, using the arbitrary name "Ethiopian" for Pollock's team ridiculed the African nation as well. Posey urged black sports editors to boycott coverage of the Ethiopian Clowns as a way to demonstrate their disgust. Pollock called Posey jealous because the Clowns made money. Arguments between Posey and Pollock continued to flair until the Negro League got involved in 1941 and ruled that all Negro League teams were forbidden from playing the Ethiopian Clowns. Playing on the same diamond with players cavorting in grass skirts and whiteface was a "detriment," they said. Wendell Smith of the *Courier* agreed. Clowning was "the kind of nonsense which many white people like to believe is typical and characteristic of Negroes." It was as damaging and demeaning as Amos 'n' Andy, he said. A year later, Pollock and the league reached a compromise. Pollock's team gave up the whiteface, the grass skirts, and the "Ethiopian" name, but they kept playing shadow ball and maintained comedy routines for pre-games, doubleheader breaks between games, and barnstorming. League owners were satisfied, and Pollock's team, renamed simply the Clowns, was admitted into the Negro League.* Posey and Smith no doubt kept their eyes on Pollock. One never knew what the white owner would have a black player do next.[64]

Toni joined the Creoles just as the team headed out for a two-week barnstorming tour through Michigan, Ohio, and Illinois. As a newcomer, she sat in the worst seat on the bus—in the back, where it was cramped and noisy, straddling a wheel well. Toni respected baseball hierarchies and recognized when to keep to herself. "I knew that there would be times when the guys would want to do things without me; even just to talk about things men had in common. I didn't think it necessary to change their lifestyles."[65] Even from her spot in the back seat, though, Toni could size her up her teammates. The Creoles were like most semi-pro and Negro League teams. They were a mix of teenage sensations just out of high school and veterans who hoped for a chance to finally make it to the majors. There was eighteen-year-old Buddy Lombard from Algiers, Louisiana, and thirty-nine-year-old Olan "Jelly" Taylor, who had joined the Creoles because he loved the game too much to give it up. Taylor was a former Pittsburgh Crawfords first baseman who had played with Cool Papa Bell and other legendary Negro League players such as Oscar Charleston, Josh Gibson, and William Julius "Judy" Johnson. Most of the Creoles players were in their twenties and thirties, and many had Negro League experience, such as Frank Evans, an outfielder who had played with the Philadelphia Stars and the Memphis Red Sox; Alfred "Buddy" Armour, an out-

---

*When the Clowns joined the Negro League in 1943, they split their home games between Cincinnati and Indianapolis. In 1946, they became known solely as the Indianapolis Clowns.

fielder and shortstop who spent seasons with the Chicago American Giants, the Homestead Grays, and the Cleveland Buckeyes; Charlie Johnson, who played with the Birmingham Black Barons; big Al Pinkston who was a St. Louis Stars first baseman; and Joe Wiley, formerly of the Baltimore Elite Giants and Memphis Red Sox who shared second-base duties with Toni. Freddie Shepard managed the team after three seasons with Birmingham as a pitcher and outfielder.*

Although they rarely admitted it, the Creoles players all shared the same worry: would they be noticed? Jelly Taylor worried that scouts would think he was too old. Buddy Lombard worried he was too young. Toni worried that scouts noticed her for the wrong reasons. While she had developed an appetite for being featured on game handbills and in stray sentences of newspaper copy even if reporters consistently got her name wrong, Toni did not want scouts to see her as a sideshow novelty. She wanted to be evaluated for her talent and commitment to the game. Toni hoped her play would attract serious attention from baseball executives like Branch Rickey who might be willing to take a chance on another groundbreaking player. She came to believe that if she were on the right team with the right manager who would give her substantial time on the field, she could prove herself. She had one goal: to become a professional baseball player without being a clown.

The Creoles enjoyed one of their best road trips of the season, with a 44–8 record, before heading home to New Orleans for a July 25 game with the Birmingham Black Barons of the Negro League. Freddie Shepard knew the matchup would bring crowds and told the press that Toni Stone would be "in good shape for the game" and that he expected her to put on "one of the finest shows of the season."[66] Toni was eager for the contest, since she knew major league scouts and representatives

---

*Teams in the 1949 Negro Southern League were the Atlanta Brown Crackers, the Chattanooga Choo Choos, the Delta Giants, the Gadesen Tigers, the Memphis Red Caps, the New Orleans Creoles, and the Owensboro Dodgers. Managers for the New Orleans Creoles included A. Hill (1948), formerly with the Negro League's Newark Eagles, Wesley Barrows, who took over in August 1949, and Felton Snow, of the Negro League's Cleveland Buckeyes, who began managing the Creoles in May 1950.

from the Negro League would be in the stands. Russ Cowans of the *Chicago Defender* reported that sixteen major league clubs were "beating the bushes for raw material of the ebony hue."[67] Traveling the South were Eddie Montage of the New York Giants and John Donaldson of the White Sox. Toni's excitement about the game was shared by Black Barons newcomer eighteen-year-old Willie Mays out of Westfield, Alabama. Like Toni, Willie's baseball dreams were fueled by growing up near a minor league ballpark. Mays followed the Black Barons, listened to radio broadcasts of the white Barons from Rickwood Field, and became familiar with the booming voice of announcer Eugene "Bull" Conner.* Toni and Willie also respected baseball veterans like Gabby Street and Pepper Batson, the former Rocking Chair catcher for the Clowns who was playing with the Black Barons. Mays thought Batson was not adequately recognized for his powerful throws to second; fans and scouts missed the exceptional skill of many clowning ballplayers, he said. Toni would have welcomed the attention Mays received from the Black Barons manager, Lorenzo "Piper" Davis. While both Stone and Mays initially had trouble hitting curveballs, Mays's batting average moved from .262 to .311 after Davis told the youngster to use his wrists and a lighter bat.

Toni's Creoles batting average hovered around .265.[68] With her playing time limited to a few innings a game and little attention from her manager, Toni had to rely on her own natural talent, observation, and advice from teammates to improve her game. Sometimes late at night when she sat around with other players "lallygagging and playing cards," she'd ask the men to help her dissect the game. "I had some buddies who would tell me things," she said.[69] Many players, like Toni, were eager for instruction, but few received coaching. Mahlon Duckett, who played for the Negro League's Philadelphia Stars, said there were simply no coaches on black teams. One man ran the squad, he said—the manager. "We had no one to teach us," he said.[70] The Creole–Black

---

*Theophilus Eugene "Bull" Connor (1897–1973) later became police commissioner in Birmingham, Alabama, and came to national attention when he used fire hoses and attack dogs against civil rights protestors.

Barons game in New Orleans was not a showcase for either Mays or Toni Stone. The Black Barons won 4–0 in a pitchers' duel.[71] After another road trip for Toni through the Dakotas and western Canada, the 1949 season came to an end with the Creoles finishing in first place.[72] The Greenville (Mississippi) *Democrat-Times* reported that Toni finished the season with a .326 average and played in seventy-eight games.[73]

Toni returned to Oakland at the end of the season. She picked up day work where she could—cleaning, carpentry, odd jobs. She was never interested in more permanent work. She'd rather stop into barbershops and ask owners if they needed help cleaning windows or sorting stock. She also sought work driving trucks or other people's cars. "Need help dumping your truck?" Toni would offer. "Want your car driven down the coast?" Dressed as she was in men's clothes, Toni made some people apprehensive, but her friendliness and open manner usually eased their suspicion. Toni was especially comfortable working with older people, older men in particular.[74] During the off-season, Toni earned enough money to maintain her independence and self-respect. Lessons in self-reliance taught by Boykin and Willa Stone were well learned. "Learn to do hair or sweep a floor," her parents preached. "You always need something to sustain you."[75] During the off-season, Toni wasn't looking for a long-term job as much as steady cash to pay basic expenses. The winter, after all, was merely a yawn between the postseason and spring training. By the following April, Toni was eager for another year with the Creoles, and she began playing pickup baseball games in Golden Gate Park. In New Orleans, sportswriter Jim Hall announced that Toni would be joining the team soon, noting that she had "received a leave of absence from a west coast college where she is a PE major."*

---

*In a 1993 interview with Kyle McNary, Stone said she completed study for her high school GED while living in California after World War II. The Minneapolis–Saint Paul *Twin City Leader* on July 19, 1941, reported that Toni was attending West Virginia State University. Officials at the University have no record of Stone's attendance, although the institution was known for its outstanding athletic program and several young people from Toni's Rondo neighborhood in Saint Paul were enrolled at West Virginia State. I have been unable to confirm or deny that Stone attended any California college.

A month later, in Saint Paul, Boykin Stone picked up the *Chicago Defender* and was astonished to find his daughter's photograph and a three-column headline stretched across page eighteen: "New Orleans' Lady Second Sacker Is Sensation of Southern League." Boykin and Willa were surprised that Toni Stone, the family's "special child," had received national recognition. Toni had started the 1950 baseball season well, and the press, if not scouts and club managers, was beginning to take note. The article described Toni's unprecedented rise in baseball and declared that she was "now displaying her greatest power with the Creoles." She was batting nearly .300, flawlessly fielded hard-hitting grounders and line drives, and displayed "a technique on second that rivals many of the males" on double plays. The article also reported that Toni had played last year in the postseason against the Jackie Robinson All-Stars in New Orleans before seventeen thousand fans. Described as a "shapely lass," Toni told reporters that she was "too busy right now for much romancing." Apparently Toni had mastered the curveball—in handling pitchers and an inquisitive press. She even managed to keep the fib going about her age. The *Defender* unknowingly perpetuated the myth that Toni was born in 1931, not 1921. Readers thought she was eighteen years old, the same age as Willie Mays. Perhaps only Toni's family and a few close readers of the *Defender* caught an inconsistency in the newspaper's text. How could a young woman purportedly born in 1931 have attended Gabby Street's baseball school in 1934?[76]

Toni was guarded about her age for a reason. Younger players were the ones making moves. Since the previous year when the Creoles met the Black Barons, Willie Mays had pumped up his batting average to .353 and signed with the New York Giants. A nineteen-year-old, Ernie Banks, who had barnstormed with the semi-pro Amarillo Colts during summers in high school had been signed by the Kansas City Monarchs. Even some black players who had made it to the big leagues regretted that their break came too late, when their skills were beginning to wane. Monte Irvin admitted he was not "half the ball-player" he'd been ten years earlier when he played for the Negro League's Newark Eagles. "I'm not bragging about what I was or trying to knock myself down about what I am now," he explained. "But between the time I was 19 and 23, I could hit a ball farther and run faster and throw harder and had better reflexes." In his thirties, Irvin regretted that the major leagues had passed him by when he was a younger man. "How I wish I could have had my chance in the majors at 23!" he said.[77] Pushing thirty herself, Toni knew she had a limited amount of time for advancing in baseball, but she also believed there were more opportunities now than there had been when segregation had a full grip on the sport.

Toni found herself at a crossroads about her future. During a series in Memphis that spring, she took stock of her options and herself. She had been playing baseball for over a decade: local teams, American Legion, barnstorming, and now semi-pro ball. Where could she go from here? The call from the Pacific Coast League that she hoped would come never materialized. No woman would ever break the gender barrier in the PCL, as Toni had hoped. She could, of course, stay with the Creoles and barnstorm in the postseason. She could quit baseball, as so many players already had, and look for permanent work in New Orleans or back in the Bay Area. She could return to Saint Paul and join her brother in her parents' barber and beauty shop business. Or she could redouble her efforts and aim—like Willie Mays—for the major leagues. It didn't daunt her that she was a twenty-nine-year-old black woman masquerading as a teenager trying to make it in America's most sacred sport. "I figured that then was the time for me to make the grade as the first woman player," she said.[78] Years later, when she looked back at that moment in Memphis, she realized it was a turning point in her life. It was there that she vowed to go as far as she could in professional baseball.

Toni's Memphis decision sparked personal results. By midseason, she had raised her batting average to nearly .300.[79] Injuries, including a bruised left arm from being hit by a pitch, kept her out of several games on a Midwestern tour. On another jump—she couldn't remember where—an injury sent her to a local charity hospital, the Sisters of the Poor. But after a quick "patch up," she "rode back to the ballpark on a policeman's horse," Toni said.[80] It was not surprising that her grit and determination impressed sportswriters.[81] One night in Iowa was particularly memorable. Creole third baseman Ralph "Big Cat" Johnson grabbed a hot line drive and fired it to Toni for the start of a double play. The lights on the field were dim, and gloves were not made well back then, Johnson said. So when Toni caught the ball, it tore through her glove and knocked her out cold. Toni lay on the ground unconscious as players yelled for water. "They poured water on that girl," Johnson said, and "she jumped up," yelling, "Let's go! Let's go!" No one had seen anything like it.[82] Women, especially, found her play inspiring. In Mississippi, a 102-year-old woman attending her first baseball game asked to shake Toni's hand and announced she was "pleased to see a woman playing."[83] The two women kept in touch, Toni said.[84] In Council Bluffs, Iowa, a former women's softball player emboldened by Toni's play approached the local men's team's manager and won a tryout.[85] For Toni, however, no attention meant more to her than the fan who sought her out during a July game in Iowa. Joe Louis, who recently had cancelled an exhibition boxing match in Georgia when local authorities refused to let blacks sit in ringside seats, was in the area participating in a golf tournament. After Toni led off the game with a single, Louis strolled over to the Creoles dugout to congratulate her.

Meeting Joe Louis may have made it seem to Toni that the vow she made in Memphis—as improbable as it was—was within reach. Just like the outstretched hand of her hero, a man she called "the champion of champions," Toni's dream felt within her grasp. Becoming the first woman to play professional baseball surely was a preposterous thought. Improbable. Naive. Some would say foolish. But Toni found it impossible to conform to someone else's notion of who she should be. "My mother had a dreamer in the bunch and that was me," she said.[86] Every night she pictured herself playing professional ball. "I imagined myself on the way to something real big with a big payoff."[87] As enormous as the odds against her were, Toni knew no other choice would be right. Nothing else felt authentic. "I had to play," she said simply.[88] "I wanted to find the heart of the game."[89]

On Deck

> No one can possibly know what is about to happen: it is happening, each time, for the first time, for the only time. . . . Everyone seemed to be waiting, as I was waiting.[1]
>
> —James Baldwin

As much as she loved the game, Toni put her baseball dreams on hold. She left New Orleans after the 1950 Creoles season ended and returned to Oakland. No one—not her teammates, not her friends back in San Francisco at Jack's Tavern, not her sister Bunny, and not her family in Saint Paul—could have predicted what she was about to do. Toni Stone was getting married.

Toni had given no indication that marriage was in her future. She displayed little romantic interest in men and rebuffed teammates who tried to make passes. When one player sexually harassed her on a team bus, she asked her manager to intervene. He told her to settle the matter herself, so Toni grabbed a baseball bat. She "hit that kid in the name of the Father and the Son," she said. "I thought I was going to have to go to jail, but I got away with it. I had to prove I was tough."[2] When Toni did socialize with men, she usually went out with a group, joining other players for drinks and cigarettes after a game. "Saturday night was good for the soul," she said.[3] She enjoyed the camaraderie, although some wives and girlfriends found Toni's friendships with the men inappropriate. They could not understand why a woman wanted to be "one of the guys" and assumed she was out to steal their men. Most of the Creole players, like her Twin City Colored Giants teammates, admitted that they did not regard Toni in romantic terms. "We didn't think of her as a girl," one said.[4] If she dated, Toni didn't let her team know. She kept that information to herself. "Dan Cupid will have to wait," she told reporters.[5] Family members said Toni rarely dressed up, put on makeup, or tried to appear conventionally attractive. Toni would wear a dress or skirt, if asked, for special occasions such as weddings or holidays. She would pose for a group photograph, and then slip out to her car where she had trousers and a shirt stashed in the trunk for a quick change.[6]

Dressing as she did in men's trousers, shirts, and shoes, many people assumed Toni was a lesbian. Cross-dressing women were commonly thought to be gay. While many considered the Bay Area a more liberal environment than other parts of the country, a cross-dressing woman still could be threatened, harassed, or even arrested by San Francisco vice squads. Local ordinances forbade anyone from impersonating with intent to deceive a member of the opposite sex. One woman admired clever cross-dressing lesbians who found a way to avoid being thrown in jail: they always wore women's underwear. "If you wore one article of feminine apparel," she said, vice squads "couldn't book you."[7] The same was true for men in drag. Men got around the ordinance by wearing "I am a boy" tags pinned to their clothing.[8] But anyone who knew Toni well would tell you that she rarely had close relationships with women. Friends and family could not recall one woman with whom Toni appeared especially intimate. She thought all women looked down on her, like her teammates' girlfriends and the stylish girls from Rondo.[9]

Above all, Toni preferred the company of older men—the old-timers who hung out at the meatpacking plants in Saint Paul, veteran ballplayers who shared baseball history with her, elderly gentlemen who frequented her father's barbershop. Toni felt at ease around them, comfortable talking about the past, and comforted, perhaps, in assuming that older men would have no sexual interest in her. Perhaps that's why she enjoyed Aurelious Pescia Alberga so much. The conversations they shared at Jack's Tavern, the way he found a place for her on the American Legion team, and his admiration for her modest celebrity all made Toni feel important. When he asked, Toni accepted Alberga's marriage proposal. The couple was married in San Francisco on December 23, 1950, at the city's Municipal Court. Alberga was sixty-seven and Toni was twenty-nine. They settled into Alberga's small Victorian home at 844 Isabella Street in Oakland.* Toni took the large first-floor bedroom and Alberga occupied a smaller one next to it. Toni called her husband "Pa." He called her "dear sweetheart."[10] Having a husband "gave me respectability," Toni said.[11]

But Alberga did not give Toni his blessing to continue playing baseball. At his request, she sat out the 1951 summer baseball season and scrounged up odd jobs around Oakland. Alberga's request was baffling. To everyone in California who knew him, Aurelious Alberga was one of the most prominent black leaders in the state. He had spent a lifetime pushing for equality. He spearheaded the California State Colored Republican League, which registered black voters. When he found out Toni was not a registered voter, he personally escorted her to City Hall.[12] Alberga helped establish the Booker T. Washington Center in San Francisco when he saw that young blacks were not provided adequate athletic opportunities. He also was one of the founders of the Northern California NAACP and would have been incensed, as other black leaders were, when reports of possible Jim Crow bomb shelters began cropping up in news articles about the Cold War.[13] As the motto of the California State Colored Republican League stated,

---

*Toni Stone's age continued to be a slippery issue even when it came to her marriage license. The December 20, 1950, license lists her age as thirty, even though she would not turn thirty until seven months later on July 17, 1951 (Stone-Alberga marriage license no. 1443, book 975, page 165, San Francisco, CA).

Alberga stood for "free, equal and un-trampled political rights for all American citizens."[14] Except, it seems, when it came to his wife.

Alberga's attempt to rein in his wife's ambitions may have sprung from two beliefs. When it came to gaining opportunities for blacks, Alberga was an accommodationist, an example of an older generation of leaders who thought that if they worked diplomatically with the white majority, more opportunities would come their way. Alberga could point to his patronage position as a bootblack in the Ferry Building as evidence that such strategies worked—at least minimally. In many ways, Alberga's worldview was similar to Boykin Stone's and the political legacy he inherited from Booker T. Washington. Blacks would gain equality by demonstrating that they were responsible, honest, hardworking, and reliable citizens; equality had to be earned by securing the respect and approval of the white majority. By continuing to "force" her way further up the ladder of professional baseball, Toni may have appeared to Alberga to be too assertive, even militant, in her desire to open doors that whites had not cracked open yet. Political leaders such as W. E. B. DuBois, who called for racial injustices to be challenged and who argued that white domination was a threat to all democracy, assumed a philosophical stance that felt threatening to men such as Alberga. It was one thing to slowly assimilate into white culture; it was quite another to demand white culture radically change. Alberga may have viewed his wife's angling for a better position in professional baseball as simply too much, too fast.

Like many other male leaders at the time, Alberga's efforts to reverse racial discrimination did not include ending sexism. Many leaders believed women could best influence political action by influencing their husbands' decisions or by demonstrating their worth in the domestic sphere. Alberga certainly knew he wasn't marrying a woman whose identity would be formed by housekeeping or childrearing. His indifference to the disenfranchisement of women wasn't rooted in a conviction that black women should not be accorded the same rights as men. He simply didn't recognize their struggles. He could not apply his understanding of racism to the prejudice that Toni faced as a woman. It was a blind spot, but a temporary one. Years later, when reflecting on the absence of women in early political battles in California, Alberga admitted that he and other men failed to reach across gender lines. "When I say [women] weren't interested," he confessed, "I mean they could have been, but we didn't take the time to interest ourselves in them."[15] Toni's family members believed there was another reason "Uncle Pescia" wanted Toni to stay away from baseball in 1951. He wanted her to help out around the house.[16] His home needed repair, and Alberga was growing physically unable to keep up with the maintenance. Toni could paint, clean, build, or restore anything. She would take on maintaining their house and marriage first, then her career.

As baffling as Alberga's edict to Toni was, her response was equally puzzling. It seemed improbable that a woman who had surmounted so many obstacles and vowed to make baseball her life could be persuaded to give it up. Gabby Street, her unlikely patron, died in February 1951, and Toni may have felt that at age thirty she belonged to an earlier era of baseball that was vanishing. Semi-pro teams such as the New Orleans Black Pelicans were folding. Even Alan Page in New Orleans was having a tough time of it. When Page had a disagreement with local park officials before one game, he abruptly removed his team from the field. Fans stormed the ticket office, jumped the fence, and swamped Page, demanding their money back. Police eventually restored order but not before Page lost his wallet and his keys.[17] If "genial Alan Page" found himself in the middle of a fracas, what could happen next to the world of baseball that Toni knew?

But more than concern about her age, worries about the future of the game, or even jitters about her safety, it was more likely that Toni took the year off to test herself. She may have looked upon her marriage and 1951 as a kind of crucible—the final test of her drive and dedication to the game. On some inchoate level, Toni may have accepted Alberga's request in order to determine if she could live without baseball and adjust to conventional life. Toni had been running from an orthodox vision of herself since she was a girl in the confessional booth at St. Peter Claver. If, after twelve months away from baseball, she found that she could not live without the game—then the vow she made in Memphis might be stronger. Tested faith is strong faith, every Catholic girl knew.

After a year, Toni had her answer: her passion for baseball was not diminished. Absence taught Toni that she relished the physical demands of the sport, needed the affirmation it provided, and grew in dignity and self-respect from doing what she loved. What emerged from deprivation was a deeper understanding of her true self. For Toni that consciousness was as certain and sharp as the crack of a bat.

Toni's temporary separation from baseball provided another revelation as well. She realized that there were other women like her who also loved playing the game. World War II and its aftermath had upended countless assumptions about what women could do. Once women proved they could work in male-dominated professions such as Bay Area shipyards, it was not long before one enterprising businessman proposed they could play baseball as well. Philip Wrigley devised a plan to form a women's professional baseball league when the major leagues were weakened by players leaving for military service. Wrigley, who owned the Chicago Cubs, contacted other baseball executives and combed the country looking for talented young women who could play the game and look ladylike doing it. They found their athletes, and in 1943 the league began with four teams in Illinois, Indiana, and Wisconsin.* A year later, Minnesota also had a team, the Minneapolis Millerettes, and by 1948 the league more than doubled in size. Wrigley placed his emphasis on building teams in medium-size cities in the Midwest, but even Chicago became part of the league

*The All-American Girls Baseball League (AAGBL), which later became known as the All-American Girls Professional Baseball League (AAGPBL), existed between 1943 and 1954. The league received attention in the motion picture *A League of Their Own*. Originally established as a professional softball league, the AAGBL gradually shifted to baseball with a smaller ball, nine players instead of ten, overhand pitching, and other modifications. Players received between fifty and a hundred dollars a week and had to attend charm school so that fans would not view them as too masculine. Athletes also had to wear skirted uniforms, which caused scrapes and bruises when players attempted to slide or field difficult ground balls.

in 1948 with the Chicago Colleens.* Toni wanted to join the growing women's league and wrote executives asking for a tryout.[18] There was one problem. The League was segregated. Black women were not included. A discussion during a 1951 AAGPBL Board of Directors meeting revealed the consensus was against the "idea of colored players unless they would show promise of exceptional ability."[19] Toni kept waiting for an answer to the inquiry she sent the AAGPBL, but never received one. When some white players later found out that Toni had requested a tryout, they were disappointed that the league had ignored her. "I don't know why we didn't have blacks," Mame Redman, a catcher for the 1950 Grand Rapids Chicks, later said. The league's executive-level bigotry bewildered her, and she empathized with the barriers Toni faced. "I felt sorry for her," Redman said.[20]

The disappointment Toni encountered as a woman seeking to play professional baseball was not new. There were, of course, other women before her who tried to make a living in the sport. A few female "baseballists" had played for short stints in front of paying fans and a curious public since the late nineteenth century. Several women also played on men's teams. Elizabeth "Lizzie" Stroud Arlington played for Pennsylvania men's teams in the Atlantic League in 1898. Lizzie Murphy played against the Boston Red Sox in a benefit game at Fenway Park in 1922.† In 1931, Jackie Mitchell famously struck out Babe Ruth and Lou Gehrig in an exhibition game between the New York Yankees and the Chattanooga Lookouts, an AA team in the Southern Association. Isabelle Baxter reportedly played second base for the Cleveland

---

*One scene in *A League of Their Own* conveys that some black women wanted to play in the AAGBL. In the scene, the Rockford Peaches team is warming up and catcher Dottie Hinson, the character played by Geena Davis, lets a ball get by her where it rolls toward a group of nearby fans. A black woman picks up the ball and eyes Davis as if to say, "May I join you?" She then fires the ball back to Davis to show she has the ability to compete. While there is no evidence that Toni Stone ever interacted with players on the Rockford Peaches exactly as the film suggests, the scene makes the point that segregation denied African American women athletes an opportunity to play professional baseball with the league.

†Outside the United States, Pearl Barnett played for the Havanna [Cuba] Stars in 1917. An African American woman, Barnett played first base.

Colored Giants in 1932 and 1933.* Frances Dunlop of the men's Fayetteville Bears played against the Cassville Blues in a 1936 Class D Arkansas-Missouri League game. Yet no woman had come as far in breaking into the ranks of men's professional baseball as Toni Stone.

That is, until a young white woman signed a contract in June 1952 to play minor league ball in Pennsylvania. Eleanor Engle was a twenty-four-year-old stenographer who played shortstop in a local women's softball league. The Harrisburg Senators, a minor league men's team in the Class B Interstate League, were in seventh place and desolate. The Senators' manager thought Engle might add punch to the lineup and pump up ticket sales. But before Engle could take to the field, baseball's minor league boss, George Trautman—Gabby Street's old friend—nullified Engle's contract, putting an end to the possibility of women in the white minor leagues. In a telegram from San Francisco, Trautman wrote, "I am notifying all clubs that signing of women players by National Association clubs will not be tolerated and clubs, signing or attempting to sign women players, will be subject to severe penalties." Major league Commissioner Ford Frick agreed. "I have consulted with Commissioner Frick," Trautman added, "and he has asked me to express his concurrence in the view that this is just not in the best interest of baseball that such travesties be tolerated."[21] Engle's career was short-lived: there would be no female "travesties" in the major or minor leagues. But Toni had heard doomsday predictions before. Some sportswriters had forecast that major league baseball would be destroyed when Jackie Robinson entered the game.†

---

*Marilyn Cohen writes that Baxter's play was limited to a few innings in a single game (*No Women in the Clubhouse: The Exclusion of Women from Baseball*, Jefferson, NC: McFarland & Company, 2009, 77).

†Jonathan Eig in his excellent account of Jackie Robinson's first season, *Opening Day*, recounts the story of Bob Cooke, a sportswriter for the *Herald Tribune*, who concurred with an anthropologist who argued that blacks had longer heel bones, which gave them greater speed. "It starts with Robinson but it doesn't end with Robinson," Cooke said in a story told by writer Roger Kahn. "Negroes are going to run the white people out of baseball. They're going to take over our game" (*Opening Day*, 67).

With the white major and minor leagues off-limits for the time being and the AAGBL ignoring her, Toni saw one viable option open to her: the Negro League. The league had lost some of its luster since Jackie Robinson integrated the majors in 1947 and a stream of younger players such as Willie Mays, Toni's former opponent, had joined him.* Owners of Negro League baseball teams were all too aware that the slump in gate receipts made it difficult to meet payrolls. One evening after a game, Buck O'Neil called Tom Baird. "How'd we do?" Baird, the owner, asked on the phone. The team won, Monarchs manager O'Neil said, 4–2. "I don't mean the score," Baird shouted back. "I mean the attendance."[22] Fans in the stands were more important than game results and standings, O'Neil found out. Many followers of black ball thought the number of teams able to draw a crowd would continue to dwindle; some thought the entire league would die, the ironic victim of integration. But men like Baird and O'Neil could confirm that the league had had its ups and downs before and had been successful in adjusting to the times and reinventing itself. Perhaps the moment for metamorphosis was again upon black baseball. Baird already had evidence that the league had become a pipeline to the majors, as Jim Hall in New Orleans and others had suggested. Baird received phone calls and letters every day from players eager to show what they could do. The Negro League, Baird pronounced, was now officially "a springboard."[23] Baird's letters to New York Yankee farm system director Lee MacPhail said as much. "Do you want me to contact you before I make any deal with the New York Giants?" Baird asked. "I feel as though I am a part of the Yankee organization and want to give you first chance at my players that your organization might want."[24] Branch Rickey, who understood the pace of integration better than most, predicted that by 1952 or 1953 every

*To many white fans, all black baseball players were Jackie Robinson. On his first airplane trip to join the New York Giants, Willie Mays placed his glove and cap on an empty seat next to him. "Are you Jackie Robinson?" the white flight attendant asked (Willie Mays with Lou Sahadi, *Say Hey: The Autobiography of Willie Mays*, New York: Simon & Schuster, 1988, 63).

minor league team—including those in the Deep South—would want to sign black players. White minor league teams would be eager to discover untapped talent, he forecast. "The only question will be, finding enough Negroes with sufficient ability to meet the demand."[25]

Born out of passion for the sport and a repudiation of racism, the Negro League had a proud tradition. Black athletes had been playing integrated baseball in the nineteenth century until 1887 when an unwritten understanding—what some called a "gentlemen's agreement"—banned future contracts with blacks in the white International League.* Baseball, like society as a whole, shifted toward more racial segregation after Reconstruction, which most people viewed as a failed effort.[26] By the turn of the century, the impact of the ban could be seen around the country; with a few exceptions, Jim Crow baseball was the rule in every state. In the wake of segregated play, Andrew "Rube" Foster, a pitcher, manager, and booking agent for the Leland Giants (later the Chicago American Giants), had been thinking of ways to bring together the jumble of black teams in the Midwest—barnstorming, semi-pro, and independent squads. On February 13, 1920, at the Paseo YMCA in Kansas City, Foster and a gathering of other black baseball executives founded the Negro National League.† Foster's monumental effort "paved the way," players said. He and the other league founders were like "the wagons going West."[27] The league began with eight teams: Foster's Chicago American Giants, Joe

*The International League was formed in 1884 and 1885 when three baseball leagues merged: the Eastern, the New York State, and the Ontario leagues. The International League reorganized many times in its history. The current AAA International League is a descendent of the earlier franchise. Current teams in the IA include the Pawtucket Red Sox, the Rochester Red Wings, and the Toledo Mud Hens. Jackie Robinson was the first African American to integrate the International League when he played for the Montreal Royals in 1946 before joining the Brooklyn Dodgers the following year.

†There are many histories of the Negro Leagues that offer thorough accounts of the leagues' fascinating past. Robert Peterson's *Only the Ball Was White: The History of Legendary Black Players and the All-Black Professional Teams* (1992) is widely considered the groundbreaking study that launched a resurgence of interest in the Negro Leagues. Other commendable accounts include Leslie Heaphy's *The Negro Leagues: 1869–1960* (2002) and Neil Lanctot's *Negro League Baseball: The Rise and Ruin of a Black Institution* (2004).

Greene's Chicago Giants, the Dayton Marcos, the Detroit Stars, the Indianapolis ABCs, the Kansas City Monarchs, the St. Louis Giants, and the Cuban Stars. Meanwhile, Thomas T. Wilson, owner of the Nashville Elite Giants, also organized in 1920 the Negro Southern League, composed of his Nashville team and competitors in Atlanta, Birmingham, Memphis, Montgomery, and New Orleans. Impressed with the success of the Southern and National leagues, Edward H. Bolden became chair of the Eastern Colored League, which included the Hilldale Club, the Cuban Stars (East), the Brooklyn Royal Giants, the Bacharach Giants, the Lincoln Giants, and the Baltimore Black Sox. Black baseball became the top entertainment for urban black residents. By 1924, the Eastern League and the National League held their first World Series competition. A series of misfortunes, however, nearly caused the death of organized black baseball. A gas leak came close to killing Rube Foster, and his subsequent errant behavior landed him in an asylum. Business pressures took a toll on Bolden, and he, too, was institutionalized. By 1928, Bolden's Eastern Colored League collapsed. Rube Foster died in 1930, leaving the National League without direction. In 1932, the *Chicago Defender* said organized black baseball was over.

Enter Cumberland Posey and Gus Greenlee. William Augustus "Gus" Greenlee was the owner of the famous Crawford Grill in the Pittsburgh Hill District. Luminaries such as Billy Eckstine, Lena Horne, and Sarah Vaughn entertained crowds, and Satchel Paige sang with the Mills Brothers during late night improvisations.[28] Greenlee was also a bootlegger and a numbers runner, and his wealth enabled him in 1930 to buy the Pittsburgh Crawfords and build it into an East Coast champion. Future Hall of Famers such as Satchel Paige, Cool Papa Bell, Josh Gibson, William Julius "Judy" Johnson, and Oscar Charleston played for the Crawfords. When Greenlee became disgusted because his team was not allowed to use whites-only locker rooms at Forbes Field, he built his own stadium, Greenlee Field, further adding to his business clout. Cumberland Willis "Cum" Posey was Pittsburgh's other black baseball powerhouse. In 1910 he organized black steelworkers into the Homestead Grays ball club, named for the industrial neighborhood southeast of Pittsburgh.* For the next thirty-five years, he built the Grays into one of organized baseball's most accomplished teams, first as a player, then as an owner. Posey earned distinction through his aggressive recruiting. He developed teams that won eight pennants and three world titles. Posey also was a vocal critic of black baseball, not only calling for an end to clowning on Syd Pollock's teams but also criticizing booking agents for unprofitable schedules.

Posey attempted to revive black baseball by organizing an East-West League, but the league collapsed after a single season in 1932, becoming another victim of the Depression. By the next year, however, Greenlee established a second incarnation of the Negro National League (NNL) that included teams in the East. In 1933, he also inaugurated the highly successful East-West All-Star game, played annually at Comiskey Park in Chicago. Teams in the Midwest and the South reconstituted themselves in 1937 as the Negro American League. With the success of Posey's Grays and stellar players such as Buck Leonard bringing attention to the game, black baseball was back on track. That is, until the prospect of integration became a reality. Judge Kenesaw Mountain Landis, commissioner of major league baseball and an ardent segregationist, died in 1945. Albert Benjamin "Happy" Chandler, former governor and senator from Kentucky and a man open to integration, succeeded him. Less than a year after Chandler became commissioner, Jackie Robinson signed with the Brooklyn Dodgers. Writing to Branch Rickey, Chandler stated, "It isn't my job to decide which colors can play big league baseball. It is my job to see that the game is fairly played and that everybody has an equal chance."[29]

---

*Pitcher Wilmer Fields claimed the Homestead area was so choked with industrial pollution that "all the houses were black or brown from smoke. . . . I could walk down the hill to eat breakfast and have to change my shirt within two hours because of the smoke" (Wilmer Fields, *My Life in the Negro Leagues: An Autobiography of Wilmer Fields*, Westport: CT: Meckler, 1992, 13).

After Robinson's signing, black baseball again was forced to reinvent itself—this time as one league, with the Negro American League absorbing six teams from the National.* By 1950, the once great teams such as the Homestead Grays and Newark Eagles were no longer financially viable. They became independent barnstorming teams or aligned themselves with semi-pro leagues. In 1952, when Toni began thinking seriously about her chances in professional black baseball, there were six teams still operating in the Negro League: the Birmingham Black Barons, the Chicago American Giants, the Indianapolis Clowns, the Kansas City Monarchs, the Memphis Red Sox, and the Philadelphia Stars. Some teams were in better financial shape than others.

Syd Pollock of the Indianapolis Clowns was in more of a whirlwind than usual.† The Clowns were the 1951 Negro League champions and had recently sold the contracts of two players to the Boston Braves. Initially Negro League teams had to fight to have their player contracts recognized by major league baseball. Some executives in the majors refused to honor players' agreements with Negro League teams, taking advantage of the league's often sloppy record keeping and stealing away players when contracts were lost or never fully executed. Other major league scouts blatantly raided black team rosters without regard to financial compensation. Newark Eagles co-owner Effa Manley led the fight to have black teams rightfully compensated.‡ Her battle made

---

*Use of the plural phrase "Negro Leagues" usually refers to the time prior to 1948 when both the Negro American League and the Negro National League were in existence. The singular "Negro League" marks the time after 1948 when only one league operated.

†The Clowns were from Indianapolis in name only. In 1950, the team did not play a single home game in Indianapolis. Syd Pollock moved the squad's home field to Buffalo, New York, for the 1951 season. "Buffalo is a great sports city," Pollock said. "It will provide substantial box office support for the Clowns" (*Louisiana Weekly*, May 12, 1951).

‡Effa Manley (1900–1981) was co-owner of the Newark Eagles from 1935 to 1948, after her husband, Abe Manley, bought the team. She played an active role in the team's management, from scheduling to payroll to equipment acquisition to negotiating player contracts. She was especially adept at marketing and promotions, often connecting Eagles games to civil rights activism. For example, in 1939 at Ruppert Stadium in Newark, she organized an Anti-Lynching Day. Manley was active in civil rights outside of baseball,

it possible for team owners like Pollock to add to their revenue by selling players' contracts. As pleased as Pollock was to see players move to the majors, he also knew he would have to fill their missing spots on the Clowns. As he looked at the team roster for the upcoming 1952 season, Pollock knew he was short on infielders. His old friend Ed Scott, who had barnstormed with the Clowns in the late 1930s, was currently managing the Mobile Black Bears, a semi-pro team. Scott had a great young shortstop who could "rip the hide off a baseball," he told Syd.[30] Pollock and the team business manager, McKinley "Bunny" Downs, thought Scotty's prospect was worth a look.

At first, he didn't look like much of a hitter. Seventeen-year-old Henry Aaron was five-foot-six and 150 pounds. "Six o'clock" was how the Aaron family described themselves: no fat and straight up and down.[31] In addition, Aaron had a quiet demeanor that led some scouts to think he was not aggressive enough. But Scotty said Aaron was one of the best wrist hitters he had ever seen; Aaron said he was built up from hauling twenty-five-pound blocks of ice. The youngster also had an odd, crossover way of holding the bat. While right-handed, Aaron placed his left hand above his right when he squared off at the plate. When Downs and Pollock watched him swing, Syd called out, "You're looking good, but when you're right handed, you grip the bat with your left hand on the bottom."[32] Even with his unconventional grip, Aaron cleaned up that day, hitting a long ball and a double or two.[33] Pollock appreciated what Scotty had seen and offered Aaron an application on the spot. "Treat the Clowns like a minor league club," Scotty urged his prodigy, "a stop on your way to the big money—$5,000 a year in the majors." Several months later, when Aaron secured his par-

---

serving as an officer of the Newark NAACP and organizing a boycott of a Harlem store that refused to hire black clerks. A daughter of white parents, Manley was raised by her mother and her black stepfather and identified herself as a light-skinned black woman. Her most notable achievement in baseball was demanding that the major leagues offer legitimate compensation for Negro League players' contracts. Among her Eagles players who went to the major leagues were Larry Doby, Monte Irvin, and Don Newcombe. She remains the only woman ever elected to the Baseball Hall of Fame. She was inducted posthumously in 2006. Her gravestone reads "She Loved Baseball."

ents' permission to join the Clowns, Bunny Downs was overjoyed. "God done sent me a miracle," Downs said.[34] The Indianapolis Clowns had their shortstop for the 1952 season.

When Aaron reported to spring training the next year—a cold and raw few days in Winston-Salem—he did not make an immediate impression on his teammates. He was respectful and shy, hardly an attention-grabbing hot shot. Even though he was young and admittedly inexperienced in the world outside Mobile, Aaron knew that veterans on the team still would be suspicious of him. Like Toni, Aaron realized that a rookie could cost a veteran ballplayer a job, and he may have cringed when his name began appearing on the team's posters. Rather than carousing with the team after a doubleheader, Aaron spent time with James Jenkins, a Bible-reading outfielder the team called Preacher. Jenkins tried to teach Aaron how to save money. Every day the older player took one of the two dollars each player received for meal money and mailed it home to his wife. Traveling with the Clowns that spring from Texas to Oklahoma, back to North Carolina, and then up the East Coast to Washington, D.C., Aaron saw sights he never thought he'd see. One scene always remained with him. After a rain-out at Griffith Stadium, the team went to a restaurant near the field. As the players finished their meals, restaurant workers gathered the plates to take them back to the kitchen. As Henry got up to leave, he heard the sound of dishes being thrown to the floor and breaking into hundreds of pieces. Young and inexperienced as he was, Aaron knew what was going on. Once a black ate off a plate, the dish was useless. "If dogs had eaten off those plates, they'd have washed them," he said.[35]

Aaron's unique crossover grip continued to serve him well that summer with the Clowns. By June 1952, he was leading the Negro League in doubles, RBIs, and home runs. Aaron's hitting and fielding were "a revelation," the *Pittsburgh Courier* declared.[36] Scouts from the Giants, the Pirates, the Reds, and the Braves were eyeing him and sending reports back to the majors. At the beginning of June 1952, both the Braves and the Pirates still were lobbying intensely for

Aaron's Clowns contract. The Boston Braves won out. Aaron finished his commitment to Indianapolis in a doubleheader at Comiskey Park, then took a single-engine plane to Wisconsin and the Braves' class C minor league club in Eau Claire. Syd Pollock gave Henry a cardboard suitcase. That was "my signing bonus," Aaron said.[37]

With Aaron gone, the Indianapolis Clowns and Syd Pollock found themselves in the same predicament they'd been in a year ago. The Clowns won the 1952 Negro League championship, their third in a row, but the team's roster and the league again were in flux. Five more players left the Clowns after the 1952 season, moving to the majors or leagues in Canada or Latin America. The fabled Chicago American Giants and the Philadelphia Stars bowed out of the league. The number of teams in the league fell down to four: the Clowns, the Monarchs, the Memphis Red Sox, and the Birmingham Black Barons. Although the league was shrinking, the number of black men clamoring for a spot on any team was far from dwindling. When executives with the semi-pro Dallas Eagles announced a tryout for black players, over two hundred men rushed the gates. The team expected fifty prospects to show up.[38] But finding players who were exceptional athletes and who could adapt to long hours on the road and the Clowns' unique brand of showmanship was difficult. Pollock knew from experience that sometimes four or five athletes had to be tried out before a suitable replacement could be found.[39] During the off-season, he signed several new players, including a shortstop, an outfielder, and a couple of pitchers. But the team still needed an addition like Henry Aaron who was sure to bring in fans. As the Creoles' Alan Page said, a team needed someone who could "hang a glittering star over his locker."[40]

Looking back years later, Syd Pollock's son thought the team should have seen it coming. "Toni Stone and Dad were destined for each other," Alan Pollock said. "Both did what they loved and nothing and nobody interfered. . . . They were two . . . lines heading to intersect." [41] The Indianapolis Clowns had played enough games with the New Orleans Creoles over the last three years to remember Toni

Stone. Bunny Downs even had come across Toni earlier in her "Tomboy Stone" barnstorming days in Minnesota. "Stay in school," Downs told her. Toni remembered Downs told her to contact him once she had more years under her belt.[42] Now, thinking about the scrappy Creoles second baseman and the impact Aaron's departure would have on their gate receipts, the men couldn't help but think Toni Stone might fit their needs. In physical size she almost was identical to Aaron. She was an inch taller and two pounds lighter. She was quick on the base paths like Henry and could run the one-hundred-yard dash in eleven seconds.* "She could run like a deer," an observer said.[43] In the field, Toni turned efficient double plays and stood firm against hard-charging base runners. She didn't have Aaron's bat—few players did—but she had wrists and arms that reminded Pollock of Willie Mays and Aaron. A smaller player had as much power as a big one, if she used timing, coordination, and reflexes. Back home in Saint Paul, one of Toni's friends remembered how strong she was. During friendly arm-wrestling matches with Tomboy, he was astonished by her taut arms and wrists—not an ounce of fat on them—all tendons and muscles. As hard and unmovable as "a cold rake," he said.[44] Besides her strength and athletic ability, Syd Pollock simply liked Toni Stone. She was sassy, he said.

The offer came to Toni when she was in Oakland. She accepted Syd Pollock's offer to play second base for the Indianapolis Clowns in the Negro League and would report to spring training in Norfolk, Virginia, in early April 1953. Aurelious Alberga may have had second thoughts about his wife returning to baseball or being used as a gate attraction, but it did not seem to matter. "He would have stopped me if he could have," Toni said, but he couldn't.[45]

---

*Toni Stone's time in the hundred-yard dash was exceptional for a woman in the 1950s, according to Christina Lee, Mount Holyoke College cross country, track, and field coach. The hundred-meter dash is now the official recorded distance for track and field events, replacing the obsolete hundred-yard dash. Florence Griffin Joyner holds the women's world record in the hundred-meter dash at 10.49 seconds. One hundred meters is slightly longer than one hundred yards: one hundred meters equals 109.36 yards (e-mail to author from Christina Lee, October 8, 2008).

Number 29

They went home and told their wives,
That never once in all their lives,
Had they known a girl like me.

—Maya Angelou[1]

Syd Pollock wasted no time in cranking out press releases announcing the signing of his new player. "Well, move over, boys," he wrote from his home office in Tarrytown, New York, "the girls have invaded another realm once regarded as the domain of the muscle and brawn set." Toni Stone, replacing Henry Aaron, would be Pollock's premier gate attraction for 1953, and Syd marshaled every detail—including underwear—to announce his new hire. "The latest masculine enterprise to fall before the advance of wearers of skirts and panties is the baseball diamond. The Indianapolis Clowns last week signed the first female baseball player in the history of the Negro American League." Pollock had promoted women baseball players before. As a young man, he created advertising for a short-lived semipro team called Maggie Riley and her Male Devil Dogs. Pollock described Riley as "baseball's $10,000 Female Wonder Girl."[2] Phrases such as "wonder girl" and later his alliterative tag for Toni, "the gal guardian of second base," were part of the language of promotion that Pollock learned from his mother's years of theater management. Up early every morning, he spent a few hours writing copy before walking to the post office, his arms loaded with press releases for promoters, baseball writers, and the Negro Association Press association. After a quick stop at a local bakery for a sugary roll, he was back at work at his roll-top desk, a reporter's green eyeshade on his head and a cigarette dangling a smoldering ash. "Toni will be the first to admit her diamond foes show her no mercy because of her sex," Pollock tapped on his old Underwood typewriter. "The pitchers throw just as hard and base runners slide into second with spikes just as high. But she likes the game and keeps coming back for more. She is positive she'll prove an asset to the popular Clowns in helping the Funmakers to their fourth consecutive . . . championship this season."[3] All those years helping his mother with theater publicity made Pollock's press releases pop, although they sounded more like Toni was making movies than making baseball history.*

Back home in Oakland, Toni's husband had become a supportive spouse. Perhaps recognizing an opportunity for Toni to achieve national celebrity, Aurelious Alberga offered his help when the Clowns contract came through. He used his past experience as a trainer to supervise Toni's daily workouts with the white St. Ignatius Catholic baseball team in Golden Gate Park. "You have a lot of wandering athletes in San Francisco," Toni said, and it was easy to find pickup games.[4] Alberga also prepared her to make a grand entrance into the world of professional sports. Alberga believed that clothes made the man. He never gave up wearing high-buttoned shoes even when they were well past their stylish heyday.[5] It may have been his

---

*What some called promotional gimmicks were not limited to the Negro League. Many believed Bill Veeck, owner of the St. Louis Browns in the major leagues, pushed baseball closer to entertainment than Syd Pollock did. Veeck also used clowns to pump up the crowd and once sent in dwarf Eddie Gaedel to pinch-hit. Another time, Veeck called on fans to help manage a Browns game by asking them to hold up placards from the grandstand calling for a "Bunt" or "Hit and Run."

idea for Toni to travel to spring training camp with a corsage neatly pinned to a stylish spring coat. When it really mattered, however, Toni had her own opinions about dress. Before the season started, Syd Pollock suggested that, instead of a regulation uniform, she wear a short skirt like the women of the All-American Girls Professional Baseball League. Toni was unequivocal, angry even. "I wasn't going to wear no shorts," she said. "This is professional baseball."[6] Short skirts were foolish if a player was expected to slide. She would have nothing of Pollock's suggestion, and she told him she would rather quit than demean herself like that. Pollock acquiesced. But a discrete clutch of carnations on her lapel was a concession she was willing to make to please her husband's sense of style. In the spring of 1953, Pollock, Alberga, and Toni Stone were all adjusting to new limits and new opportunities.

So were McKinley "Bunny" Downs and Albert "Buster" Haywood. Downs, the team's business manager, and Haywood, the Clowns' manager, had a lot to say about Toni as they rode the team bus to Norfolk, Virginia, for spring training. Every season, the Clowns bus offered a kind of long-distance taxi service from Pollock's Tarrytown, New York, home to training camp. "Big Red," the Clowns' five-year-old Flxible bus, spent the winter in a Westchester County barn about fifteen miles from Pollock's home office. In early April, Haywood arrived from his home in Virginia, dusted off the bus, and drove it to Syd's. There, Pollock's sons earned extra cash by readying the bus for the long baseball season. The next day, Haywood drove the bus to Bunny's apartment in Harlem. When residents saw Big Red parked on the street, the sidewalks filled with well-wishers. As one bystander said, "half of Harlem" turned out to say good-bye to the Clowns. After gathering up Downs and a few players who lived nearby, M. H. Wilson, the quiet, dignified bus driver—or "Chauff" as the team called him—began the journey. Chauff steered the bus out of Manhattan, past Newark, into Philadelphia, down to Washington, D.C., and on into Norfolk—picking up other players and their duffle bags along the way.[7] The nearly four-hundred-mile trip gave Downs and Haywood plenty of time to air their views on Toni Stone.

The Clowns were fortunate that all three men at the top of the organization got along so well. They were an unlikely trio: Syd, the white Jewish team owner; Bunny, the Negro League second baseman turned pragmatic business manager; and Buster, the diminutive former catcher for the Clowns who valued passion on the field above all. In spite of their differences, each respected the jobs the others had to do. "Bunny [is] Syd's right hand. I'm his left," Buster said.[8] Their friendships also extended to their families: their wives attended games together, visited in the off-season, and watched over each others' children. Yet when it came to Toni, the men disagreed, at least initially. Syd believed in her athleticism and thought the risk of signing her was worthwhile. "It would do black baseball no good to draw fans, then disappoint them," he said. Bunny needed no convincing that she would help with the team's financial bottom line. Pollock's team policy called for Bunny to carry cash from each game's receipts in a money belt. He only had to feel the belt to know if ticket sales were up or down, and he knew better than most that since Jackie Robinson integrated the Dodgers, Negro League receipts had gone down. But Buster Haywood was not sure Toni was the answer. Good baseball was all about hustle, he believed, not gate attractions. Ray Neil, the Clowns' second baseman, was the team's premier player. If he played as well in 1953 as he had in previous years, he could win the batting title. Why did Pollock want to put the team and Neil's statistics in jeopardy by putting a woman at second? Pollock reassured Haywood by having Neil keep his bat in the lineup and moving the infielder to the outfield during the innings Toni played second. But Buster Haywood did not buy their strategy. "I didn't like it," he said, admitting he didn't think Toni could handle the challenges on and off the field. "She had the experience," he said, "but playing with a bunch of men was a different story."[9] Apparently Haywood chose to ignore Toni's nearly two decades of playing on men's teams. Most fans did not expect the Clowns to repeat their championship in 1953. The team had lost three of its best pitchers, a fourth was at the Milwaukee Braves' training camp, and the Clowns' top base stealer was a holdout.* And one had only to step inside the bus to recognize that new players were needed. Big Red smelled of horse liniment, a sure sign that the Clowns' legs were aging.[10]

Toni flew from Oakland to Washington, D.C., before continuing to Norfolk. As she stepped off the plane, she knew immediately that playing in the Negro League would put her in the spotlight far more than semi-pro ball had. Photographers were already waiting and snapped pictures as she exited the airport gate. The armloads of Pollock's press releases had worked. "Toni Arrives!" black newspapers later declared under a photograph of Toni looking surprised.[11] By the time she made it to training camp, the number of photographers had multiplied and was joined by a crush of reporters, film crews, theatrical booking agents, television scouts, and major and minor league representatives—all elbowing each other to get a look at her. Admitting she felt like a "goldfish," Toni was at once disoriented and excited by the attention. Children especially were taken with her. Little girls in checked dresses and boys eager to hear her advice gathered around her during practice; some shyly reached out to touch her bat. Other children back in Oakland sent a box of candy to Toni for good luck. Sounding confident, Toni told reporters, "I know what I am doing and what I am in for. I don't want anyone playing me easy because I'm a woman and I don't plan to play 'easy' against them. I'm out here to play the game and I'm sure I can take the knocks as well as anyone else."[12]

---

*Two of the pitchers who left the Clowns in 1953 were James and Leander Tugerson, who signed with the Hot Springs [Arkansas] Bathers, becoming the first black players to integrate the Cotton State League. League officials and other teams in the league said segregation had to be upheld and that black players could not play against white teams in the South. Mississippi Attorney General J. P. Coleman got into the debate and ruled that if the Tugersons pitched against white teams in his state, he was sure "such proposed exhibitions would violate the public policy of Mississippi." The Tugerson brothers, Air Force veterans who accounted for over twenty wins with the Clowns in 1952, became the subjects of editorials in black newspapers across the country. "[Georgy] Malenkov, Joe Stalin, and Adolph Hitler could play ball in Mississippi if they were good enough to make a team," the *Chicago Defender* wrote in an April 11, 1953, editorial. "But a black boy who fought to keep Mississippians safe from the Nazi hordes is denied this privilege."

Syd Pollock, however, set Toni up for some knocks from the Clowns when he fabricated facts in his press releases, most notably her salary details. "Stone has inked a contract with the Clowns, reportedly earning $12,000 for her first season's work," he wrote.[13] If Toni were indeed earning twelve thousand dollars, she would have been the highest paid player in the Negro League, earning more than many players in the majors. Jackie Robinson signed with the Dodgers organization in 1947 for six hundred a month and a thirty-five-hundred-dollar signing bonus.[14] In reality, Toni earned much less: three hundred dollars a month and the usual two dollars a day for meal money, which didn't go far. "I stayed hungry all the time," she said, and especially missed her mother's lemon pie.[15] Later, if asked, Toni would set anyone straight about what she really earned.* But she was not so forthcoming about her age; the lie she had begun telling in San Francisco continued. Syd either truly believed she was twenty-two years old when he signed her or chose to overlook that she was a decade older. Everyone in baseball knew that a player was in his prime between the ages of twenty-five and thirty. Toni would be expected to run and hit like a twenty-two-year-old athlete, not one who was approaching middle age.

The two weeks spent working out at Golden Gate Park had served Toni well.† Those weeks were nearly all the preseason warm-up she would get. Official spring training with the Clowns amounted to only two days of practice before departing for a month of games with semi-pro teams and a few Negro League matchups across the South. The

---

*According to Pollock's son, Syd increased Toni Stone's salary during the 1953 season to $350 a month and eventually $400 a month, making her the highest paid Indianapolis Clowns player (Alan Pollock with James A. Riley, editor, *Barnstorming to Heaven: Syd Pollock and His Great Black Teams*, Tuscaloosa: University of Alabama Press, 2006, 243).

†Toni told her family that in her early days in the Bay Area, she played pickup games with the DiMaggio brothers. In 1992, Stone repeated the story to *Oakland Tribune* columnist Miki Turner. Stone told Turner that she shagged balls in Golden Gate Park and worked out with Vincent DiMaggio. I have been unable to confirm or deny Stone's story (Maria Bartlow-Reed interview with the author, March 10, 2008; Toni Stone interview with Miki Turner. Turner's interview notes shared with author July 10, 2009).

official opening day for the Negro League would take place in Beaumont, Texas, on May 15 against the Monarchs. The scant two days in Norfolk gave Toni barely enough time to try on her navy blue uniform—a team color Pollock had personally chosen because it didn't show grime and could be worn day after day. The uniform was not new, and it was certainly not designed to fit Toni's female form, but it was regulation. Toni respected that Pollock made good on his promise. Reporters, eager for every detail, wrote that she wore an "oversize 42 shirt . . . to accommodate her 36 inch bust."[16] Toni would be number 29, the starting second baseman for the Indianapolis Clowns. She understood the deal Syd and Bunny had struck with Buster: she would rarely play complete games, bowing to Ray Neil after the fourth or fifth inning. Still, she had a spot on the team and she vowed to make the most of it. "I've got my own ideas," she said. "Who knows? Maybe I'll be the first woman to play major league baseball. At least I may be the one who opens the doors for others. A lot of things can happen, you know. There's always got to be a first in everything. Before 1946 nobody thought Negroes would be in the big leagues. But we got 'em in there today. A woman might have a chance also. Maybe it will be me."[17]

If Clowns players resented Toni occupying a position on the team, were jealous of the spotlight shining on her, or were angry at her reported salary—they kept their opinions to themselves. Pollock set the tone for the club's public comments. "This girl is no freak," he said. "[A]nd although I would not deny that her publicity value is very great to our team and its games, we expect her play to help us a lot."[18] One of the scouts getting a first look at Toni at Norfolk was impressed by more than her ability to bring in crowds, too. "She's better than a lot of men who show up at Spring training," he said.[19] On Sunday, April 12, the exhibition season started. In Oakland, Toni's husband sat down to write, bringing Toni up to date on the publicity about her that had been circulating in the Bay Area. "My Dear Sweetheart," he began. "I forgot to enclose the clippings of Alan Ward [*Oakland Tribune* sports columnist] that I thought you may want, also Sis told me that a few days before you left she heard a nice talk by Ira Blue [San Francisco radio announcer] over the air about you but forgot to mention it." Life was quiet around the house, he said, with only their dog to keep him company. "Fuzzy stays close to me and almost asks what became of you." He wondered how Toni was getting along with her team and closed on a hopeful note. "Hope you get a hit in first game. Love + Kisses Poppy."[20]

Toni's first game would be the beginning of a relentless and grueling schedule. Ahead of Toni were eight months of baseball, from April through the November barnstorming postseason. The team would play nearly every day, including two games on Sundays and occasionally a third in another city. They would travel four hundred miles between games without a stop. "Travel date" was a white term, players said. With Chauff at the wheel, Toni, Bunny, Buster, and the rest of the team boarded Big Red. Syd Pollock stayed at home. Jim Crow laws forbade a white man from riding a bus with Negroes. He would remain in Tarrytown tapping out press releases on his Underwood typewriter.*

Cold rain washed out games in Virginia, and Toni sat on the bench shivering in weather that reporters complained felt more like football season than baseball. Skies cleared as they moved to North Carolina. Syd always made sure the season began and ended in tobacco country where black workers, who were needed to plant and harvest the crop, had money to spend on baseball.[21] The crowd in Elizabeth City, North Carolina, was the first to see Toni rip a single and earn her first two RBIs. Two days later, in Windsor, she hit another single, grabbed two more RBIs, and later in another game topped off her North Carolina tour by sneaking behind a runner at second and tagging him in the pickoff.[22] But the long bus rides and cold weather may have been to blame when leg cramps forced her to sit out a few contests. She hated the idea of not playing, but found it nearly impossible to run. "Boy,

---

*Pollock was forcibly removed from the Clowns bus in the early 1930s when Alabama troopers insisted he obey state segregation laws (Alan Pollock with James A. Riley, editor, *Barnstorming to Heaven: Syd Pollock and His Great Black Teams*, Tuscaloosa: University of Alabama Press, 2006, 88).

have I had the charley horses," she said. "Once I hit a two bagger and when I turned first and started for second, my leg knotted up and down I went."[23] By the time the team hit Miami at the end of April for doubleheader play against the Monarchs, Stone was back in the lineup regardless of the strain.* Haywood admitted that Toni had been hobbled by injuries, but said he was sure that her play had not weakened the team's infield "one iota."[24] Haywood's comments may have been Pollock talking, but even Buster could not deny that Toni played with passion. As a catcher, he played with such fierceness that he sustained injuries. When he crouched to receive a pitcher's throw, Haywood always kept his throwing hand next to his mitt. If he needed to throw the ball to second base in a split second, his throwing hand was right where it needed to be. It was a questionable strategy: all five fingers on his throwing hand had been broken. But playing all out was one of the reasons fans loved the Clowns. No one ever would forget the standing ovation the team once received in Chicago after a particularly vigorous infield practice. As Pollock had predicted, curious fans did come out to see Toni's fervent play. Crowds filled the small ballparks in Virginia and North Carolina. In the season's first larger venue in Miami, the local black recreation commissioner called Toni and the Clowns "the best drawing card in Negro baseball."[25] It was still uncertain whether Toni and the Clowns would interest fans in the big industrial cities of the North and the Midwest, but the team would soon find out.

The Miami game also gave the Clowns their first look at the Monarchs' new shortstop, Ernie "Bingo" Banks. The 1953 season was actually a return to the Monarchs for Banks, who had held a spot on the team before serving for two years in the military. The Monarchs manager, Buck O'Neil, loved Banks's rangy play that allowed him to go to his left or right, but a scouting report observed a weak throwing arm. He "doesn't gun it," the report said.[26] On the field, Banks was not flashy in other ways as well. "I want to outsmart the other

---

*Since the Negro League season did not officially begin until May 15, 1953, preseason games with other league clubs (the Monarchs, the Memphis Red Sox, and the Birmingham Black Barons) were recorded as exhibition games.

team," he said. "I don't yell at umpires or get into fights."[27] When a later manager tried to get him to "holler more," Banks said, "I holler. I holler a lot, but I don't have growl in my voice so nobody hears me."[28] Banks's subdued behavior on the field also translated into patience at the plate. Rather than the wild swings that Negro Leaguers often used—sometime to dramatic effect—Banks was restrained. "He can wait on a pitch until the catcher's almost ready to throw it back to you," one opponent said. Toni respected Ernie Banks. "I liked his ways," she said, and remarked that he seemed like an old man even though he was young.[29] Banks had a wisdom and maturity about him, she observed. Toni would see a lot of Banks during the season and vowed to study his play. He was studying her, too, and noticed the way other players occasionally shunned her. "Human beings are the only ones that can make life complicated and unpleasant," Banks later said. Toni had her priorities straight, it seemed to him: her actions on the field were more about self-respect than flashy play, he said.[30]

From Florida, Pollock routed the team through Georgia, Alabama, Mississippi, and Louisiana for more preseason play. They continued to meet up with Banks and took on the Negro League's Memphis Red Sox later in the tour. In New Orleans, Toni brought fans to their feet when she singled in a run and later started a double play that squelched a Kansas City rally.[31] With every game, the crowds grew larger and Toni attracted more press attention. Even teammates who begrudged a woman on the team acknowledged that Toni could hold her own on the field, increase gate receipts, and keep their salaries from shrinking. "She put fans in the stands," pitcher Rufus "Zippy" McNeal admitted.[32] "I think it brought more women to the game," Toni said. "Curiosity, if nothing else." She especially enjoyed when fans stayed after the game and asked to meet her or patted her on the back. The personal connection with fans moved Toni, perhaps because she remembered the ways the Rondo girls once scorned her. "I was so glad they'd touch me," she said.[33]

The route Pollock constructed—through Louisiana and the Deep South—was intentional. Not only did Syd suspect that fans who

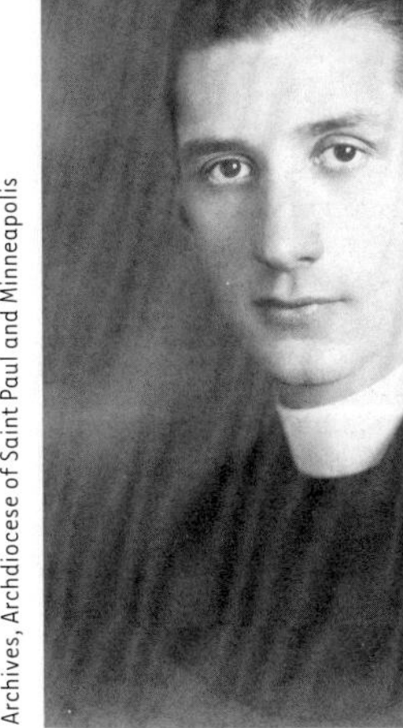

Archives, Archdiocese of Saint Paul and Minneapolis

Father Charles Keefe.

Courtesy of the Stone family

Boykin Freeman Stone.

GIRL ATHLETE

Fifteen year old girl athlete, Marcenia Stone, 257 West Central, St. Paul, native of Bluefield, West Virginia, was awarded a letter each for tennis, high jump and diamond-ball at the First Annual All-City Emblem Dinner of Junior High School Girls Athletic Association held at the Y. W. C. A. June 10.

Miss Stone, who was honor guest at the dinner, is the first girl in 18 years to receive three letters for one year's work. She won her first medal in 1932 for running and has worked hard and participated in numerous field meets since that time as well as taking part in other athletics, always taking away honors. Among her medals is a trophy cup for Twin City Girls Track won at Humbert High School.

The girl athlete gives much credit to Miss K. H. Wheeler, teacher at Hammond Jr. High, who has aided her in every way to become proficient in athletics, as well as other teachers, Mrs. Engan, Miss Hinckley and Miss Smitz.

Courtesy of the Stone family, first published in the *Minnesota Spokesman–Recorder*, June 25, 1937

Tomboy Stone excelled in baseball, basketball, golf, hockey, ice skating, swimming, tennis, and track. One local newspaper reported that "Miss Stone" is "always taking away honors."

Charles Evard "Gabby" Street.

Red Powell/Reggie Pettus Collection, in *Harlem of the West: The San Francisco Fillmore Jazz Era* by Elizabeth Pepin and Lewis Watts, Chronicle Books, 2005

Jack's Tavern, San Francisco.

Toni Stone on the San Francisco Sea Lions, 1949.

Photo by Don Perry, courtesy Don Perry Collection. Hogan Jazz Archive, Tulane University

Louis Armstrong's appearance in the 1949 Mardi Gras Zulu parade, which sparked controversy.

(right) The San Francisco Sea Lions' posters highlighted their two gate attractions.

Jay-Dell Mah/www.attheplate.com

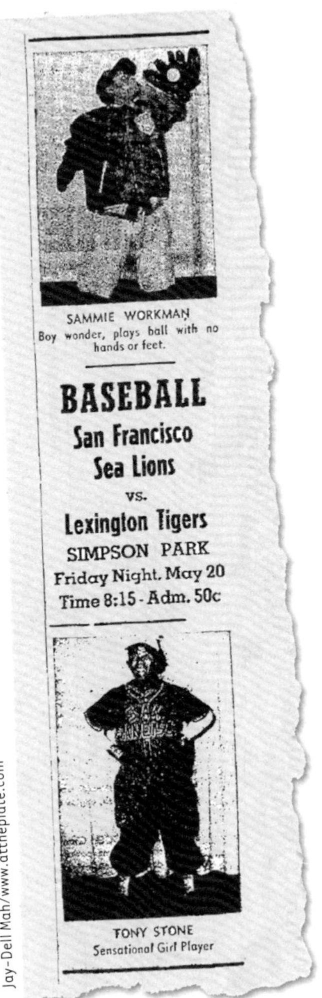

SAMMIE WORKMAN
Boy wonder, plays ball with no hands or feet.

BASEBALL
San Francisco
Sea Lions
vs.
Lexington Tigers
SIMPSON PARK
Friday Night, May 20
Time 8:15 - Adm. 50c

TONY STONE
Sensational Girl Player

Ernest C. Withers Estate, courtesy Panopticon Gallery, Boston

From left to right: Negro Southern League president Dr. W. S. Martin, A. B. Harvey, Toni Stone, an unidentified promoter, and public relations representative Matty Brescia at the 1949 Negro Southern League All-Star Game.

Minnesota Historical Society

Toni Stone met Joe Louis during her 1950 season with the New Orleans Creoles.

Courtesy of the Stone family

Courtesy of the Pollock family

(above) Aurelious Pescia Alberga.

Indianapolis Clowns team owner Syd Pollock gave Henry Aaron his start in the Negro League.

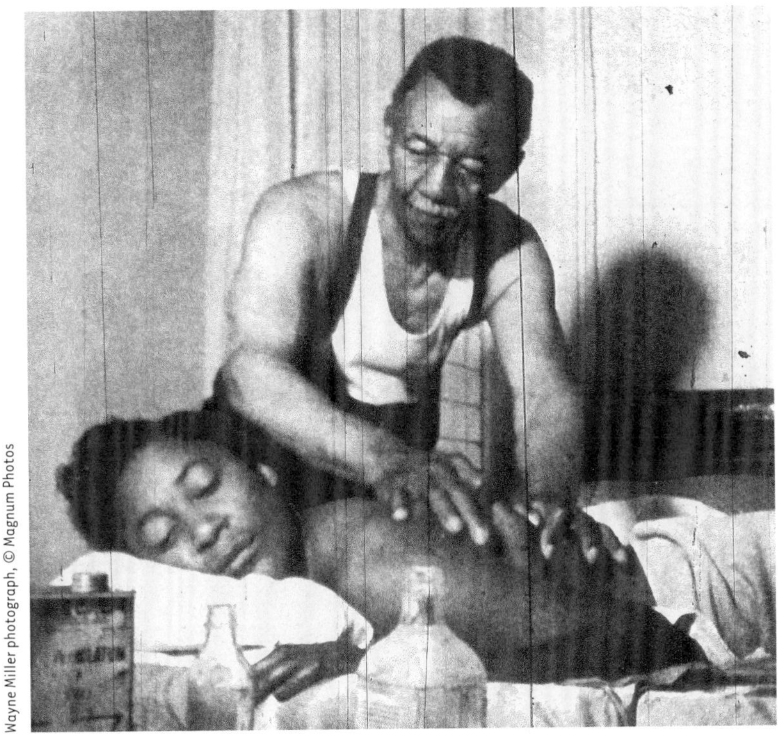
Wayne Miller photograph, © Magnum Photos

Toni with her husband, Aurelious Pescia Alberga.

Wayne Miller photograph, © Magnum Photos

Toni with Buster Haywood, manager of the 1953 Indianapolis Clowns.

Courtesy of the Pollock family

1953 Indianapolis Clowns Toni Stone (middle), second baseman Ray Neil (left), and outfielder Henry "Speed" Merchant (right).

Courtesy of the Pollock family

The 1953 Indianapolis Clowns finished third in the Negro American League. Toni Stone is fourth from left in the front row.

Wayne Miller photograph, © Magnum Photos

Toni Stone, *Ebony* magazine 1953.

Jackie Robinson with Indianapolis Clowns business manager McKinley "Bunny" Downs.

Connie Morgan at her tryout for the Indianapolis Clowns with Jackie Robinson.

Negro Leagues Baseball Museum

Pitcher Mamie "Peanut" Johnson, 1954.

Negro Leagues Baseball Museum

Kansas City Monarchs manager, Buck O'Neil.

National Baseball Hall of Fame Library, Cooperstown, NY

Satchel Paige.

Minnesota Historical Society

In the early 1970s, the San Francisco Giants invited Toni to throw out the first pitch.

When Baseball's Hall of Fame and Henry Aaron recognized Negro League players in 1991, Toni Stone became overcome with emotion.

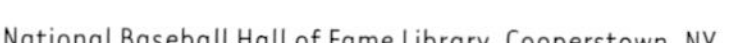
National Baseball Hall of Fame Library, Cooperstown, NY

remembered Toni from her Creoles days would turn out to see her, but he also did his best to avoid stops through the Appalachian states. The Clowns hated mountain travel. "Don't book us through the Smokies this year," players begged Pollock. "Don't want to ride those cliffs."[34] As good a driver as Chauff was, the tight curves and sheer drops were dangerous for a large bus traveling late at night on narrow two-lane roads. Chauff was supposed to sleep during games so that he would be ready for a twelve-hour drive after the last out. But Wilson loved dominoes more than sleep, and he often sat high up in the stands during a game, flipping dominoes when he should have been napping.[35] To help Chauff navigate the roads and keep him company at night, a player volunteered to ride "milk can." A metal milk keg was wedged into the top of the stairwell across from the driver. As copilot, "Milk can" was responsible for calling out every road sign, curve, or potential danger to the driver. Players took shifts sitting milk can, although the team clown, King Tut, who knew nearly every road on the tour, was the mainstay.* No one made jokes about the dangers of travel, even though in all their years on the road the Clowns had only one serious accident. Once, on a rural stretch of Indiana road during the 1947 season, the main fuel tank ran dry. Chauff pulled over to switch on the auxiliary tank. The players set up flares to warn oncoming motorists. The next day's pitcher was asleep in his assigned spot—the long seat at the rear of the bus. When Bunny looked up to check on Chauff, he saw what looked like a car full of drunks, wildly careening down the road toward them. "Man's gonna hit us!" Bunny yelled. The car swerved and hit the rear of the bus, sending the pitcher crashing to the floor, where his knees slammed into a metal support

---

*The Clowns' team comedians were King Tut (Richard King), Spec Bebop (Ralph Bell), and later Ed Hamman. They performed before the game and in between innings and did not play baseball on the team. Tut was a vocal critic and cheerleader for the Clowns. At times he berated them as the "sorriest bunch I ever saw" and later praised them as "the best baseball club ever." King Tut was similarly opinionated about Toni Stone, often telling her, "Shit, woman. You can't play no ball. You ought to be home washing dishes" (Alan Pollock with James A. Riley, editor, *Barnstorming to Heaven: Syd Pollock and His Great Black Teams*, Tuscaloosa: University of Alabama Press, 2006, 114, 244–245).

post. The bus didn't fare any better: the crankcase, the motor block, and the storage compartment door were all severely damaged. Pollock was tied up in lawsuits for years.[36] Given all the miles they traveled, some veteran players and perhaps even Chauff himself believed it was only a matter of time until a serious accident happened again.

The same day fans were cheering for Toni in New Orleans, national weather forecasters based in Louisiana warned of vicious storms that were lining up in Texas and heading east. The team was heading in that direction, bound for Texas after the game. Later that day, an F5 tornado—the most destructive in Texas history—ripped into Waco, killing 114 and injuring nearly 600. The storm struck the downtown area near the ballpark, flattening buildings but leaving light standards around the field untouched. Over 200 businesses and 150 homes were destroyed, including the town's large Dr. Pepper bottling plant. The tornado reminded Toni and the Clowns that long jumps in bad weather posed another threat to traveling ball teams. Unlike major league clubs, which traveled by trains or airplanes and whose salaries were not dependent on playing every game, Negro League squads pushed, sometimes carelessly, in order to make it to the next town. "Shuckin' corn, hoeing taters, picking cotton, ain't no tougher than this business," Buster said.[37] In its many years as a traveling squad, the Indianapolis Clowns ran up more miles than any other team. They boasted that they had never missed a booking. "Join the Clowns. See the world!" was the team's ironic motto. Pollock kept track of the miles as well as the dangers and used both as promotional copy in the team's program book. "The Clowns have traveled 2,110,000 miles. Once played in a town with a population of 476 and had 1,372 fans at the game. Largest crowd 41,127 in Detroit. Smallest 35 in Lubbock, TX during a tornado. Have had the same bus driver for 17 years, worn out three buses and 19 sets of tires."[38] While fans reading the book might have found the statistics amusing, there were others, including Toni, who recognized the dangers. When the Clowns reached Texas a few days after leaving New Orleans, the state was still reeling from the tornado. Seeing the devastation in Waco, no one felt comforted to learn that storm forecasters predicted the summer of 1953 would be a bad one.*

On Friday, May 15, the Clowns kicked off the official start of the Negro American League season in Beaumont. They lost to the Monarchs 4–2, squeezing out only four hits. Toni walked twice and handled every fielding opportunity "without a miss" according to published accounts.[39] Ernie Banks received one of the Monarchs' two errors when he overthrew first base and forced an unearned run.[40] But the game in Texas was only a warm-up for what everyone considered the true opening of the season, the home opener against the Monarchs in Kansas City. From Waco, the Monarchs and the Clowns pushed on to Oklahoma, then Kansas, and finally into Missouri for the big game. Toni thought Opening Day festivities for the New Orleans Creoles had been exuberant. She could not imagine what might unfold in Kansas City. The Monarchs' businessmen watched closely, too. No one knew for certain if crowds would be smaller than last year or if there would be renewed interest in black baseball in this first test of the Midwestern market. The Monarchs hoped that the seventeen-thousand-seat stadium would attract fourteen thousand fans, an improvement over the previous year's twelve thousand. Everyone watched the gate that Sunday morning.

The first indication of what was in store for Toni and the future of Negro League baseball was the hurried young waitress serving breakfast to *Chicago Defender* sports columnist Russ Cowans. She couldn't wait for him to gulp down his coffee, pay the bill, and be gone. She had to get to the game. Fans started lining up outside the stadium at 11:00 A.M. for a game that didn't begin until 2:30. By noon, traffic was

---

*Forecasters were right. On June 9 while in Hopkinsville, Kentucky, the Clowns received word of another storm following them. The day before, 115 people had been killed in Flint, Michigan. As tornadoes moved across the Great Lakes and into New England, one touched down in Worcester, Massachusetts, on June 9, causing ninety-four deaths and nearly 1,300 injuries. The debris field from the storm was so vast that people fifty miles away reported seeing first oak leaves, then rags and shingles, and finally insulation and clapboard planks rain down. Pieces of a frozen mattress were found in Boston Harbor nearly an hour away from Worcester. The year 1953 proved to be the worst season for tornado deaths in U.S. history.

snarled and "Sold Out" signs began appearing on makeshift parking lots filled with out-of-state cars. Then the parade began. A police escort wailed its siren as seven hundred people—majorettes, marching bands, politicians, and businesspeople—began the slow route to the stadium. Some of the dignitaries admitted they were sleepy. A celebratory banquet had gone late the night before, saluting old-timers and welcoming Toni and other members of the Monarchs and the Clowns to the 1953 season.

As she always did, Toni basked in the attention. She admitted that sometimes she played the part of a big shot. "I'd get a $20 bill and get it all in ones and have one five that I'd wrap around and it made me look like I had big money," she laughed.[41] Everyone seemed caught up in the spectacle. "The fervor of interest is hard to describe," one diner said, recalling years past when stars like Cool Papa Bell and Josh Gibson came to town. Newspapers sensed the same excitement and thought Toni Stone might be a new catalyst. Cowans called her "the greatest star attraction to hit the loop since Leroy 'Satchel' Paige." This year would be different, baseball promoters thought. Even the Cincinnati Reds' general manager, in town to scout major league prospects, agreed. "I believe some Negro League teams quit too soon," he said.

As the parade entered left center field, the drum major at the head of the line could see that the fans filled the park and overflowed to a grassy slope outside the field. Hundreds more stood on ramps around the stadium or outside, hoping to get in. Families brought picnic baskets and cool thermos jugs for the long afternoon. Syd Pollock had come in from New York for the game and served as catcher for the ceremonial first pitch. But once the teams got down to playing, the game did not go well for the Clowns. The Monarchs scored one run in the first, another in the second, and exploded for five in the third. The Clowns' pitchers, Percy Smith and Ted Richardson, had difficulty locating their pitches, and by the game's end the team had managed only three runs on eight hits. Toni Stone did not fare well either. In her first at bat, she fouled off two, then swung wide and missed a curve for a strikeout; her second time up, she hit a grounder to first base for an easy out. She had no chances in the field. The final score was 8–3. It was the Clowns' sixth straight loss to the Monarchs in league play.

The following day two stories dominated black sports news. Over twenty thousand fans had attended the Opening Day in Kansas City, a figure larger than promoters had hoped for and significantly greater than in recent years. And Toni Stone was the main attraction. Even though she did not make any sparkling plays in the field or pound the ball, simply the fact that she played competent baseball against professional male athletes was newsworthy. "The only girl playing in league baseball had an appeal," *Kansas City Call* sports editor John L. Johnson wrote. "And the fact that she elects to play the difficult second base position instead of choosing a nice soft berth in right or left field, arouses the interest of the curious." Toni Stone earned "the plaudits of the crowd," another writer noted, "in every park in which she has appeared so far this season." Another was struck by her serious devotion to the game and called her a veteran player. Even white columnists commented on her play. Dorothy Kilgallen observed, "Metropolitan baseball scouts are more than a little interested in a twenty-one-year-old Negro lass—name of Marcenia Lyle (Toni) Stone, who played second base for the Indianapolis Clowns. She belts home runs as easily as most girls catch stitches in their knitting, and the sports boys are goggle-eyed." Nearly every account of the game acknowledged that Negro baseball appeared healthier and more alive than in recent years and gave Toni credit for enlivening fan interest. "Who says the Negro American League is dead?" the *Pittsburgh Courier* asked. "You can't make fans in this city [Kansas City] believe it."[42]

The next week, over ten thousand fans came out to see the Clowns and Black Barons series in Birmingham—the largest crowd Rickwood Field had seen in five years. Later, in St. Louis, fourteen thousand fans attended the game. When Clowns second baseman Ray Neil received an offer to play AA minor league ball with the Beaumont Texas League, he turned them down. The pay and perhaps the crowds were better in the Negro League. At the end of May, Syd Pollock had an announcement to make. A Japanese league had offered to purchase Toni Stone's contract for twenty-five thousand dollars, but Pollock said "his girl infielder was not for sale at any price." Pollock said he would consider negotiating a tour of Japan for the Clowns after the season was over and would guarantee Toni's appearance.[43] Cities where the Clowns had not scheduled games in years, such as Louisville, contacted Pollock to arrange an appearance. On a swing through Tennessee, the Clowns played the Memphis Red Sox. During infield practice, Toni bare-handed a line drive and the ball sliced open her palm, requiring four stitches. The injury forced her to sit out five games, although the day after the accident she appeared in full uniform, ready to play, and argued in the dugout with Buster Haywood. She wanted at least to take infield practice, but Haywood refused, saying her hand needed time to heal. Toni obeyed her manager's order although she did not like it. All too often, Haywood recognized, Clown players stayed in the game with injuries that jeopardized their health.[44]

As the crowds continued to turn out to see Toni play, it was inevitable that critics would also emerge. The only surprise was who fired the first shot. Wendell Smith, the *Pittsburgh Courier's* influential columnist, had fought for the integration of baseball and traveled with Jackie Robinson during his first season with the Dodgers. In a June 20, 1953, column, Smith publicly ridiculed Toni Stone. "Maybe the guy was tired of baby-sitting or couldn't find the can opener, but whatever the reason, he was justified when he cried out: 'A woman's place is in the home!' That undisputable statement rings true, we think, in the case of a baseball player by the name of Toni Stone." Acknowledging that Toni had revived the league, Smith went on to belittle the league. "It is indeed unfortunate that Negro baseball has collapsed to the extent it must tie itself to a woman's apron strings in order to survive," he wrote. Smith cited Stone's statistics, including seventeen at bats, but not the complete two months' season thus far. Many statistics for Negro Leaguers were based on league games only, even though the Clowns played the Monarchs, Red Sox, and Black Barons many other times during the season. Smith judged that Stone had a .217 average for her seventeen visits to the plate. "That's not much of an average to write home about but you'll have to admit, it's not bad for a dame." Twenty-two other Negro League players had batting averages below Toni Stone, according to Smith. "Any guy who can't out-hit a fraulein shouldn't be permitted to play in the Little League which is an organization for tykes and midgets," he wrote. Smith wondered whether a .217 average was inflated to begin with, speculating that scorers perhaps patronizing her would say, "She's a cute little thing, let's call it a hit."[45]

"I ask for no favors," Toni had said earlier in the season. "I'm playing a man's game and I want no special considerations. I'll get my share of the hits."[46] If she read Wendell Smith's comments, the insults would have been nothing new. "There are people who try to make it hard," she later said. "There are people who call you names."[47] Over the years, Toni had found a way to inoculate herself against people like Smith. "I've heard so much cursing in my life and have been called so many bad names," she said. "It doesn't bother me at all."[48] Profanity she could take, but ridicule cut deeper. Smith's disparagement was only beginning. The centerpiece of his column was a lengthy fictitious dialogue between Toni and her husband, presenting Alberga as a henpecked subordinate and Toni as a makeup-wearing, man-crazy, wardrobe-conscious, department-store bargain hunter. No one who actually knew her would ever have recognized the "Toni Stone" that Wendell Smith mocked.

> Husband: How did the pitcher on the other team look today?
>
> Mrs. Stone: I'm telling you that guy's just about as handsome as they come. When that big, strong beast looked down at me when I was batting, I got so excited I didn't know what to do. I won't ever get a hit off him. I get so weak when he looks at me. I can't generate enough strength to bunt. What curves he has! . . .

Husband: Some bills came today and one of them is for $350.

Mrs. Stone: I know . . . I went downtown yesterday and purchased a new glove . . . a silver mink glove. It's really something. I'm the envy of every woman in the stands on Ladies Day.[49]

The contrast could not have been greater between Wendell Smith's assessment and a sports column that appeared at the same time. Fay Young, the *Chicago Defender's* sports columnist, wrote about female tennis star Althea Gibson. In 1950, Gibson broke the color barrier of the U.S. Nationals and went on to challenge racial restrictions at the French Open and Wimbledon. While both women were trailblazers facing significant odds, Gibson was not breaking into a male domain and into a team sport that depended on—at least—the begrudging support of others. Wendell Smith viewed Toni as an interloper, not a pioneer. Even when Syd Pollock—perhaps opportunistically—began turning out press releases that placed Toni's play in a larger social context, many baseball observers remained unswayed. "Continuing to make headlines is the Clowns' 22 year old second baseman," Pollock wrote, "the first girl fielder to be signed and break down the prejudice against women players" in the Negro League.[50] Dr. J. B. Martin, league president, also began using Toni as an example of the league's commitment to equity. The Negro League "does not even bar a person because of sex if that person can play baseball," he wrote in a syndicated column. "The Indianapolis Clowns are featuring a woman at second base this season."[51] Yet Martin never backed up his comments with action that took Toni seriously, by advocating, for example, that she be allowed to play as many innings as her statistics warranted rather than being pulled midway through the game.

Despite Wendell Smith's ridicule (or perhaps because of it), fans continued setting ballpark records to see Toni Stone. At Briggs Field in Detroit over Father's Day, the Clowns and the Monarchs split a pair with attendance that matched the 1940s heyday of the Negro Leagues. Over twenty-six thousand watched Toni "hold up her share of play at second base."[52] Later that month, at a doubleheader in

Toledo, Toni pulled a ligament in her shoulder lunging for a line drive in another game against Kansas City. The injury was bad enough to send her to the hospital, and after she struck out in pain several nights later in Chicago, Haywood sent her to an emergency room again. Gordon "Hoppy" Hopkins, the Clowns' utility infielder, said Toni's arm was in a sling. But posters were up all over town announcing her appearance, so Bunny told her to put on her uniform and play. "And she did," Hopkins said.[53] Perhaps worried about further injuries to his star female player, Syd Pollock in July signed Doris Jackson as an "understudy to Toni Stone," according to reports in the *Washington Post*.[54] Jackson, a sixteen-year-old from Philadelphia, had attracted attention playing at a local recreation center.[55] "I hope you do not permit the other gal you say they are breaking in to worry you for one minute," Toni's husband wrote. "After all they have built you up and it is you the fans are looking to see play."[56] But Toni rebounded. Jackson apparently left the Clowns; her name was not in any lineup for the remainder of the season.

In fact, Toni went on a tear, hitting her stride and feeling healthier than she had all season. In Muskegon, Michigan, she got the Clowns' only hit in a Kansas City shutout, but the single did not go over well with her teammates. "When I came back to the dugout, not one player shook my hand or acknowledged what I had done," she said.[57] Several days later, while playing against a white national semi-pro championship team, she slashed a line drive single in the first inning and a double to left in the third. One of Toni's teammates may have thought the only way to stop Toni from overshadowing the men on the team was to injure her. According to Hoppy Hopkins, third baseman Willie Brown took too long getting a grounder over to Toni at second, and his throw positioned her for a spike. Bunny Downs didn't like what he saw; Brown's play looked like sabotage. After the game, when players were showered, dressed, and in their seats on the bus, Bunny stood and faced them. "Ain't no need to naming names," he said. "We all know what happened. This lady's putting money in our pockets. We don't want her hurt turning double plays. You men all expendable. She ain't. 'Nuff said."[58] While Downs's warning may have curbed some of the sabotage Toni experienced on the field, it was not the end of the harassment she received from her teammates.

At midseason, Kansas City was on top in the standings and Indianapolis was in the cellar. The Clowns' Ray Neil, however, led the league in hitting with a .416 average; Ernie Banks was close behind. Toni Stone had raised her average to .302, according to the Howe News Bureau.[59] A few weeks later, Neil and Banks were still in the number one and two spots, but Toni had risen to fourth in the league with a .364 average.* Toni's impressive hitting interested others besides Syd Pollock. A man approached Pollock and told him to talk to Louisville Slugger. "They'll make a special bat—put her name on it." Toni was thrilled, but Buster vetoed the idea. "The bats we've got are good enough for her," she heard him say.[60] By mid-July, the Clowns had returned to the East Coast for their second loop around the country, this time with games scheduled in bigger ballparks: Griffith Stadium in Washington, D.C., Connie Mack in Philadelphia, Forbes Field in Pittsburgh, and back to Griffith. Only New York and Boston remained unscheduled, and Pollock was working on possible games at the Polo Grounds or Yankee Stadium. After touring the urban centers, the team moved on to play in smaller cities before turning west: Reading, Wilmington, Newport News, Richmond, Chattanooga, Nashville, Columbus, Toledo, and finally St. Louis. The long season and the difficult travel schedule took their toll on everyone. Clowns pitcher Percy Smith dropped out with a knee injury after sliding into second; outfielder Verdes Drake broke his arm in the D.C. game; Speed Merchant, the team's other star outfielder, wrenched his knee in Memphis and got benched; pitcher Ted Richardson fractured his ankle and was out for two weeks. "We had no doctors," Toni said.

---

*Statistics released by the Baltimore *Afro-American* for July 11, 1953, also included the following information for Neil, Banks, and Stone. Neil achieved his average based on playing in twenty-six games with ninety-three at bats. Banks appeared in twenty-one games and had seventy-three at bats. Stone appeared in twenty-five games with thirty-six at bats. See also Marilyn Cohen, *No Girls in the Clubhouse: The Exclusion of Women from Baseball.* Jefferson, NC: McFarland & Company, 2009, 85.

"They'd just throw out that soreness in their arms [or] just slide over the swap positions when they got hurt."[61] Teams relied on home remedies such as "coal oil"—kerosene with a teaspoon of sugar—for colds and flu, and goose grease—drippings from a cooked goose—as a treatment for aching arms or legs. When a player suffered a deep spike wound and there weren't any bandages or ointments around, someone would find soot from a coal stove and smear the gash with the black paste, then place a spider web over the dressing to seal it.[62] All the Negro League teams had athletes too hurt to play. The Black Barons were so decimated by injuries that they hired two former players from the defunct Philadelphia Stars. Ernie Banks, after being scouted by major league scouts at nearly every Monarchs game, was no longer in the lineup, sidelined for two weeks with injuries.[63]

During the Negro League midseason meetings in Chicago, league executives and club owners, including Syd Pollock, heatedly discussed Toni Stone. Pollock complained that pitchers threw Toni too many curveballs, knucklers, changeups, and screwballs. "She's a woman but she's capable," Pollock's son remembered his father arguing. "Just have your pitchers throw her fastballs only." Birmingham Black Barons owner William "Soo" Bridgeforth and Tom Baird, owner of the Monarchs, accused Pollock of trying to compromise the integrity of the game. Pollock countered that if Toni were injured, fans would not return. "Then you can't afford your teams. The league dies, and all these great pitchers got no place to pitch." The club owners and club president Dr. Martin felt pressured. They voted, unofficially, to throw "hard but straight" to Toni. When Pollock also asked the group to forbid pitchers from aiming at her head, intentionally hitting her, and brushing Stone back, they agreed as well, unofficially. No one, it seems, asked Toni her opinion of the proposition or of the league's vote. Had she known that Pollock asked pitchers to play her differently, she would have been incensed. Toni always wanted her experience in baseball to be professional. That meant treatment that was equal and fair. She also would not stand for being patronized. "Don't worry," she had told reporters at spring training. "I can take care of myself."[64] Ironically, when Pollock and his son watched Clowns games during the rest of the 1953 season, they didn't think pitchers threw to Toni Stone any differently. Toni got "the same rotation or pitches as anyone else," Pollock's son said, and "we saw her hit the dirt more than once later that season."[65]

That July, *Ebony* magazine published a five-page story and photo spread on Toni that unfortunately did not help her efforts to be viewed as a professional baseball player. The feature had been in the works for several months and included photographs from spring training as well as staged shots of Toni washing windows at her home in Oakland, stepping out on the town, and receiving a rubdown from her husband. "Toni Stone is an attractive young lady who could be someone's secretary," one caption read. The article was a mixture of fact and fabrication. Her years with the Saint Paul teams, the San Francisco Sea Lions, and the New Orleans Creoles were accurately presented, but the story also included false or misleading details made to enhance her education and femininity. "She studied for a time at St. Paul's "McAllister [sic] College," the article said, and she is "an excellent housewife and cook." Perhaps eager to please Syd Pollock or simply wanting to appear higher paid than she was, Toni told reporters that for two years she had refused Pollock's offers to join the team. "I felt I wasn't ready, but when he said $12,000 for the season, I reached for my fountain pen." The feature may have gained Toni notoriety, but it treated her desire to play baseball as a curiosity. It certainly did not help break down or even identify the serious barriers she faced. Years later, she looked back on the feature as a mistake and wished she had not participated in it. "I was young," she said, "and they were capitalizing on me."[66]

Second thoughts about her participation in the *Ebony* feature may have led Toni to be less available when a woman reporter in St. Louis wanted to sit in the dugout with her in the July game at Busch Stadium and talk about what it meant to be a woman in a man's world. As she stepped out of the first aid room—her improvised locker room for changing into her uniform—Toni saw the reporter waiting for her. "Oh, no," she said, refusing to be interviewed, "not until after I have played." She's superstitious that way, Buster said. If the team wins with her sitting on the right side of the dugout, she'll sit there every night, he explained. Toni coached first base during the initial game of the doubleheader, and was animated with Clown runners on first and third. But when the Monarchs ended the rally with a double play, Toni stormed back to the dugout, sputtering to no one in particular. "You bring them in. I can get them on base but not farther."[67]

Also watching the game from the dugout was Deseria "Boo Boo" Robinson, who had joined the team four days earlier as another Toni understudy. Robinson, a twenty-three-year-old former player for the Capehart team, a semi-pro squad from Fort Wayne, Indiana, appeared shy and nervous and looked to Buster every time the reporter asked her a question. Like Doris Jackson, who had joined the Clowns two weeks earlier in Washington, D.C., Boo Boo would be gone before she had time to make an impression.

Game two was terrible for Toni. She committed two errors and struck out twice. And even worse, Syd Pollock had come in from New York to watch. Back home in Tarrytown, his "Girl Player" folder was thick with letters of inquiry and applications.[68] With all the publicity Toni was receiving, other women wanted to play with the Clowns or take her job. Despite the rousing ovation fans gave Toni at Busch, she could not forgive herself the mistakes. After her second strikeout, Toni returned to the bench and started to cry. "She takes the game too seriously," Pollock said. "She knows the crowd came to watch her give a show as the only woman in the league and she was trying awfully hard to make one for them." Trying too hard was a criticism Toni had heard before. She sat alone on the bench for the rest of the game and remained "very quiet," the reporter noted.[69]

On Saturday, August 8, Big Red was nearing Jefferson City, Missouri, en route to a doubleheader in Kansas City. The matchup would be the second time since Opening Day that the two teams had met in Blues Stadium, and Bunny expected another big crowd. Toni and the Clowns were tired from a quick jump to Buffalo and Pittsburgh earlier in the week and were trying to nap as they always did when the bus droned on. Another line of fierce storms had rolled through the Midwest two days before, and the damage still could be seen. A few hours to the east, hurricane force winds had knocked down a highway patrol radio tower in St. Louis. In a business district, glass from broken windows littered the sidewalks, and the ground was still saturated from half an inch of rain that had fallen in five minutes. The downed trees and debris created a "jungle-like scene."[70] The Clowns were glad that the bad weather did not seem to threaten their game in Kansas City. They were eager to play, and the season was turning around for them. Now in second place in the second half of the Negro League season, they were playing ball well above .500. Syd Pollock had returned to New York after the St. Louis trip and gotten busy with press releases, using a new phrase for promoting Toni. "She is murder minded in her effort to aid the team," he wrote, "a tough sister on defense [who] asks no odds from men hurlers when she goes to the plate."[71] Hyperbole again blurred the line between fact and a good phrase.

Everyone on the bus was in his usual seat: Ted Richardson, the next day's pitcher, slept in the long back seat, stretching out his legs so they wouldn't cramp. Bunny Downs sat near him where he could eat his ritual meal in peace—a concoction of pork and beans, sardines, onion, and bread. Spec Bebop, the team's dwarf comedian, rarely sat. If he perched on a bus seat, his short legs did not reach the floor and his limbs became numb, so Bebop stood most of the time.

Charlie Rudd, a former driver for the Birmingham Black Barons, was at the wheel. He had relinquished driving to Chauff some years ago but pitched in when the Clowns needed him. After four months on the road, Chauff welcomed relief from four-hundred-mile days. Already the team had been driving for hours that morning. Around ten-thirty, they approached the Osage River Bridge, a two-lane crossing south of Jefferson City. As usual, the milk can sentry sat perched next to Rudd, but there weren't many directions to call out—just a narrow country bridge over muddy water. As Charlie steered Big Red onto the bridge, he saw a panel truck at the opposite end, politely waiting to give him a wide berth. "Fashion Cleaners," he read as he aimed the bus between the truck and the guard rail.

Behind the truck was a large tractor-trailer, its driver impatient that Fashion Cleaners had stopped. Unable to see what was holding things up, the tractor-trailer shifted into gear, swung around the cleaners' truck, and accelerated onto the bridge. That's when Milk Can saw it. By the time the tractor-trailer's driver realized the Clowns bus was coming dead on toward him, it was too late. Charlie slammed on his brakes, but he couldn't stop in time.[72]

Keep on at It

Looks like what drives me crazy
Don't have no effect on you—
But I'm gonna keep on at it
Till it drives you crazy, too.

—Langston Hughes[1]

Charlie Rudd was covered in broken glass, but he was alive. Big Red, too heavily damaged to move, sat wounded and gasping on the bridge. The drivers of the tractor-trailer and the laundry truck opened their doors and edged out to inspect the crumpled piles of metal that their vehicles had become. No one was seriously injured—thankfully—not even Milk Can, who, like Charlie, was cut and bleeding. As soon as they could get to a phone, Bunny Downs and Buster Haywood started making calls. Bunny reported the accident to Syd Pollock, who made quick arrangements for a charter bus to pick up his battered team and take them to Kansas City. Buster called the Monarchs office and tried to have the next day's doubleheader dropped, rescheduled, or at least reduced to one game, but wasn't successful. A doubleheader meant double gate receipts, and neither team could afford to cancel. The next day the Clowns limped onto the field, rarely got a runner on base, and dropped both games. Like most of her teammates, Toni played only one game, too sore to make it through two. She sat out the first game, went 0 for 2 in the second, got irritated when the Clowns shortstop yelled her off an easy popup, and then dropped the ball, allowing Ernie Banks to take first base.

It was a long afternoon. The Clowns looked "not up to their best in body or mind," one sportswriter observed in generous understatement. With bruises, jangled nerves, and more than three months on the road still to go, Toni must have felt that the jubilant Opening Day had been a dream. Only a fraction of the fans who had overflowed Blues Stadium for that matchup at the beginning of the season now returned for the doubleheader.[2] Gone was the euphoria. Ahead was the grind. August, September, October, and November would reveal much about both the league's future and Toni's determination. There would be good news and bad.

The good news came from Sam Lacy and the *Pittsburgh Courier.* Before the Clowns' wreck, Lacy had taken in the team's games in Washington, D.C., against the Birmingham Black Barons. His sports column appeared a week later and focused on his impressions of Toni Stone. Lacy admitted he had felt skeptical about a woman playing professional baseball. He even confessed that he attempted to trick her into believing he was only interested in "an informal chat." In fact he was sizing her up, evaluating her femininity, her sexuality, and her grit. He even grabbed the glove out of her hand to determine if it had extra padding. By his own admission, Lacy had a "reputation for kicking the props from under the building," and he expected to find that Toni's foundation was flawed. What he discovered, however, surprised the jaded reporter and upended the assumptions he and other sportswriters had about Toni Stone. "She's no dummy," Lacy declared. He found her wise to Syd Pollock's hyperbolic prose and wise to his own attempt to entrap her. Lacy was astonished to discover that Toni was married. She "measure[s] up as a gal in every respect," he said and wrongly cited "Al Berger" as her husband. During warm-up practice, Toni could feel Lacy's eyes on her: he was trying to catch her flinching when teammates threw hard at her. Toni's strength surprised Lacy—the way she took intentional hard throws, heightened press and player scrutiny, and quietly went about her work on the diamond. He respected her resolve. "What you're doing is something no other woman has ever done before you and fearfully few are likely to do after you," he wrote. To this "hardboiled newspaperman," Lacy confessed, Toni Stone was no gimmick.[3]

Then bad news came from Chicago. Comiskey Park had been home to the Negro Leagues' fabled East-West All-Star game for over two decades. All the greats had played at Comiskey: Satchel Paige, Josh Gibson, Buck Leonard. During the peak years of the leagues, the ballpark stands were filled with smartly dressed couples, some of whom had traveled on trains especially chartered for the game. Toni was slated to play for the East team, representing the Clowns. Russ Cowans of the *Chicago Defender* predicted that, with all the players hoping to get into the game, Toni would play an inning or more "based on her magnetic drawing power . . . particularly [for] those gals who remain in the grandstand."[4] But when the teams were announced, Toni didn't make the cut. Players were chosen for the game based on ballots fans sent in, and apparently Toni did not receive enough votes. The game on Sunday, August 16 also was a disappointment. The East, managed by the Clowns' Buster Haywood, lost the game 5–1. And even with scouts from at least sixteen major league clubs in the stands, the reports on some of the standouts were not good. The word on Ernie Banks was "good field, no hit." Even the Monarchs' traveling secretary, a bird dog for the Yankees, did not recommend him for a move to the majors. But the biggest disappointment was the crowd itself. It was the smallest East-West attendance in almost ten years. Some observers wondered if the location of the game was a problem—that Chicago fans were no longer interested in the game. Others thought two all-star contests should be held: one in Chicago and another in Kansas City. A few critics argued that the game itself had become passé, damaged by unprofessional management, poor promotion, inadequate press, and the lack of an official scorer. "The ruse of race pride is no longer valid for its success," opponents argued. Even league president Dr. J. B. Martin admitted there were problems, citing that liquor bottles were found in the stands and fans hurled rowdy jeers at league umpires. Frustrated and seemingly out of ideas for improvement, Dr. Martin invited fans to write him directly with advice.[5]

The disappointment of the East-West game prompted another round of debate about the future of the Negro League. The results were surprising. As dismal as the turnout had been at Comiskey Park, many observers remained optimistic that the league could survive as a feeder system to the majors. Moreover, Toni Stone's continued magnetism brought new fans to the game who might be converted to the league. Some credited Stone with carrying the Negro League on her back in 1953 and giving other players a shot at the majors. Without her, they argued, the league would have folded, and young stars like Banks would never have been considered by scouts. Players and owners owed Toni Stone a lot, Cal Jacox of Norfolk's *Journal and Guide* wrote. She was the Negro League's "badly needed shot in the arm" and proved that black baseball "is too valuable an asset . . . to be allowed to wither on the vine."[6] Syd Pollock needed no convincing that signing Toni had been the right move for the Clowns, whether Buster Haywood liked it or not. Pollock's 1953 team set attendance records among all other Negro League teams; while the crowds were not the same as they had been in the flush of May and June, Syd had hopes that gambling on a woman at second base would continue to pay off. Pollock started making plans for the postseason, including the possibility of games with Jackie Robinson's integrated All-Star team. Toni Stone and Jackie would make a perfect marquis matchup, he thought, especially if Toni were healthy. Just to be assured there would be a woman on the team, Syd pulled out his "girl players" folder again and read through letters of inquiry to determine if any other female player measured up. He might need a backup.

Toni had already seen a couple women come and go on the Clowns. "Ole Syd . . . had a gang of [women] standing up, trying them out," she said. "He was hoping he'd get one."[7] But no woman stayed for longer than a few games. Perhaps the league was too competitive, or the women soon realized that they had not been educated to understand the game's fundamentals the way that the men had. Always a student of the game since the days she read baseball books in Saint Paul's libraries, Toni earned the praise of reporters who noted her "fine baseball mind" and awareness of what she didn't know.[8] Once when Ernie Banks was running toward second base with Toni covering the bag, Banks aimed his sliding foot at the ball and kicked it out of Toni's hand as she tried to apply the tag. "That was something I should have learned in high school," she said. "I learned something from it and told [Banks] it wouldn't happen again."[9]

Occasionally, when Pollock scheduled the Clowns in a city where another team was playing nearby, Toni asked if she could take in a few innings so that she could study the game. Bunny "would let me go for a half hour or so," she said, and the other Clowns would wait for her on the bus.[10] Nobody else wanted the extra study. Toni believed women who dreamed of playing professional ball had to be skilled and smart to overcome detractors—like Buster Haywood—who thought they had no right to play. Over the months that Toni played with the Clowns, a chasm began to develop between Buster and Bunny Downs. "Buster wouldn't want Lena Horne if Lena Horne could play second like [Ray] Neil, hit like Josh [Gibson], run like [Speed] Merchant, talk like J. B. Martin and dance like Bojangles," Bunny said.[11] Buster's aversion to women in baseball was so intense, Toni knew she needed more than skill to succeed. To earn the respect of men like Haywood, women had to "put their heart and soul in it," she said. They had to want it and work twice as hard as any man to get it. Pollock's son, Alan, who occasionally traveled on the bus when the team was up North, caught a glimpse of Toni's determination in an unlikely moment. Late at night when the bus stopped for a bathroom break, the men lined up beside the road to relieve themselves. Alan watched as Toni walked into the woods alone and disappeared into the darkness. It had to be lonely, he thought, for a woman to travel night and day on a bus with nearly two dozen men.[12] Some of her teammates, the ones who did not begrudge or belittle her ambition, could not understand how she kept at it. "Nothing comes easy," Toni would say.[13]

Toni had to persevere through additional challenges, trials she shared with her teammates. On a daily basis, every member of the Indianapolis Clowns confronted humiliations as blacks living in Jim Crow America. Nowhere were those struggles more pointed than in restaurants and hotels down South. The Jim Crow stories were legion: service refused, contaminated food, smashed plates and cups. But the Clowns met discrimination with resolve and creativity. In places where the team knew white hotels would refuse them, Syd made arrangements in advance from the home office. But sometimes rooms were not available or schedules changed at the last moment, and Bunny would have to consult his book of addresses of black establishments. When the Clowns ran out of suggestions from their usual sources, Chauff could always pull out The Negro Motorist Green Book—a publication nearly every black family used when traveling in the segregated South. The Green Book was the work of New York City travel agent Victor Green, who in 1936 began a listing of hotels, taverns, service stations, barbershops, and night clubs that would serve black clientele. "Carry Your Green Book With You. You May Need It," the cover read.

When the Clowns traveled below the Mason-Dixon line, they knew not to expect service in white restaurants, but sometimes those establishments were the only places serving food. One player would have to knock at the back door of a restaurant and ask if it sold food to blacks. "Shoot!" Toni said. "You'd have somebody go to the old back . . . windows and the old sandwiches were cold."[14] When white comedian Ed Hamman joined King Tut and Spec Bebop as part of the team's entertainment midway through the season, his wife often accompanied him. The couple drove along the same route as the Clowns bus. Joyce Hamman would offer to buy food at white diners and bring it to the team's locker room before a game so the Clowns wouldn't have to play hungry. Sometimes, however, she was thwarted by restaurant owners who suspected what she was doing. "Ain't gone to be no integration by proxy" was an all-too-familiar refrain.[15] Along the Mason-Dixon line, restaurants would serve black clientele but in a decidedly hostile atmosphere. The Clowns had their own policy when it came to bigoted "partway" table service in border towns. They knew waiters and waitresses would not overtly refuse them but would ignore the team, so they devised the "three strikes and you're out" rule. After waiting for five minutes or more for service, players would flag down a waiter. "In a minute," the waiter would say: strike one. More time would pass and another attempt would be made to get some attention. "Be right there," was the reply: strike two. After more time passed with more neglect from the waitstaff, one final attempt would be made. "Coming, coming," a waiter would respond: strike three. That's when the Clowns would gather up the silverware, pocket the utensils, and walk out the door. Later, when the team reached their favorite black hotel in Indianapolis, they would present the owner with gifts of Jim Crow table service.[16]

Felix "Chin" Evans, a Clowns pitcher, became famous for his response to the smashed dishes that so deeply disturbed young Henry Aaron when the team tried to eat in Washington, D.C. Chin had heard the sound of crashing plates so often in one D.C. restaurant that he came prepared on a later visit. When he purposefully walked toward the restaurant for lunch, a teammate grabbed Chin and tried to steer him in another direction. Chin went in anyway, alone. Just as everyone suspected, an infuriated host threw a menu at him and stomped off, muttering about the "nigger ball club" whose bus was parked outside. Chin ordered, ate, and shooed the waiter away when it came time to clear the dishes. He didn't want the server to appear "like a servant haulin' off a colored man's trash," he said. The bill for Chin's meal came to under one dollar, but he handed the bigoted host a twenty-dollar bill. "Pretty big tip for a nigger clown," the host replied. It wasn't a tip, Chin explained. It was a "waste riddance fee." That's when he reached into his pocket and brought out a hammer. Chin pulled the tablecloth up over the dishes, swung the hammer, and smashed every plate, cup, and saucer. "Just throw the nigger dishes out in the nigger tablecloth and keep the change," he said and walked out.[17]

The treatment the Clowns received at Jim Crow restaurants infuriated them, but the team's experience with hotels was often miserable and occasionally terrifying. Tired and dirty from being on the road, Toni and her teammates would dream of a clean bed. It was the little things that she missed, Toni said, like being able to wash out her underwear. "You could kinda feel a little like home" when that amenity was available, she said.[18] When black hotels were not available, the team stayed in boarding houses, rooming establishments, or private homes. Teams had to find these accommodations before local curfews for blacks went into effect. One player remembered playing one town in Mississippi where the local police announced the game would have to be over by 10:00 P.M.; black men were not allowed on the streets after that hour. The team played fast, got back on the bus, and returned to Memphis in sweaty uniforms and without any dinner. They simply couldn't risk stopping anywhere for food.[19] And Ed and Joyce Hamman later received bomb threats at their own home because Ed was involved with a black team.[20]

While threats against blacks occurred less frequently than they once had, ball clubs like the Clowns and the Monarchs were always vigilant travelers. They never became complacent or beguiled into a false sense that they were safe. On the Monarchs bus, team manager Buck O'Neil made a ritual of offering advice and warnings based on recent news reports whenever the team pulled into a new town. Like the Clowns' King Tut, Buck had seen nearly every stretch of road, and he knew from experience which businesses would welcome black men. He realized he had young charges under his supervision, some of whom came from the North and might be naive or uninformed about the reach of Jim Crow. When the Monarchs arrived in one Kansas town, Buck got up to offer his usual speech. But this one was more serious than usual. He told his ballplayers that there had been a recent lynching. Buck told his team, "Just get dressed, go to the park, and play." Ernie Banks found it odd that the white fans who cheered for him from the stands could threaten him on the street. Then there was that most ridiculous of charges: "reckless eyeballing."[21] The mere phrase "reckless eyeballing" was laughable, he thought, but he also knew that a white woman could report any black man—even have him thrown in jail—if he looked at her a second too long. "Those were dangerous times," Toni later said.[22]

For Toni, finding comfortable and safe accommodations was the most difficult challenge of life on the road. Sometimes rooming houses would offer her—but not the men—a place to stay. "I told [the proprietors] 'thank you very much' and got back on that old bus and went to sleep," she said. Toni believed refusing a room under those conditions was an important show of respect toward her teammates. "They're my brothers," she said. "And we stick together."[23] Asking Toni where she slept was a favorite question of reporters. Everyone was curious about her sleeping arrangements and whether her teammates took advantage of her sexually. Toni had a practiced, if not always truthful, response. "I found that this wasn't any headache," she said. "At first, the fellows made passes at me, but my situation in traveling around the country with a busload of guys isn't any different from that of the girl singers who travel with jazz bands. Once you let the guys know that there isn't going to be any monkey business, they soon give you their respect."[24] Of course Toni did not mention that showing there would be no "monkey business" sometimes meant taking a baseball bat to the head of a teammate as she had on a bus ride years before. But Toni's comparison of her life to that of jazz musicians was appropriate. They were both willing to accept rough accommodations, loneliness, and isolation for steady work doing what they loved. But there was one difference. People were used to female singers traveling with jazz bands: Billie Holiday, Alberta Hunter, Ella Fitzgerald. Few people, however, expected to find a woman on a men's baseball team. If hotel proprietors in small towns had not read about Toni Stone in the *Defender* or in magazines, they made assumptions about why she traveled with the men.

What Toni did not tell reporters but confessed to her family years later was that those assumptions hurt. But she found a way to take advantage of them. At times hotel proprietors assumed Toni was a prostitute traveling with the men in order to serve their sexual needs. They refused to let her stay and gruffly directed her to the nearest brothel.* Her teammates, Bunny, and Buster either would not or could not successfully defend her. That's how she discovered the underworld of prostitutes' hospitality. "They took me in," Toni said. The "sporting girls" gave her a clean bed to stay in and a meal to eat. Perhaps Toni saw something in the women that reminded her of her own outsider status; perhaps they saw some of the same in Toni's unconventional life. They liked each other, and when Toni returned the women would have a car waiting for her. They sometimes attended her games, followed her in the sports pages, and encouraged her to take her responsibility to the race seriously. "You got to represent," they told her.

Toni developed a network of brothels throughout the South where prostitutes took care of her, sometimes washing her uniform during the night and leaving it folded on the dresser for when Toni awoke the next morning. After Toni complained of the discomfort of taking hard throws to the chest (some intentionally), the women sewed padding into her navy blue Clowns shirt, hoping the extra padding—something sports columnist Sam Lacy never saw—would keep her safe. Some mornings Toni would wake to find a few dollars beside her uniform—extra money to make the two-dollars-a-day meal money she received from the Clowns go further. Those mornings weren't the

---

*Scholar Henry Louis Gates Jr. said that whites steering blacks to brothels was "another way of relegating blacks to second-class citizenship and ascribing to them questionable morality" (e-mail to author, October 17, 2007). Journalist Robin Roberts, in her book *From the Heart: Seven Rules to Live By*, wrote that a brothel was once an accommodation of last resort for her parents. "In the Air Force, my dad's division, the all-black Tuskegee Airmen, was segregated from the white divisions in the early days. And my dad wasn't always treated with the respect he was due. Once, after serving in Japan, he was transferred to an Air Force base outside of Dallas. My parents arrived about nine p.m., assuming there would be accommodations for them. They were stopped at the gate to the base, and the guard said, 'You'll have to go into Dallas. There is no housing available to you.' And he was very pointed when he said 'for you.' My parents drove into Dallas and had no luck finding lodging. Finally, a black proprietor took pity on them and said, 'I do have one place . . .' It was a room in a brothel. The doorbell rang all night" *(From the Heart: Seven Rules to Live By*, New York: Hyperion Books, 2007, 65–66).

first time that Toni had encountered the kindness of prostitutes. Before she turned to the church for help finding a permanent room in San Francisco, she found temporary housing in the attic of a prostitute's home. "She was a 'wrong woman,'" Toni said, "but a beautiful human being. She taught me many things . . . the walks of life. I had no crime with her."[25] Realizing many people thought otherwise, Toni was quick to come to prostitutes' defense. "They were good girls," she said. Like other times in her life when Toni expressed respect and even tenderness for social outcasts, she sounded as though she might be seeking respect herself. As confident and driven to play baseball as she appeared to be, Toni could be wounded by incivility and humiliation.[26] She heard the jeers: "Why don't you go home and fix your husband some biscuits!"[27] Playing professional baseball might simply be too hard and maybe it wasn't the right thing for her to do, she sometimes thought.

But there were other women athletes who admired Toni and were eager to follow in her path-breaking footsteps. Eighteen year-old Mamie Johnson was a pitcher for the semi-pro Alexandria (Virginia) All-Stars and the St. Cyprian's recreational league in Washington, D.C.* Like Toni, Mamie grew up playing baseball with the boys. As a child in rural Ridgeway, South Carolina, she learned baseball from her uncle and practiced pitching by throwing at crows on a fence. Her ball was a rock wound with twine and sealed with heavy masking tape. She made bats from tree limbs. First base was a pie plate. Second was a broken piece of flowerpot. Third was a tree root near a lilac bush, and home plate was the lid from a five-gallon bucket of King Cane syrup. Mamie lived with her maternal grandmother while her mother, who had once played baseball herself, worked as a dietician in Washington, D.C. Mamie's father, a construction worker, was not an active presence in her life. When her grandmother died, young Mamie went

---

*Mamie Johnson's birth date has been listed as 1932 in Indianapolis Clowns publicity material and 1935 by the U.S. Public Records office. In my interview with Mamie Johnson [Goodman], she said she was born in 1935, and I have used that year as her birth date.

to live with an aunt and uncle in Long Branch, New Jersey. One day she wandered into a police precinct in New Jersey and asked about playing for the Police Athletic League (PAL) baseball team. The PAL organization in Long Branch had never had a black ballplayer on the team and certainly not a female one, but the lieutenant invited her to try out. Once she started pitching well, the team accepted her. Mamie played with PAL through high school and then moved to D.C. where she lived with her mother. She married and started playing recreational baseball in the lots across from Howard University.[28]

Playing baseball was a passion for Mamie—much more than working at an ice cream shop in the District. "The more I played, the better I got and the more I wanted to play," she said. When her friend Rita Jones—a first baseman for the St. Cyprian's team—heard on the radio that the All-American Girls Professional Baseball League was holding local tryouts, the two young women made plans to attend. After locating the baseball field, they looked around and saw that all the players were white. "You think they're going to let us try out?" Rita asked. Before they could put on their baseball gloves, AAGPBL players and organizers gave them a stare that communicated everything. "They looked at me like I was crazy," Mamie said. She and Rita understood immediately that they were not welcome. The experience marked Mamie. "It dawned on me," she said. "They think we're not as good as [they] are."[29]

Mamie returned to Washington and continued playing with St. Cyps on Sundays at Banneker Field. One afternoon, Bish Tyson, a sometimes bird dog for the Clowns, watched the five-foot-four-inch teenager pitching. He liked what he saw, but the risks with Mamie were substantial. She had played on local men's teams, but she lacked high-level playing time and had not been out on the road with a team. Her experience could not be compared with the depth of Toni's background. Nevertheless, Bish thought Mamie was worth a look and contacted Bunny Downs, telling him he had found a player worth evaluating. Bunny arranged for Mamie to meet the team in a September swing through D.C., take some cuts off Clowns pitchers, and serve up some fastballs to Toni Stone, Gordon "Hoppy" Hopkins, and other Clowns players. After conferring with Syd Pollock and Buster Haywood, Downs offered Mamie a noncommittal postseason spot with the Clowns when they barnstormed for two months in the fall. Within days, the young woman quit her ice cream shop job and was on the Clowns bus bound for Norfolk and barnstorming games against the Negro League All-Stars. "Honestly, to be frank," Mamie said, "I slipped away." Her husband did not appear to have a voice in her decision, either. "It didn't make any difference because I was going to play anyway," she said.[30]

About the same time Mamie joined the Clowns for postseason play, another young woman, inspired by Toni Stone, approached the team. Connie Morgan had read about Toni in *Ebony* magazine and announced to her grandmother that she was going "to write to Toni Stone and see if I can get on a baseball team."[31] But her grandmother did not take Connie's ambition seriously and shrugged it off "like a pipe dream," Connie said. The young woman did write a letter, and Toni passed it on to Bunny Downs. When the Clowns traveled to Baltimore for the start of their postseason barnstorming tour, Syd invited Connie to drive from her home in Philadelphia for a tryout. Connie Morgan was a standout with local softball and basketball teams.

Like Toni, Connie had honed her athletic skills at community centers. No one really knew where she got her athletic talent. Her parents, Vivian and Howard, were not particularly athletic. Her father was a window washer and her mother worked for the local Sea Farer's Union.[32] The couple had six children: two boys and four girls. The oldest of the siblings, Connie tried to interest one sister in basketball, but the younger girl did not stay with it. When Connie entered Bartram High School in Philadelphia, a neighborhood youth worker saw her playing softball and asked if she would be interested in joining a recreational league. Connie joined the Honey Drippers and played with them for nearly five years. A right-handed hitter, she batted around .370 and played every position except pitcher.[33] But as the girls on the team neared the end of their high school years, most of them lost interest in softball. The "girls got so they didn't want to play anymore," Connie said. None of the girls in her class ever heard of athletic scholarships to college and "no one offered me" one, she said. A good student, Connie enrolled in the William Penn School of Business in Philadelphia after she graduated from high school and took typing and bookkeeping classes to prepare for a career as a secretary. While enrolled at William Penn, Connie read the article about Toni Stone and wrote her letter. Her parents were proud that their daughter had taken a step toward playing black baseball, but were "shocked," Connie said, when the Clowns invited her to Baltimore.[34]

On October 9, nearly a month after Mamie Johnson joined Toni on the postseason tour, Connie Morgan appeared at the Baltimore stadium for a tryout. Some thought Syd Pollock was just as interested in Connie's cute appearance as he was in her athletic skills.[35] A petite, attractive eighteen-year-old "gal guardian" in the infield would be in marked contrast to Toni with her rough hands, fiery disposition, and bowlegged walk. Syd wanted the newcomer to try out in Clowns flannels and arranged for some photographs to be taken of Connie just to see how she would look as an official team member. Buster Haywood told Connie to take up position at third base and then hit balls to judge her fielding and throws to first base. Haywood and others thought third base "was too hot a corner for me," Connie said, and Buster put her on second instead. Toni watched from the sidelines, keenly aware that second was her spot in the infield. She felt nervous, even usurped—like some of the old-timers on the Clowns who six months before wondered why Syd had gambled on a woman from the New Orleans Creoles.

The greatest pressure was on Connie, however. Few players could ever say they had a tryout in front of Jackie Robinson, Luke Easter, Pee Wee Reese, and Gil Hodges. Robinson's All-Stars had responded to Syd's earlier invitation and signed to travel throughout the South, playing games against the Clowns, the Negro League All-Stars, and other teams. Robinson and his teammates watched Connie and commented on "her good arm."[36] Bunny Downs, seeing an opportunity to have Connie photographed with Jackie, asked Robie to pose as though he were offering "batting tips" to the young woman. Robinson complied and stood with the teenager, who looked dutiful and stunned next to her hero. Haywood told Connie that Syd Pollock would be in touch with her later. She returned home to Philadelphia in her grandmother's DeSoto, "surprised that [the Clowns] wanted me."[37]

Nobody took a photo of Jackie Robinson with Toni Stone. Toni thought Syd would have wanted one. He always wanted her to sell photographs of herself in the stands or after games. It was a chore that Toni disliked and one that she felt diminished her stature as a professional baseball player. "I shouldn't have to do that, you know," Toni said.[38] Then there were problems with Toni's mail. All of her fan mail and professional inquiries were routed through Pollock's Tarrytown office. Toni believed letters from other teams—asking if she might be interested in joining them for a higher salary—never found their way to her. "They say, 'We sent you a letter so and so and so.' I never got it. I know there were a lot of people wanted me to try to play for them. You know, more opportunities." Then there were the comments she began to hear from the Clowns management. "Oh, she's chesty," Toni said she heard—too full of herself, too ambitious and unyielding. "Things looked like they just got rougher," she said. [39]

The Clowns and the Jackie Robinson All-Stars continued their play throughout the South, sometimes also playing against Roy Campanella's All-Star team. In Memphis and Birmingham, local Jim Crow ordinances forbade whites and blacks from playing on the same team. Birmingham Sheriff Bull Connor warned that if the Robinson All-Stars fielded a team of whites and blacks, there would be "big trouble." Many of Jackie's white major league players stayed away, afraid for their lives. Robinson believed that paying fans were entitled to a game and did not challenge the ordinance. Instead, he supplemented his team with other black players, including Willie Mays. Critics of Robinson said he should have defied Birmingham's Jim Crow rules and refused to play the game. Later in the season, Robinson rethought his position. He pledged to field another integrated barnstorming team next season and donate his earnings to charity.[40]

Debate among those who believed prejudice should be faced down intensified in 1953. When Robinson and the All-Stars pulled into Baton Rouge the evening of October 25, the city was still spinning from the successful bus boycott that summer. Baton Rouge's city-parish council had voted earlier in the year to raise bus fares, an increase that affected mostly black passengers, who rode the buses more frequently than whites. Reverend T. J. Jemison, the pastor of Mt. Zion Baptist Church, denounced the increase and also called for an end of segregated seating on buses. Although black passengers paid full fare, he said, they were forced to sit in the back or stand while "white" seats up front remained empty. The Baton Rouge Council amended the seating policy to allow blacks to occupy bus seats as long as they didn't sit in front of or alongside whites. Yet no one enforced the policy, bus drivers threatened to strike, and the Louisiana attorney general stepped in to declare the new seating ordinance unconstitutional since it violated the state's existing segregation laws. Angered, Reverend Jemison and others formed the United Defense League (UDL) and called for a boycott of the city's bus system. Thousands of black residents began participating in nightly UDL meetings across Baton Rouge. Five days later, black and white leaders negotiated a compromise allowing bus riders of any race to sit wherever they wanted, except for the first two rows, which were reserved for whites, and the last two rows, for blacks. One young man who took special interest in the successful bus boycott was Martin Luther King Jr., who had recently completed his theology degree at Crozer Theological Seminary in Pennsylvania. Reverend King and his new wife, Coretta, were preparing to take up his new ministry at the Dexter Avenue Baptist Church in Montgomery, Alabama.

When the postseason with the Jackie Robinson All-Stars ended, Toni's husband knew she was upset with the addition of Mamie Johnson, and the prospect of Connie Morgan, on the team. "At the end of your contract you understand you are free to do what you want, though I say look before you leap," he warned her. Alberga thought that the Clowns might be in a better financial position than other Negro

League clubs and encouraged Toni not to make any quick decisions. "Dear, you have shown good judgment in the past and I am sure you can do it again," he wrote.[41] With the season concluded, the Howe News Bureau posted the Negro League's final results, showing that the Kansas City Monarchs had won both the first and the second half of the 1953 season. The Clowns finished third out of the four teams. Although Buster Haywood feared Toni's play at second base for the Clowns would affect Ray Neil's batting average—it did not. Neil won the Negro League batting title, hitting .397. Ernie Banks came in third at .347. In the last days of the season, Banks signed with the Chicago Cubs. The Bureau reported that Toni Stone hit .243 in league play, with seventy-four at bats over fifty league games. "All of her hits were singles, except for one double," it stated. Toni also stole one base, had three RBIs, and posted a .852 fielding percentage.[42] What the Bureau did not record, however, were statistics from the nearly one hundred non-league games and other barnstorming contests that Toni and the Clowns played during the majority of the 1953 season. In some respects the Bureau numbers represented only a portion of any player's record. Most sportswriters believed a Negro League player's statistics for the full year—rather than just the league-sanctioned games—were higher than what the Howe News Bureau reported.

Toni returned to Oakland and her husband for the first time in over eight months. She was exhausted, and Alberga was ill. In January, Syd Pollock wrote with concern for Alberga's health, adding that he knew Toni regarded her husband as "a guiding light and inspiration in your endeavors and future success." Syd informed Toni that the Clowns' contracts for the 1954 season would be mailed out in February and reminded her that the team had a "right to her services" for the upcoming year. He asked that she tell him as soon as possible if she intended to return for the next year.[43]

Toni could not make up her mind. She was worried about her husband, ground down by the road, and disturbed about several new developments. The hiring of Mamie Johnson for the barnstorming season made her feel as though the team had less interest in her, the potential of Connie Morgan at second base would reduce her playing time, and the lack of respect that Buster Haywood showed her was apparent not only to Toni but to others as well. Sam Lacy of the Baltimore *Afro-American* reported that "late summer rumors said Buster chafed at having to use Toni as box office bait."[44] The 1953 season was the only year Buster ever got angry at his friend Syd Pollock, he said. Haywood complained, "She wasn't a ballplayer and I'm playing to win."[45] Syd's January letter temporarily eased Toni's distress on one score: Buster Haywood would not be managing the Indianapolis Clowns in 1954. The forty-four-year-old Haywood might stay on as a substitute player or the club chauffeur, Syd informed her, but Oscar Charleston—the legendary former Negro League slugger—was taking over the reins. The Monarchs coach, Buck O'Neil, was typical of many ballplayers who thought Charleston was the greatest ballplayer who ever lived. "He was like Ty Cobb, Babe Ruth and Tris Speaker rolled into one," O'Neil said.[46] Players also said Charleston was an excellent coach who could teach anyone how to lift his game.

But Pollock confirmed Toni's concerns about Mamie Johnson and Connie Morgan. Syd told her he was hiring both young women for the upcoming season and intended to use only one of the women in the lineup at a time. The team couldn't risk "letting the public down when injury crops up," he said, "which occurred so many times last season when [we] only had you to fall back on." Pollock offered Toni $350 a month—down $50 from her 1953 high of $400. He realized the offer was less than she had been making and opened the door for Toni to consider other possibilities. Syd offered to contact Tom Baird, owner of the champion Kansas City Monarchs. Baird and O'Neil had agreed that the only woman they would consider was Toni Stone. They offered to sign her for $325 a month. Neither Pollock's offer nor the possibility of going with Kansas City for even less money was a choice that pleased Toni, and she did not immediately reply to Pollock's letter.[47]

Later that month, Toni heard from her strongest advocate on the Clowns, Bunny Downs. Toni had written to Downs after receiving Pollock's offer and asked for his advice. "It was a real pleasure to hear from you," Bunny said, "as I am beginning to feel as though I was the forgotten man as far as some people I do claim as my personal friends." Bunny had taken the liberty of talking with Syd about Toni's contract. "I think a person deserves every cent he or she can get for services rendered. So make up your mind what you estimate your services are worth and explain to Syd and see what terms are satisfactory to all concerned." Bunny seemed to be as surprised with the change in Buster Haywood's position with the team as Toni must have been. "Every thing changes in this world," he wrote philosophically, "so we have to try and be ready for anything that may arise." He then zeroed in with his most candid advice. "Before you arrive at your salary terms do a lot of thinking for YOUR future," he wrote, "and then talk it over with Mr. Alberga, then explain your side to Syd."[48]

Bunny Downs was right. Toni understood that the decision was about her future and that she needed to figure out what she wanted and how to negotiate for it. In 1954, she would be thirty-three years old, not the twenty-three-year-old that the new coach, Oscar Charleston, would think she was. She would no longer be the only woman in the Negro League and would have to share the spotlight with two nineteen-year-olds. In addition, the Clowns made it clear that she would not play every day. Toni knew baseball skills only improved with practice, and it gave her a fit, she said, to be "bench jockeyed."[49]

So many possibilities she dreamed of had come true. She was playing professional baseball in the Negro League. She heard cheering crowds at Griffith Stadium and Forbes Field. And she had held her own against future major leaguers and seasoned pros. But, like Mamie Johnson said, the more she played, the more she wanted to play. Toni wanted to go as far as she could in baseball. If wild propositions like being traded to a Japanese team for twenty-five thousand dollars a year had not come true, maybe others that she could not even imagine would. Toni had to decide if she would take Syd's offer, the Kansas City Monarchs' proposed $325, or some other option that she could not recognize yet. The choice was hers to make. "You have always treated me right and looked out for my interest," Toni wrote to Bunny in a return letter.[50] The question Toni faced that January was: what exactly did she want?

A Baseball Has 108 Stitches

It's a long old road, but I know I'm gonna find the end.

—Bessie Smith[1]

Toni decided to keep playing baseball. She signed with the Kansas City Monarchs for the 1954 season. The decision came down to two issues: Syd Pollock's resolution that the Clowns would have only "ONE" [girl] in the starting lineup" and Bunny Downs's advice to think about "YOUR future."[2] Those two capitalized words stuck in Toni's mind and convinced her that joining the Monarchs was the right choice. As much as she felt the previous season had not ended well, she left the Clowns on good terms and expressed her thanks in painstakingly deliberate words. "I trust you will believe me when I say that I fully appreciate all that [y]ou have done for me and the interest shown in me likewise," she wrote Syd.[3] But Toni couldn't stay with the Clowns and compete for attention with Connie Morgan and Mamie "Peanut" Johnson. She felt she stood a better chance of being noticed with Kansas City. The decision to jump also turned—as it always did—on money. Syd's offer was lower than what he had paid her a year before. After negotiation with Tom Baird, Toni persuaded the Monarchs owner to increase her salary to four hundred dollars a month with the prospect of a two-hundred-dollar bonus at the end of the year. Toni accepted Baird's terms and told him she would do her best to cooperate, noting she had heard only "good things" about Monarchs manager Buck O'Neil.[4] Toni's most candid comments were reserved as usual for her old friend Bunny Downs. "A change would do me good," she wrote, adding, "I shall always remember how nice and considerate you was to me and I [want] you to know that I shall always remember you for the same."[5] As Bunny readied the Clowns bus for the annual spring training trip to Norfolk, Toni went to the TWA office in San Francisco to pick up the airline ticket Baird had reserved for her. Dress warmly for Kansas City, he advised. "Weather is very cold here now."[6]

Baird's concern for Toni's comfort was the only hint of cordiality in his stiff correspondence. Thomas Y. Baird was not a warm man, certainly not beloved in the way that former Monarchs owner J. L. Wilkinson was.* "Wilkie," as he was affectionately known to his players, made the team into a legend, owning the Monarchs for twenty-eight years until age, ill health, and the slow demise of black baseball forced him to sell the franchise. The origins of the Monarchs reached back to 1912, when Wilkinson and a partner organized the All Nations team, a squad featuring players of many racial and ethnic backgrounds. "Direct from their native countries, Hawaiians, Japanese, Cubans, Filipinos, Indians, and Chinese," promotional material read.[7] The team also included one woman player, May Arbaugh, who was billed as "Carrie Nation." When arriving in a new town to play baseball, the All Nations team would also host a dance, organize a wrestling squad, and provide music performed by the athletes. The

*James Leslie Wilkinson pitched for an Iowa semi-pro team until a broken wrist ended his playing career. In addition to owning the Monarchs, Wilkinson also served as the secretary of the Negro National League and treasurer of the Negro American League. He was elected to baseball's Hall of Fame in 2006 when he was acknowledged as "the man most responsible for saving black baseball during the Great Depression" (http://web.baseballhalloffame.org/hofers/detail.jsp?playerId=506642).

team was not all sideshow, however, and they played some of the best black teams in the country, including Rube Foster's Chicago American Giants. After World War I, Wilkinson reorganized All Nations as an independent semi-pro team and located in Des Moines before finally settling in Kansas City. Pitcher John Donaldson suggested the name "Monarchs" as a way to project the athletic supremacy the team hoped to achieve. In 1920, the Monarchs became a member of the newly constituted Negro National League. As the only white owner at that time in black baseball, Wilkinson used his race to make profitable financial bookings—bookings that racism would have made difficult to negotiate for black baseball executives. Newt Allen, a former Monarchs infielder and later team manager, said Wilkinson was "one of the finest men I've ever known. . . . You could go to him in the winter and get half of next summer's salary."[8]

Besides being respected by the black community for his fairness and decency, Wilkinson was also admired as an innovator. He urged teams to move away from train travel to buses so that they could play in the small towns the railroads did not reach. Wilkinson's most memorable innovation was a portable lighting system that made night games possible. In 1930, Wilkinson—with financing help from Baird—bought a "Sterling Marine 100 kilowatt generator with a 250 horsepower, six cylinder, triple carburetor, gasoline-drive engine" from the Giant Light Company of Omaha, Nebraska. Twelve men used the mobile generator to install forty-four portable floodlights on tall poles in the beds of Ford trucks to flood the diamond with light. The innovation, overwrought contraption that it was, ushered in a new era and new revenue to baseball. Five years later, when President Franklin Delano Roosevelt flipped a switch in the Oval Office to illuminate stadium lights at Crosley Field in Cincinnati, he was following a vision that Wilkinson and the Negro Leagues had already made a reality.[9]

In July 1947, Wilkinson and several of the Monarchs players were involved in a car accident in Chicago. Wilkie ruptured the retina in his left eye and later became virtually blind. The following year, he sold his 50 percent ownership of the team to co-owner Tom Baird, retaining the right to organize a second, separate squad called the "Kansas City Monarchs Traveling Team" as well as the right to negotiate with his friend and former Monarchs player Satchel Paige. When Wilkinson handed over the reins to Tom Baird, the Monarchs had won eleven pennants and two Negro World Series and had sent more players to the major leagues than any other franchise. Next began the Baird era for the Monarchs.[10]

Tom Baird had been involved with baseball long before he became the owner of the team.* As a teenager, he played for local championship teams near White City, Kansas. A fracture to his right knee, suffered during the off-season when he worked as a railroad brakeman, ended his playing career. Baird turned to managing and promoting area semi-pro teams. He ran the Peet Brothers company team and booked visiting squads in the Peet Brothers Billion Bubble Park.† Later he owned the T. Y. Bairds, a longstanding team in Kansas City's white municipal league, who were occasional opponents of the African American Topeka (Kansas) Giants.[11] In the 1930s Baird promoted both the House of David team and the Monarchs and arranged for the two teams to barnstorm against each other, with Babe Didrikson playing for the House of David team. After Babe Ruth retired from the Yankees, Baird tried unsuccessfully to woo him to one of the teams he represented.

In 1946, when Jackie Robinson left the Monarchs to play with the Brooklyn Dodgers' farm team, Baird threatened to sue Branch Rickey for failure to compensate the Monarchs for Robinson's services. The black press descended on Baird, interpreting his action as a white man trying to protect his investments and standing in the way of integration. Baird later publicly supported Robinson's move, but complained,

---

*Thomas Y. Baird was born in 1885 in Madison County, Arkansas, and later moved with his parents to Kansas City, Kansas. After his railroad accident—which left him with a limp for the rest of his life—Baird opened a billiard parlor and began his involvement with the business of baseball (David Conrads, "Biography of Thomas Y. Baird," Kansas City Public Library, Missouri Valley Special Collections, 1999).

†The Peet Brothers company later became Colgate Palmolive.

like Effa Manley of the Newark Eagles, that the majors outright stole players from Negro League teams. But above all, Baird was a businessman, and most blacks viewed him as an undependable ally. That attitude certainly was underscored by his membership in the Kansas branch of the Ku Klux Klan.

Like Gabby Street back in Toni's Saint Paul days, Baird was a white, middle-class Protestant Southerner who aligned himself with the Klan during its resurgence in the Midwest. Their local headquarters were in the same building as his office, and observers later suspected that Baird joined the Klan for business reasons. He believed Klan members could help advance his professional ambitions. He worried that if he did not join, his billiard business would suffer. But Baird also believed that whites were superior to blacks and did not question racism's assumptions. For example, when Toni left the San Francisco Sea Lions, club owner Harold "Yellowhorse" Morris found himself on a Canadian prairie without a team, looking for help. Morris asked Baird to recommend him for a potential Chicago Cubs scouting job since the two men knew each other from Yellowhorse's years as a Monarchs player. Baird wrote to the Cubs' farm director with what he thought was a compliment. Yellowhorse Morris, he wrote, was "above average in intelligent [sic] for a Negro." When major league clubs came looking for players who didn't look "too black," Baird did not question their racist assumptions and offered "an intelligent looking Negro, in fact he might even pass for an Indian," and another who looked "like a white man from the stands." Baird accepted Jim Crow stereotypes while simultaneously profiting from the labor of his black players.[12]

The sterile tone of Baird's letters to Toni indicated that her relationship with her new boss would be nothing like Syd Pollock's gregarious intimacy. There would be no easy "Dear Toni" and "Cordially, Syd" exchanges, no "Kindest regards to your hubby" or concerned inquiries about the family's health. Bob Motley, an umpire who worked for many Negro League teams, had occasion to compare owners and recognized the sharp contrast between Baird and Pollock. Baird was unfriendly, he said, was all about money, and only looked at blacks in terms of how he could profit from them. Syd "wasn't looking at what I could do for him," Motley said. "Pollock looked at the person I was and what I wanted to do in life."[13] There was no doubt that Pollock was a businessman, but he cared about the Clowns players and—at the very least—treated Toni and the other players with courtesy and respect.

Before the Clowns and the Monarchs began spring training, Syd wrote to Toni and asked if all details with the Monarchs had been resolved to her satisfaction. He also had been in touch with Baird to check on Toni's contract and make sure she would be playing in the 1954 season. In his letter, Pollock closed by asking for advice on an even more personal matter than her contract; he asked about her bra. "I'm having difficulty locating a place to make me up some sort of protective bra for Connie and Mamie," he confessed. "Am sure you use one, and maybe you can give me some information." He asked for specifics on who to contact and how much such special underwear might cost.[14] Obviously Syd was not aware that the prostitutes who so often had provided her with a place to stay had also helped Toni adapt her uniform for rugged play. If he had known, the enterprising and open-minded Pollock might have contacted the sporting girls himself.

In the middle of April, before boarding the Monarchs bus for spring training in Virginia, Toni stayed for a few days at Kansas City's Streets Hotel in order to—at the team's suggestion—practice with boys in the local Jackie Robinson baseball camp. She spent afternoons in warm-up drills with the teenagers, then returned to Streets for some rest and evening entertainment. Toni was familiar with Streets, having stayed there when the Clowns played the Monarchs. Like most players, she enjoyed the lively jazz scene in the hotel's Blue Room and reacquainted herself with some of the musicians with whom she had become friendly. The 18th and Vine district was the home of jazz saxophonist and composer Charlie Parker, and the alleys behind the clubs were Bird's early practice rooms. Connie Morgan's younger brother, Sonny—who was starting out as a jazz musician with his own group in Philadelphia—was typical of many musicians who looked upon KC as a musical mecca.* In Kansas City, jazz and baseball were two parts of a cultural whole. "You couldn't toss a baseball without hitting a musician," one player said. "And you couldn't whistle a tune without having a baseball player join in."[15] Toni loved the beat of the Blue Room and the flair of Kingfish, the locally famous bartender.

One member of the Monarchs Toni was sure to spot at the Blue Room was her new manager, John Jordan "Buck" O'Neil. O'Neil lived permanently in Kansas City, not far from the Streets Hotel, and he loved jazz almost as much as he loved baseball. To him, the two delights "were the best inventions known to man." O'Neil first embraced baseball as a way of escaping life in the Florida celery fields—farm work that the Sarasota native detested. *There has got to be something better than this*, Buck thought as he hauled boxes of celery from hot fields of muck. With the support of his parents and local teachers, Buck became a first baseman in 1934 and—as a teenager—began playing weekends with semi-pro teams around Florida. Semi-pro led to barnstorming, including time on Syd Pollock's Ethiopian Clowns. But when Buck made it to the Monarchs in 1938, he found his home. He won the Negro American League batting title in 1946 and, after serving in the Navy during World War II, moved to managing the team in 1948. Managing a baseball team fit Buck O'Neil perfectly. He took great pleasure in studying the game, and was skilled in teaching techniques to younger players. When he once observed old Rube Foster conducting team strategy with a Meerschaum pipe, he was inspired. Foster "signaled his players and coaches with smoke rings," O'Neil remembered. "Smoke rings!" Buck said he "spent a lot of time trying to figure out Rube's system," but he never could. O'Neil also spent enough time around players in the white leagues to admire the unique

*Howard "Sonny" Morgan (1936–1976) was a jazz percussionist with an interest in West African and Caribbean music. Morgan led his own band in Philadelphia from 1953 to 1960, then worked with musicians including Willie Bobo and Max Roach. He also arranged music for dance groups, including Geoffrey Holder's Negro Ensemble Company, was a side musician for Count Basie and others, and performed on the 1969 soundtrack for the film *Slaves*.

quality of black ball. There were differences, he said. White players depended on powerful home runs while black players "were fast and aggressive with lots of stealing, bunting, hit-and-run play." They "brought speed, intelligence, unbridled aggressiveness on the basepaths," he said. To those who said the Negro Leagues could not compete and that the best players were in the majors, O'Neil had a good-natured but pointed response: "Bring 'em on." [16]

Anyone who spent time with Toni and Buck would tell you they had much in common. First there were their backgrounds and similar routes to the Negro League: caring parents, supportive teachers, and weekend, semi-pro, and barnstorming teams. They both were gifted storytellers with a deep respect for Negro League history and a hunger for remembering the past. They also were among the oldest members of the Monarchs—over thirty—the age by which most Negro Leaguers already had found their way into the majors or found their way home. But the most significant quality that made them similar was comportment. Both Buck and Toni had a way of surviving in baseball without losing their self-respect. In a profession that broke many—the months away from home, the temptations of the road, the frustrations of an unforgiving sport—they could commit to the game while maintaining their dignity. If a person at a Blue Room table looked closely at Buck, for example, he could see O'Neil having as much fun as the other men laughing and drinking around him. But if he really studied the skipper, he also would notice that the highballs Buck kept drinking never seemed to take effect and that O'Neil left Streets as sober as when he walked in. "I never did drink," Buck confessed later. He and Kingfish had a pact: the bartender would serve Buck a tall glass filled with cracked ice and a slice of lemon, and then pour water into it. "I'd sip at that and act the fool like the other people," Buck said. "We had a ball."[17]

For Toni, the greatest challenge was making her teammates understand that she was dedicated to playing baseball and was not interested in sexual relationships with them. During the hours he rumbled along on the team bus with the Clowns, umpire Bob Motley watched the way Toni drew the line. "Someone must have talked to her," Motley said, because everyone recognized that Toni was there to play and not play around. Maybe it was her parents, he thought. Toni "was well bred" and mature enough to recognize potential pitfalls to her career. She knew that if she wanted to be taken seriously, she needed to "carry herself like that," Motley said.[18]

To many who knew them, integrity was the essence of Buck O'Neil and Toni Stone—a truthfulness to who they were. There was one more quality they had in common. Playing baseball gave them absolute joy. With the 1954 Negro American League season about to start, Buck and Toni would find out if it would always be that way.

Even with a dismal showing at the East-West game, the 1953 season set league records for attendance. In fact, the previous year had been so financially successful that Negro League President Dr. J. B. Martin approved two new teams to join the new season's league roster: the Louisville Clippers and the Detroit Stars. The addition of new teams and the hirings and firings on existing teams meant five new managers would begin the season. The Memphis manager moved to become skipper of the Clippers, leaving a vacancy with the Red Sox. Seeing the opening, Buster Haywood asked for his release from the Clowns and left for Memphis. After all his years with Syd Pollock, Buster could not accept the prospect of being demoted to the Clowns' chauffeur.

With Haywood gone, the Clowns had to search for a replacement and—as usual—Pollock's choice made the headlines. Buck O'Neil, who had seen many great Negro Leaguers in his day, believed the Clowns' new manager, Oscar Charleston, was the best baseball player who ever lived. White ballplayers in the major leagues wished they could sign him during his playing days. Old John McGraw, manager of the New York Giants, once infamously said he wished he could "calcimine" Charleston with whitewash.[19] In the 1920s and '30s, Charleston played for an illustrious string of teams: the Pittsburgh Crawfords, the Homestead Grays, and the Indianapolis ABCs, and he posted a .357 lifetime batting average with 151 home runs. After his playing career was over, "Charlie" managed the Philadelphia Stars until 1952 when the team bowed out of the league. A mercurial man, Charleston had a volatile temper and could be insolent on the diamond. After the game, however, he was approachable. His personality was "so calming," one observer said, "you could have mistaken him for a man of the cloth."[20] Toni respected Charleston and envied the Clowns players who would be under his generous tutelage. Connie Morgan was one of them. "He was my mentor," Morgan said. He showed her how to run the bases and slide. Morgan was also on the receiving end of Charleston's courtesy when he paid a visit to Philadelphia to meet with her grandmother and assure her that Connie would be properly looked after on the road.[21]

After brief spring training in Norfolk, Toni and the Monarchs played preseason games against the Clowns across the tobacco road circuit before heading down to larger crowds in Florida. With the first games came press releases and a chance for both the Monarchs and the Clowns to introduce their new women players. Just as he had done with Toni, Syd inflated the salary figures for Peanut Johnson and Connie Morgan, reporting that Connie was making ten thousand dollars a year and Peanut five thousand. The two women also attracted attention for their early play in North Carolina. Johnson pitched scoreless innings in Winston-Salem and Wilmington, while Morgan had hits in Greensboro and drove in a run in Rockingham.[22] Staged photos of Connie Morgan, taken the previous year at her tryout, cropped up in black newspapers across the country: Connie Morgan and Jackie Robinson, Connie Morgan and Gil Hodges. Syd's press releases called her a "bonus beauty."[23]

Toni did not begrudge the young woman's time in the spotlight; after all, she had helped put her there. She did, however, resent the staged photographs the Monarchs arranged. Seated in front of a makeup mirror with glove and ball on a vanity, Toni looked pained as she pretended to apply powder to her face. Just as she had done with the *Ebony* photo shoot a year before, she went along with the charade, but she disliked making the compromise. She gave in to the publicity because she knew the attention made her more valuable to the sport and might help increase her salary. At least there were a few newspaper articles that portrayed her in a more serious light. The *Atlanta Daily World* reported on her move to the Monarchs, noting that as the first woman in the league last year, she had conducted herself well. She had courage, the newspaper said.[24]

After a Saturday night game in Spartanburg, South Carolina, the Monarchs boarded their bus for an all-night trek to Miami. They were glad the game had been shortened by rain since the ride to Miami would be over seven hundred miles down the eastern spine of Florida. The night was hot and—with no air-conditioning on board—the team's uniforms hung limply in the sticky air. Everyone wanted to look good for Miami. Playing in a large city meant that players took extra pains to appear clean and sharp. Sometimes if they arrived at a field ahead of schedule, they would spread their uniforms on the outfield grass and press them with their hands so that their shirts and pants would look almost ironed. A big crowd meant they made other attempts at enhancement, too. Some players would wear double or triple pairs of socks—even in the heat—so that their legs would seem bigger and more muscular. The better for scouts in the stands, they thought.[25] Toni believed that the gear that helped her win a spot on the Monarchs was good enough, and in fact she still played with the same old glove she had bought with spare change in Saint Paul. Other players found it odd that she always carried her glove with her. She never stashed it in the equipment compartment under the bus. Maybe she feared the glove would get mixed up with the others; perhaps she worried that someone would steal it. Whatever her reason, Toni kept her glove right next to her so that she didn't have to worry.

The next morning, the bus labored in the heat twelve miles south of St. Augustine. The Monarchs' driver shifted into "grandpa gear," as players called it, trying to take the strain off the clutch and brakes. Umpire Motley smelled something smoldering and looked out the window. A farmer must be burning off crops, he thought. Hearing the team needed to take a bathroom break, the driver eased the vehicle off the road. Just then, outfielder Doc Horn saw smoke rising inside the bus. "Fire!" he yelled, and players scrambled for the door. Toni grabbed her glove and ran with the others. With everyone safely out, Toni watched clouds of smoke fill the bus as a teammate opened the luggage compartment below, hoping to retrieve their equipment. When the door opened, flames roared out. Within seconds the entire bus was engulfed. "Spontaneous combustion," someone said. A few players tried to re-enter the bus to find their belongings, but turned back coughing and singed from the heat.

Everything was lost: two grosses of baseballs, all the equipment, everyone's clothes and personal belongings. The team waited beside the road for help, but no one stopped. Finally, after half an hour, a local sheriff pulled up and ambled over to the team. The white officer looked at the bus and the black team and told them he'd get help. Then he slowly walked back to his vehicle to radio the dispatcher. Sherwood Brewer, who shared second base duties with Toni, heard the sheriff make the call. "Nothing serious," he heard the sheriff say. "Just a bus burning up with niggers on it." It would be another two hours before help arrived.[26]

Tom Baird arranged for a new bus and equipment to meet the Monarchs, and after the Miami date the team retraced its steps back through the Carolinas. In Charleston, on Mother's Day, the Clowns and the Monarchs squared off with all three women facing each other for the first time. Their play rewarded curious crowds, but not in the way Toni wanted. Mamie Johnson held the Monarchs scoreless until Toni ripped a single to the outfield. Straying too far off base, however, Toni misjudged Peanut's ability to make a quick move. When the small right-handed pitcher fired a pick-off throw to the first baseman, Toni was embarrassed and out.[27]

The official league opener came a week later on the road in Memphis against Buster Haywood's new team. The day brought perfect temperatures, and the Monarchs and the Red Sox expected a good crowd. But promoters had not accounted for competition of a different kind and carelessly scheduled the game on the same day as the annual Cotton Makers' Jubilee.* With black residents attending parades and all-day parties, fewer than two thousand fans opted to go to the game. To add to their dejection, Kansas City lost to the Red Sox 15–8. The next day, in Sikeston, Missouri, the Monarchs' luck changed. A young pitcher, Jim Gilmore, who had recently returned from a hitch in the army, threw a perfect 4–0 game for Kansas City. Things were looking up for the home opener at the end of the month.

When the big weekend arrived, Kansas City was in a "dither," Russ Cowans of the *Chicago Defender* observed, and the old magic of Negro League baseball seemed to have returned. On Saturday, the Monarchs took practice down the hill from Blues Stadium at the old Parade Park. From the practice field, Toni could look up the hill toward the stadium and Lincoln High School. Those two symbols—sports and education—stood like sentries to a future for many black youth. Fifteen years before, Toni had chosen sports as her route forward, as unlikely a path for a young black girl to follow as aiming for the White House. But she had gone far, and now she was in Kansas City, home to the greatest black baseball franchise in the world. That evening as Toni readied herself for the annual home opener banquet, she looked forward to spending time with Bunny and Syd and being introduced as a new member of the Monarchs. But the Booster Club president, a man Cowans described as "a sprightly old coot who knows all the tricks of whipping up the enthusiasm," was more impressed with Clowns manager Oscar Charleston than he was with Toni or the other new players. In a way, it seemed as though the banquet celebration was all about the past, not the future of black ball. Oscar Charleston was "one of the greatest ball players ever to put his feet in baseball shoes," the booster declared. Toni, Mamie, Connie, and the other players could not help

*Like New Orleans' Mardi Gras, the Memphis Cotton Carnival was both a social and a civic celebration. In the early 1930s, city leaders thought a celebration might bring pride and revive the sagging city and organized the first event. White krewes paraded on floats, many of which were pulled by black men. After a young black bystander asked his parents "why all the Negroes were horses," black community leaders organized their own separate event, the Cotton Makers' Jubilee. The two events briefly merged in the 1980s. Today the celebration suffers from a declining reputation.

but feel overshadowed. When she went back to her room at the Streets Hotel that night, Toni hoped the change she told Bunny would "do her some good" would pay off tomorrow.

But the next morning, when Toni looked out across the streets below, the day was anything but bright. Overnight storms had moved across the Midwest, and rain was coming down hard. Hundreds of teenagers milled around Blues Stadium, wondering if their drum and bugle corps would perform during the home opener festivities. About an hour before the game, the rain finally let up—but the field was soaked and too wet for bands and beauty queen floats. Shortly before the ceremony was to begin, boosters announced that the opening show was scrapped. Although the Monarchs won the game 8–5, both teams felt they had lost. The game was filled with errors and miscues, some no doubt caused by the slippery field conditions. Kansas City catcher Juan Armenteros broke his finger trying to hold onto a wet foul tip. Fans complained about missing the pregame excitement and about the game's sloppy play. Tom Baird and Syd Pollock lost more money than they could afford. Just over seven thousand fans attended the game—a deeply disappointing number compared with the previous year's nearly twenty thousand. There were other reasons besides the rain for the small turnout, some said. For the first time in the Monarchs' history, the game was broadcast over local radio. On such a dank day, even neighborhood boys who usually sneaked into the game for free found they would rather stay home and listen on the radio. Peanut and Connie never made it into the lineup. Only Monarchs second baseman Hank Baylis seemed to have a good day. He went two for three and scored three runs. Toni watched his success from the bench.[28]

The most significant event in May 1954 was not the home opener washout but the news two weeks earlier out of Washington, D.C. In a unanimous decision the U.S. Supreme Court declared separate educational facilities were inherently unequal and in violation of the Fourteenth Amendment to the Constitution. The landmark *Brown v. Board of Education* decision overturned a century of laws that denied black children equal education and upended the old *Plessy v. Ferguson* ruling that had ushered in Jim Crow laws that stretched from schools to streetcars. As a Southerner, skipper Buck O'Neil knew all too well how deeply Jim Crow education hurt. When he graduated from eighth grade in Florida, O'Neil hoped to continue high school. But there were only four high schools across the state open to blacks, and O'Neil's local Sarasota high school was not one of them. "I cried for two days,"[29] Buck said when he was denied enrollment in his hometown high school. Later, his family asked relatives in Jacksonville if Buck could live with them and attend one of the state's black high schools nearby. O'Neil moved over 250 miles away from his parents to go to school. He graduated, then stayed two more years in Jacksonville to attend Edward Waters College.*

In delivering the opinion of the Supreme Court on the *Brown* decision, Chief Justice Earl Warren wrote that segregation's "impact is greater when it has the sanction of the law; for the policy of separating the races is usually interpreted as denoting the inferiority of the negro group." Although she was able to attend public school in Saint Paul, Toni still encountered the seep of bigotry in countless ways, and legally sanctioned racism made her feel embittered at times. She admitted that she found it difficult to sing the national anthem and acknowledge the flag. To her, the rituals represented the disjuncture between the ideals of democracy and the U.S. government itself. While Toni always voted and in fact called casting her first ballot "one of the most beautiful things in the world to me," she found the flag and the national anthem insincere representations of an incomplete promise, and the hypocrisy of the act infuriated her. "The blacks were always looked down upon and [the government] looked upon us as second-class citizens," she said. Politicians, "the high and mighty, would fly the flag and sing 'God Bless America,'" but the words meant nothing. "Shit!" she scoffed.[30] Without the full reality of equality, displays of patriotism were empty gestures to her.

---

*In 1995, Sarasota High School awarded O'Neil an honorary high school diploma.

Toni also was quick to point out that the Supreme Court lagged behind professional baseball, and the *Brown* ruling was just catching up when it came to ending segregation. Seven years before the court's ruling, Jackie Robinson integrated the Dodgers. Many felt Jackie had a greater impact than all the politicians on Capitol Hill. "Baseball has done more to move America in the right direction than all the professional patriots with all their cheap words," Monte Irvin of the New York Giants said.[31] But just as the wheels of the courts moved slowly, so too did progress in baseball. Many fans naively assumed that, once Robinson integrated baseball, the floodgates would open. But in 1954 there were only thirty-seven blacks among nearly four hundred players in the major leagues. The floodgates had produced only a trickle. The week that the Supreme Court handed down the *Brown* decision, four teams—the Phillies, the Red Sox, the Tigers, and the Yankees—had yet to sign even one black player.

The pressure on black players to represent the race had not vanished either. Toni's friend Ernie Banks almost cracked from the stress when he joined the Cubs.* Bandleader Lionel Hampton and singer Pearl Bailey used to remind Banks that they were watching his behavior. They would pull him aside and say, "Hey, young man . . . you're playing for a whole lot of people, you gotta be the best. And we're gonna check on you to make sure you do not get into trouble." At times Banks had second thoughts about playing under such stress. He'd say to himself, "I don't want to do this. I really want to quit.

---

*In 1954 the following black players appeared on major league rosters: Brooklyn Dodgers Jackie Robinson, Roy Campanella, Don Newcombe, Junior Gilliam, Sandy Amoros, Joe Black; Milwaukee Braves Bill Bruton, Henry Aaron, Jim Pendleton, Charley White; New York Giants Willie Mays, Monte Irvin, Ruben Gomez, Henry Thompson; Chicago Cubs Ernie Banks, Gene Baker, Luis Marquez; Cincinnati Reds Nino Escalera, Charlie Harmon; Pittsburgh Pirates Curtis Roberts, (Luis Marquez, traded midseason), Sam Jethoe; St. Louis Cardinals Tom Alston, Bill Greason, Brooks Lawrence; Cleveland Indians Larry Doby, Al Smith, Luke Easter, Dave Hoskins, Jose Santiago, Dave Pope; Chicago White Sox Minnie Minoso, Bob Boyd; Philadelphia Athletics Bob Trice, Joe Taylor, Vic Power; Baltimore Orioles Jose Heard; and Washington Senators Carlos Paula. Teams without black players included the Philadelphia Phillies, Detroit Tigers, New York Yankees, and Boston Red Sox (*Kansas City Call*, May 21, 1954; Larry Lester e-mail to author, September 3, 2009).

God! This is too much." But then he'd think about the sacrifices Robinson had made. Jackie's "urgency for progress" inspired him to dig in and play to the best of his abilities. Robinson's insistence, Banks said, "drifted into my life. It drifted into Henry's" [Aaron's], too. As odd as it may have seemed to others who watched him integrate the Chicago team, Ernie Banks came to regret that he was not more involved with mounting challenges to racism. Banks sometimes felt as though he were standing on the sidelines, apart from the people who were jailed for protesting unjust laws. "I was playing baseball," he'd say. "That was the struggle."[32]

The rising call for civil rights that Banks heard around him made many supporters of Negro League ball more keenly aware that a segregated league might not survive. Besides the disappointing number of fans at the Kansas City home opener, Toni had other worries as well. Buck added several new players to the roster, including two infielders. The additions were a bad sign to Toni, who was already sharing second base duties with Baylis and Brewer—the latter of whom, like Toni, was over thirty and trying to stay in the lineup. Toni would have to double up now with two more players: an eager eighteen-year-old and a young college graduate. Traveling through Canada playing games against the Clowns, Toni spent more time on the bench than she did in the field. It wasn't that O'Neil did not respect her. Toni "was a pretty fair player," he said. "She ran well and knew what she was doing around the bag." He certainly did not dispute her ability to bring in new fans. "The women really came out to watch," he said.[33] But Buck thought others were better at producing runs and even put himself in the lineup—at age forty-two—before he sent Toni in. During June games, O'Neil inserted himself in the lineup as a substitute for the team's ailing catcher and even took to the mound once in relief.

When she did get into the game, Toni was cold and batted a miserable .105 during league games. Syd Pollock's words from the previous year's game in St. Louis came back to mind. She was trying too hard; her swings were forced and overeager. She also was gaining weight. Toni had packed on twelve pounds above her 135-pound playing weight. She placed herself on a two-week diet, cutting out bread and sweets.[34] The more she sat, the more frustrated and restless she became. During off-hours, she was no longer satisfied with watching others play or studying baseball books. "That's not going to get it," she fumed—angry at herself as much as she was with others. "You have to execute your ability," she said.[35] It was as though she had lost what once came naturally for her.

By the end of the first half of the season, the Monarchs were in last place, with June's only bright spot another perfect game. This time a twenty-three-year-old right-hander earned the accolades, blanking the Clowns 6–0 in Cincinnati. "Speedy, young ambitious ball hungry kids" were dominating the team, Buck said. [36] Many of the new players were Cuban and had played the year before for the Havana Cuban Giants, a team that served as the Monarchs' farm team. "They wanted the young ballplayers, especially the Latins to be seen by the major league scouts," Toni said.[37] The standout youngster for the Monarchs was a twenty-year-old first baseman from Havana, Francisco "Pancho" Herrera, who was hitting over .300 and knocking 450-foot grand slams. The Clowns also were stocking up on young players and added a seventeen-year-old infielder and an eighteen-year-old pitcher to the team. Outstanding players such as the Clowns' Ray Neil, who had grabbed the league's batting title in 1953 and shared second base with Toni, knew they would be overlooked by scouts who considered them too old. The line on Neil was that he "can't be considered a Big League prospect because he has celebrated at least 30 birthdays."[38] Even Jackie Robinson wondered if 1954 would be his last season. At thirty-five, Jackie was dubbed the "graying old man" by reporters.[39] Club owners such as Syd Pollock and Tom Baird almost put a higher priority on signing a young rookie than on winning the Negro League championship. A talented young rookie certainly stood a greater chance of bringing the team financial rewards if he turned out to be major league material. Even convincing a young player to sign was considered a success as some teenage prospects felt they no longer needed to use black ball as a stepping stone to the big leagues. Baird offered a fifteen-year-old sensation out of Omaha a contract with the Monarchs, but the young pitcher turned him down.* As more black players entered the major leagues, "the Kansas City Monarchs were not the be-all and end-all for a Negro ball player," Bob Gibson, the Omaha pitching sensation, said.[40]

But just when Toni despaired at being benched, new opportunity gave her hope. Thanks in part to the excitement she had generated among fans during the last season's play, Syd and Baird were able to book the big stadiums for July: Connie Mack in Philadelphia and even the colossus of stadiums, Yankee Stadium in New York City. The Monarchs had trudged through so many small towns during the 1954 season: Creston, Iowa; Sikeston, Missouri; Holt, Alabama. Even if Toni had played in more games, few people would have noticed. Back in Norfolk, sports columnist Cal Jacox wrote that "as far as the baseball fan in the Southeast is concerned, the [Negro League] does not exist. Negro baseball has the strange habit of groping in the dark in its relations with the public and this year appears to be no exception."[41] But with the Philadelphia and New York bookings, fans in big cities who had never seen her play finally would get a chance to see "the much publicized infielder Miss Toni Stone."[42] Syd Pollock knew the Philadelphia game would be especially important to Connie Morgan, and he gave her a handful of complimentary tickets to distribute to family and friends in the area. Students from William Penn business school were giddy with excitement and looked for their classmate before the game. They found her in the Clowns dugout out and descended on Connie with warm wishes. Connie said they "spoke to me and hugged me and kissed me and wished me good luck."[43]

Weather for the Sunday doubleheader at Yankee Stadium could not have been better. The warm summer day brought peak crowds to area beaches. Both Baird and Pollock had been reporting brisk sales for

---

*Bob Gibson went on to become a powerful right-handed pitcher for the St. Louis Cardinals. During his sixteen-year career he posted 251 wins against 174 losses. His ERA was 2.91 and he threw 3,117 strikeouts. Bob Gibson was inducted into baseball's Hall of Fame in 1981.

the game as the announcement had circulated for weeks in black newspapers from the Midwest to the East Coast. But promotional talk of hot-selling tickets did not translate into big gate receipts. Seventy-five hundred fans watched as the Clowns and the Monarchs split the twin bill. While some were surprised that the crowd was as large as it was, attendance did not compare to the number of fans attending the Brooklyn Dodgers and New York Giants games that afternoon. Six times the number of home fans crowded their games to cheer Jackie Robinson, Don Newcombe, Monte Irvin, and Willie Mays, who was back with the Giants after his stint in the army. If fans cheered Toni at Yankee Stadium and if she did well at the plate, no one knew. Reporters wrote nothing about her play. Connie Morgan and Peanut Johnson received no mention, either. The bench jockeying and Toni's mounting frustration gnawed at her and affected her play. "I did myself in," she realized.[44] The game Toni hoped would turn things around for her garnered less attention and attracted fewer spectators than the amphitheatre concert of Jerome Kern and Oscar Hammerstein music over at City College. The great black baritone William Warfield "brought down the house as expected," the *New York Times* reported, with his rendition of "Ol' Man River." What made the performance especially memorable, the newspaper said, was its "easy, unforced delivery."[45]

For Toni, the rest of the 1954 season was labored. The week after the game in Yankee Stadium, she celebrated her thirty-third birthday. It was not much of a celebration. After the long haul from the East Coast, she was back in Kansas City again for a night game against Buster Haywood and the Memphis Red Sox. Buck gave Toni a rare start and she led off the batting order. But again she could not find her intuitive swing. Toni went 0–2 with a grounder and a strikeout. By cruel contrast, the rest of the team enjoyed a slugfest, and the Monarchs won the game 8–0.[46] When she returned to her hotel room later that evening, she tried to console herself by rereading the birthday card Alberga had sent from Oakland. A few days later, in Salina, Kansas, she sat down and wrote her husband. She told him her injured finger was healing, but the hot summer weather was almost unbearable. Recently, she wrote, the team played in 118-degree heat. She avoided telling Pa the worst and did not mention how small irritations were growing larger and engulfing her. Not a word, for example, about the nightly bathroom aggravation. "Two boys would be going in the tub," she later said, "two a piece." After their shift, another set would go in. The rotation continued until sometimes as late as midnight with Toni still waiting to get her turn. "When they got through there was no hot water for me," she said. She tried to talk with Buck about it and asked to be placed on another floor where she would have a better access to the bathroom, but nothing changed. While she knew she had to get along with the team, there were moments when the men's behavior felt like intentional harassment. "Things could have been a little more comfortable," she said. "I know when I was goin' to go into this, it was goin' to be tough." But the mounting irritations hurt, she said. The team seemed to "figure any way to keep me miserable." One old-timer in Peoria, seeking to offer Toni comfort, took her aside and said, "There's gonna be days when you feel like killing yourself." The degradation, the frustration, the long, physically exhausting days could bring a player to the breaking point. One afternoon after a warm-up practice when teammates teased her by purposefully hitting balls she couldn't reach, Toni hit her limit. "I just got real angry," she said, and after the game she wandered by herself into a liquor store. Toni bought a bottle of Mr. Boston's—an "old cheap bottle of liquor," she said—and sat on a curb and drank until she got drunk. She felt that all the years of struggling to play baseball had amounted to nothing. "I could of just died," she said.[47]

When voting results came in for the East-West game in August, Toni's name was not on the roster. The news broke her spirit. For the second year in a row, fans did not choose Toni to be among the Negro League All-Stars. Connie Morgan was not selected either, and Mamie Johnson was no longer in the running. The Clowns released Peanut, the Norfolk (Virginia) *Journal and Guide* reported. "You know I have played hard Poppie to go to the East & West game," Toni wrote to her husband. "My name was not on the list." Her disappointment cascaded into disillusionment about her entire career, and she could no longer hide her despair. "My years in Negro baseball [have] not meant anything," she wrote. "The owner has capitalized me . . . that's all." To Toni, team owners and players seemed interested only in money—"peddling flesh," she called it.[48] They were not focused on improving their abilities or winning championships. The Monarchs had come to conduct themselves less like a team than a collection of independent agents out to get the best deals, she thought. Why would it matter to self-interested players if a team won a championship, Toni asked? They only wanted to move out of the Negro League and on to the majors. "Baseball is a business," she wrote, "and now I have to capitalize for myself." Toni told Pa she would look into barnstorming at the end of the season and then added in a small script at the bottom of the page, "Don't nobody want to win a champ?"[49]

The rest of the Monarchs began to feel the weariness of the road as well. In a game against the Clowns in Joplin, Missouri, the teams committed eleven errors before a meager crowd of fourteen hundred fans. Players looked "lackadaisical" and "worn out," the *Kansas City Call* reported. Later, in a game with Detroit, a reporter observed that "both teams displayed a half-heartedness in the field that left several fans wondering." During a rainout in Kansas City, even the groundskeepers were so exhausted that they "abandoned their job in the downpour" and left the field looking like a lake.[50] Fatigue spilled over into spite as well. Buster Haywood was so fed up with an erratic pitcher he gave the youngster a handful of bills at a rest stop, instructed him to buy the team sandwiches, and then drove off without him.[51] In locker rooms before a game, Buck O'Neil could hear opposing players sharpening their steel cleats in hopes an aggressive slide would slice a Monarch guarding the bag. "Hey, Buck," they would yell between locker room walls. "Hear that?"[52] Umpire Motley knew players also placed rocks in their gloves for aggressive tags. They would smash loaded gloves across the face of an opposing runner, hoping to stun or disorient him, he said.[53] Motley even saw spite turn to violence one night on the Monarchs bus when Hank Baylis came charging after him with a knife after what the infielder thought had been a bad call during the evening's game.[54]

Then there was the incident with Toni at home plate. Always intense when she was at bat, Toni flew into a rage when she was called out on a pitch that she believed was a ball. She jumped on the catcher's back and the crowd went wild with delight. Everyone in the stands thought Toni's explosion was trumped up and part of the show, as amusing as King Tut's clowning. What they didn't know was what the catcher said as the ball flew over the plate. "Pussy high," he yelled as the ump called her out. Days later, Toni did not know what angered her most: the wrong call, the catcher's demeaning attempt at a joke, or the pleasure Buck O'Neil seemed to get in telling the story over and over again.[55]

On Saturday, August 28, Doc Young, a columnist for the *Chicago Defender*, delivered the season's final word on women in baseball. "Toss 'Em Out," the headline read in a stinging indictment of Toni's entire career. "Girls should be run out of men's baseball on a softly padded rail," Young wrote. "When Miss Stone, who appears to be a woman of unusual athletic ability, was signed last year, the report was . . . that she had earned her chance with three years of professional competition." But she was a joke, Young said. Her presence threatened men's morale and made them feel "pretty silly." Men who praised her tenacity were disingenuous, he said, and only looking out for their own jobs. If a girl is athletic, let her play a feminine sport such as tennis or maybe wrestle with other girls, Young suggested. "When the time comes that a woman's affections depend on her batting average, the world will be a sorry place in which to live," he wrote. "It's thrilling to have a woman in one's arms, and a man has a right to promise the world to his beloved—just so long as that world doesn't include the right to play baseball with men." The entire social order could be toppled if women like Toni Stone were allowed to keep playing baseball. "This could get to be a woman's world," Young warned, "with men just living in it!"[56]

By the end of 1954, the Monarchs were in last place, and the Clowns had won both the first and the second half of the season. Toni's official line in Negro League games was a .197 average with thirteen singles and doubles in seventy-one times at bat. She posted three RBIs, walked seven times, and struck out eight.* Once again, there was no record of her performance during the majority of contests that were not sanctioned Negro League games. Kansas City signed to barnstorm for a month throughout Missouri and Kansas until autumn made playing baseball in the Midwest too cold. The season closed with increased grumblings and occasional flare-ups on the bus, some between Toni and the Cuban players. She resented that the Cubans seemed to dominate the roster and believed they were on the team only because they would play for less than black players. The altercations were not Toni's finest moments and revealed how grasping she had become. Just as many men begrudged her desire to play baseball, Toni also at times diminished the ambitions of Cuban players. After one argument, Toni stood up and asked which players on the bus were with her. No one said a word.

When the end finally came, it occurred in the most mundane of circumstances. Toni found Buck and some of the players in a garage trying to coax one more trip out of the Monarchs bus. While she could not say exactly why, Toni felt as if she was standing at an impasse. As the men crowded around the bus, she asked for a word with O'Neil. They started talking but the conversation descended into bickering. Later, Toni could not remember what the two fought about. They could have argued about the bench jockeying or the forced twist of her swing or even Buck's delight in retelling the "pussy high" story. She could not retrieve the specifics. When other players in the garage joined in and the exchange grew hot, Toni looked to her skipper for defense. But Buck "stood there and looked simple," she said. "Did not do nothin' in my defense," she said, "in my defense

---

*Connie Morgan hit .178 in league games with seven singles, a double, and one RBI in forty-five at bats. She stole one base, walked seven times, and had eight strikeouts (Alan Pollock with James A. Riley, editor, *Barnstorming to Heaven: Syd Pollock and His Great Black Teams*, Tuscaloosa: University of Alabama Press, 2006, 258).

whatsoever." The moment staring face-to-face with Buck O'Neil froze in Toni's memory for the rest of her life. It was as if everything in her life changed in that single instant. All she could say later was that "something was missing."[57] It was not that she had lost O'Neil's support, as angry as she was with him. In truth, she had lost something much deeper. Standing in a dirty garage in the outskirts of the Midwest, Toni Stone lost what she never thought would abandon her. She lost her joy for the game.

At the end of the season, Toni turned in her uniform to the Monarchs bus driver. She collected her four hundred dollars for the last month's pay, but did not receive the two-hundred-dollar end-of-the-year bonus from owner Tom Baird. In October word came that the Philadelphia Athletics, a major league team, would be moving to Kansas City and taking up residence in Blues Stadium. Trying to sound optimistic, Tom Baird declared that the city was big enough for two teams, but others worried that the new Kansas City Athletics would be the death of the Monarchs. Connie Morgan returned to Philadelphia and re-enrolled in accounting courses at William Penn business school. She would not be with the Clowns the next season. While she enjoyed traveling with the team, Syd's press releases said her real objective was "to be a top-flight worker in a business office."[58] Just weeks after the close of the 1954 season, word came that Oscar Charleston was dead. The big man— some said he was so strong he could tear the horsehair off a baseball with one hand—had died of a heart attack at age fifty-seven. A few months later, Wendell Smith reported that Syd Pollock's Indianapolis Clowns were "throwing in the sponge," dropping out of the Negro League to play independent ball the coming season. Bunny Downs gave Syd his notice and quit as the Clowns' longtime road manager. His diabetes had grown worse, and he couldn't look at one more year riding on Big Red. "Bus baseball ain't right for anybody as old as I am," he said. "It's downright intolerable." Buck O'Neil began making calls to friends in Chicago. If the Monarchs ever go under, associates told him, let the Cubs know. There might be a job for him in the majors.

In Oakland, Toni's older sister, Blanche, and her daughter Maria visited from Saint Paul. The Stone women loved California, and Alberga was at his most courtly squiring them around the Bay Area. There was talk that Blanche, Maria, and even Toni's mother might actually move to the West Coast. Willa Stone wanted to start a new beauty parlor in Oakland and had ideas about buying an apartment building. All the changes swirled around Toni like an approaching thunderstorm. She packed her baseball glove and put the cleats that Gabby Street had given her back in their worn box. The trip back to Oakland seemed exceedingly long. "I got tired," she said. "I got so tired."[59]

Happiest Day of My Life

After you get on first base it takes a lot of cooperation and understanding on the part of your teammates to get you all the way home. That goes for baseball or the everyday business of living in a democracy.

—JACKIE ROBINSON[1]

Bunny Downs could not stop thinking about baseball. Even though he'd told Syd Pollock he was finished with the Negro League, he kept dreaming about making plays and scoring runs. Downs's wife said that when he was sleeping, Bunny's legs would kick and pump as if he were still running the bases. "Throw the ball!" he would shout.[2] To many fans, black baseball seemed to exist only in dreams. In 1955, the Kansas City Monarchs had their worst financial year in the team's history, and Tom Baird was trimming everything, including meal money. Now, instead of buying a roadside dinner of crackers, sardines, an onion, and a can of beans, a player had to forgo one "side dish." By the end of the season, Baird could no longer make the numbers work and sold the team to Ted Rasberry of the Detroit Stars. The storied franchise that had won seventeen pennants and two World Series and sent twenty-one players to the majors relocated to Grand Rapids, Michigan, and left Kansas City forever.*

Pollock had seen it coming. "It's sad," he said. "The Monarchs and the Birmingham Black Barons miss dates because they can't afford bus repairs or don't have enough players after a non-payday. Used to be a bus league. Now it's a broken-down-on-the-side-of-the-road bus league."[3] Near the end of the 1955 season, Pollock suffered a heart attack, and several months later he moved his family and the Clowns operation to Hollywood, Florida. Even Jackie Robinson was beginning to feel the time had come to move on. He confessed to being "fed up." His batting average was down, he was sitting on the bench, and he was sick of battling the front office, the press, and his aging body.[4]

Toni made up her mind to stay in Oakland and not return to the Monarchs. Her husband was nearing seventy, and she thought he needed her care. "He helped me," she said. "Now, it's my turn to help him."[5] In truth, she had no other choice. The majors continued their ban on women players. The Negro League was dying, and even the segregated All-American Girls Professional Baseball League had folded. After two decades of fighting with others to let her play, Toni now faced a battle with herself. She had to find a way to let go of baseball and let it not ache so much. "Not playing baseball," she said, "hurt so damn bad I almost had a heart attack."[6]

As much as the demise of Negro League baseball unsettled athletes, it also affected others connected to the sport such as grounds crews, ticket sellers, ushers, public address announcers, maids—even clubhouse boys. Blacks who found employment with teams such as the Monarchs or the Clowns were not apt to be hired by the major

---

*The Kansas City Monarchs also hold the distinction of having fourteen former players and club owner J. L. Wilkinson enshrined in baseball's Hall of Fame. The players are Ernie Banks, Cool Papa Bell, Willard Brown, Andy Cooper, Willie Foster, Pop Lloyd, Jose Mendez, Satchel Paige, Jackie Robinson, Bullet Rogan, Cristobal Torriente, Turkey Stearns, Hilton Smith, and Willie Wells.

leagues. Ernest Withers was a photographer based in Memphis who sold his baseball photographs to the *Chicago Defender* and other newspapers. He shot the last picture of Josh Gibson in 1946, covered Toni in her days with the Clowns, caught Connie Morgan with Willie Gaines and Bebop before a game at Martin's Stadium, and chronicled scores of players from Paige to Mays. Withers knew that black weeklies did not want "Sunday-to-Sunday pictures of ballgames," so he tried to capture a more evocative, almost historical perspective of the game—"what black baseball looked like."[7] When the market for Negro League baseball photographs dried up in 1955, Withers took on other assignments, such as a September court trial in Sumner, Mississippi.* A young black boy from Chicago had been murdered that summer after he reportedly whistled at a white woman. His lynched body was brutalized so savagely that the funeral operator sealed the casket. Emmett Till's mother, Mamie Till Bradley, thought differently. "I want the world to see what they did to my baby," she said, and ordered the casket open. When photographs of Till's mutilated body circulated through the black press, the public was horrified. Withers was the only photographer covering the trial. He seized a dramatic shot of Emmett's great-uncle, Mose Wright, pointing from the witness stand at the killers.† When Emmett Till's murderers were acquitted by an all-white jury, Withers gathered all his trial photographs and published them.

Over years of finding the right angle, developing prints in his family's bathtub and drying them in the oven, Ernest Withers had captured images many Americans did not want to see. The individual photographs were extraordinary, but the accumulation of the shots

---

*Ernest Withers (1922–2007) took some of the most iconic photographs of the U.S. civil rights movement, including images of the 1962 integration of Ole Miss, the funeral of Medgar Evers, the Little Rock Nine, and Martin Luther King Jr. at the Lorraine Motel after the 1966 March Against Fear. Withers also documented the Memphis music scene and photographed Ray Charles, Sam Cooke, Aretha Franklin, Elvis Presley, Tina Turner, and others.

†Roy Bryant and J. W. Milan, the acquitted defendants in the Emmett Till murder trial, later boastfully confessed to the killing in *Life* magazine.

conveyed meaning as well. If one lined up all of Withers's photographs—from the faces of Negro League players to that Mississippi courtroom—a relationship emerged. The passion and dignity of black baseball players seemed to make way for the resolve of Mose Wright. It was as if seemingly nonpolitical acts—blacks wanting to be taken seriously as ballplayers—helped create a broader canvas for subversion. Some years later, Martin Luther King Jr. wrote that images of the early Civil Rights movement—such as the ones Ernest Withers recorded—revealed a profound social inequity that had been unobserved in dominant American culture. They exposed injustice, Reverend King said, "imprisoned in a luminous glare."[8] Ninety-five days after Emmett Till's murder, Rosa Parks refused to give up her seat on the bus to a white patron. Her action ushered in the Montgomery bus boycott led by Reverend King, the newly elected president of the Montgomery Improvement Association. "When that white driver stepped back toward us," Parks said, "when he waved his hand and ordered us up and out of our seats, I felt a determination cover my body like a quilt on a winter night."[9]

The wave of mounting purposefulness that fueled Rosa Parks and later the Little Rock Nine and the black college students integrating Woolworth's lunch counters in Greensboro, North Carolina, did not embolden Toni Stone. Without baseball, she lost sight of her dream and watched from the sidelines as the Negro League community vanished—a community that had both thwarted and sustained her. Had she found the words to articulate how her struggle to play professional baseball was connected to the growing civil disobedience around her, she might have found a purpose. But she let her vision slip and could only see a dead-end street, while others such as Parks and King were imaging a new world. Even though her mother, sister, and niece had moved permanently to Oakland, Toni felt alone. Blanche was busy finding a job as a nurse. Her mother, amicably separated from Boykin Stone, started investing in Bay Area real estate. Aurelious Alberga took Toni's niece, Maria, under his wing. Ever the dapper gentleman, "Uncle Pescia" knew just the right place for Maria to find a better cut of school uniforms and proudly escorted her across the bridge to San Francisco to supervise a proper wardrobe. The Isabelle Street house became the Stone family headquarters, but more often than not Toni would not be found laughing and making plans with her family. She would retreat to the basement amid the stored antique furniture, yard tools, and boxes of baseball mementoes. It was as if rereading the old *Chicago Defender* newspaper clippings was the only way Toni could remember who she had been. "Just don't forget who you are," Toni would say to herself, her voice cracking. "Don't forget, Toni, who you are."[10]

In moments of weakness, she thought a bottle of Jack Daniels helped. Sometimes she could be persuaded to join her sister Bunny in showing Maria the sights. Once she took the teenager to the Fillmore, where Toni had begun her climb in professional baseball. Maria sat at the Texas Playhouse and rubbed her hands across the bar with its shiny veneer of embedded silver dollars. No one in the Fillmore or at Jack's Tavern remembered Toni anymore. The reaction was even worse after the Giants moved to San Francisco. Toni would mention to sandlot baseball players that she had played with Willie Mays, and the athletes looked at her as if she were crazy. These rebuffs made Toni short-tempered, often morose. When Alberga saw the cloud descending, he took the dog for a walk and simply got out of her way.

Maria observed that when others forgot or had never heard of her aunt's accomplishments, Toni almost ceased to exist. It was as if the authentic Toni disappeared under a carapace of disappointment. Some thought Toni was like the dining room table that she obsessively covered. The table was a family joke. It was a beautiful piece of mahogany furniture, probably shipped from one of the family homes in Saint Paul. But Toni insisted that the table be covered, first with a pad, then plastic sheeting, a lace tablecloth, and a final surface of placemats. The "thing kept growing and growing," Maria recalled. No one could remember what the mahogany looked like. Trying to insulate herself from pain may have been one of the reasons Toni talked so frequently with the priests and nuns at Oakland's St. Francis de Sales church. She had turned to the Catholic church as a girl when she wanted to run away from home and again when she was stranded in San Francisco without a job or a place to stay. Just as she had with Father Keefe in Saint Paul, Toni unburdened herself to clergy at St. Francis de Sales and asked why life was so difficult. Sitting in the Oakland church seeking answers may have spun Toni back to Milwaukee and a game with the Clowns. "Ladies and Gentlemen! Miss Toni Stone," the announcer would proclaim as Toni ran out on the field to applause. The routine was always the same: she would play a few innings and then be pulled from the lineup. The frustration of sitting on the bench overwhelmed Toni that day in Milwaukee and she left—simply walked out of the stadium by herself. As she often did, Toni went looking for a church and found one nearby. Her memory of the moment clouded over the years, but she later said she entered the sanctuary, sat down in a pew, and "cried and cried" until her shoulders shook. "'Do I need to play harder?'" she asked God. "Do I need to pray harder?"[11] She never heard an answer.

Desolation either devours or it subsides, and Toni was fortunate to slowly rediscover pieces of herself. The nuns and priests at St. Francis found the same answer for Toni that Father Keefe had offered her nearly thirty years before. By the 1960s, Toni returned to baseball: she began coaching a neighborhood baseball team for teenage boys—the Isabella Hard Heads—and gathered donated equipment from area Catholic churches. She also started playing men's recreational ball and tagged around some lesbian teams that began cropping up in the Bay Area. "I kept active so I wouldn't lose my mind," she said, and continued to play recreational ball for the next twenty years.[12] To get out of the house and earn pocket change, Toni worked in local hospitals, provided home health care, and rode her bike everywhere around Oakland. People called her by her old Saint Paul name, "Miss Tomboy Stone," either forgetting or ignoring her baseball moniker and her married name. She made friends, and neighbors offered to cook holiday meals for her since Toni never developed culinary skills beyond sardines and crackers. She insisted, however, on paying for the cooked dinners, adamant that no one should be exploited for their work. Few realized how sorely earned her principle was.[13]

Satchel Paige once remarked that "we don't stop playing baseball because we get old. We get old because we stop playing baseball."[14] Coaching the Isabella Hard Heads and playing neighborhood ball sustained Toni for many years after the Negro League. In 1966, support of another sort came from a surprising voice. That year Ted Williams was inducted into the Hall of Fame in Cooperstown. The Red Sox slugger took the occasion to chide major league baseball for overlooking great black players. "The other day Willie Mays hit his 522nd home run. He has gone past me and is pushing ahead, and all I can say to him is, Go get them, Willie," Williams said. "Inside this building are plaques to baseball men of all generations, and I'm privileged to join them. . . . And I hope someday, the names of Satchel Paige and Josh Gibson in some way can be added as a symbol of the Negro players that are not here only because they were not given a chance."[15] Five years later—after Commissioner Bowie Kuhn and a ten-member committee surveyed the Negro Leagues' top players—Satchel Paige was inducted into the Hall of Fame. The occasion addressed years of neglect, but Paige was not sanguine, saying his selection turned "a second-class citizen to a second-class immortal."[16] Paige's comment and the criticism of Ted Williams did, however, translate into increased attention on Negro Leaguers by the Hall and the public at large. Most important, the enormous social changes forged by Martin Luther King Jr., Fannie Lou Hamer, and Malcolm X brought sustained attention to the legacy of slavery and Jim Crow. Countless others—sometimes without their even knowing it—also helped drive forward the goals of the civil rights movement.

Speaking about unnamed and unrecognized trailblazers, Robert Kennedy observed in 1966, "Few will have the greatness to bend history, but each of us can work to change a small portion of events, and in the total of all those acts will be written the history of this generation."[17] One consequence of the movement's actions was a rediscovery of African American history—the history that Toni had yearned for when she was a schoolgirl in Saint Paul. In 1970, Robert Peterson's *Only the Ball Was White: A History of Legendary Black Players and All-Black Professional Teams* served as a pivotal early text for baseball fans who had never heard of Rube Foster, John Henry Lloyd, or Buck Leonard. Analyzing baseball both as a sport and as a political entity, Peterson wrote that "Negro baseball was at once heroic and tawdry, a gladsome thing and a blot on America's conscience." A work of staggering research, the book only briefly mentions Toni Stone. "The Indianapolis Clowns reached the height of ingenuity in 1953," he wrote, "when they had a girl named Toni Stone as their second baseman." Peterson cited the "reported" twelve thousand dollars that Toni earned, her four to six innings of play in most games, and her "credible" .243 batting average.[18]

Only the Ball Was White released a wave of renewed interest in the Negro Leagues, just as it also pointed to a way of life that vanished when some tight-knit black communities disintegrated after segregation. Gone were the Sunday mornings when church services let out early so that parishioners could make it to the Monarchs game on time. Gone were the thriving urban centers that featured black-owned nightclubs, restaurants, movie theaters, miles of record stores, dress shops, and five and dimes. Gone were many of the black newspapers that had advocated on behalf of the community. One Monarchs player admitted he had "a bitter sweet feeling because I remember that a lot of people lost their whole way of life. That was another of those ironies, the hardest one," he said. "Not only did a black business [Negro baseball] die, other black businesses did, too. . . . The Streets Hotel had to close because it couldn't compete with the Muehlebach Hotel downtown."[19]

In the 1960s, under the guise of "urban renewal," black communities from San Francisco to New Orleans to Kansas City were decimated to make way for highways, industry, and gentrification. Toni's old Rondo neighborhood in Saint Paul was one of them. The construction of Interstate 94 tore right through the heart of the community, displacing families, destroying neighborhoods, and literally erasing the word "Rondo" from maps. Residents watched with sadness as bulldozers demolished churches and homes, including one residence near the ballpark where the Stones had lived. Those who stayed around Rondo no longer recognized their streets and lost track of their friends.

"A lot was lost when the Negro Leagues went belly up," novelist John Edgar Wideman wrote. The neighborhoods, social life, and identity that disappeared along with segregation made it difficult to remember the character they uniquely offered. Speaking of baseball, Wideman observed that "what was contained in those institutions was not simply a black version of what white people were doing, but the game was played differently."[20] Stealing bases, hitting behind the runner, taking advantage of a bunt—were all trademarks of black baseball. "There's two kinds of ball," Toni said. "I learned black ball. You had to think or get killed."[21] Negro League players who moved to the majors also brought showmanship with them—or tried to. When Ernie Banks first reported to the Cubs, he laced up his shoes with the bright yellow laces the Monarchs wore. The Cubs' clubhouse personnel thought Banks's laces were too flashy, "did not fit the style of everyone," and suggested he change. Teammates and fans, however, loved Willie Mays's wild dashes that sent his cap flying. "When I first came up to the Giants in 1951," he remembered, "I never lost my cap." It fit perfectly. After some time with the Giants, Mays began to think about the showmanship of the Negro Leagues and decided he needed a gimmick. "I started wearing a cap that was too big for me," he confessed. "Every time I ran from first to second and wheeled to my left, that cap would simply fly off just as if I'd been running so fast I'd run out from under it." The same was true for stealing a base. When Willie called time to retrieve his hat, "the moment's delay would keep the fans worked up and make the opposing pitcher think a bit more about the spot I'd got him in," Mays said.[22] "Some people call it 'show business,'" Toni said as if confronting critics. "But I call it plain hard baseball."[23]

Even with a renewed interest in the Negro Leagues, some fans and even a few players distanced themselves from the past.* In 1985, St. Louis Cardinals outfielder Vince Coleman admitted he "don't know nuthin" about Jackie Robinson and bristled when asked about the

---

*The Boston Red Sox were the last major league team to integrate when they signed second baseman Elijah Jerry "Pumpsie" Green in 1959.

pioneer's legacy. Coleman's ignorance created a firestorm among former Negro Leaguers, including one who responded, "If I would have been there, I would be serving time now because I would have tried to kill him. [Coleman] is making millions of dollars now for all the sacrifices Jackie had to make."[24] Yet while most players and fans recognized the importance of Robinson, few realized that Toni Stone, Connie Morgan, and Mamie "Peanut" Johnson had once played alongside him. Like Toni, Peanut Johnson and Connie Morgan remained largely forgotten after playing in the Negro League. They created lives outside of baseball and lost touch with each other. Johnson returned to Washington, D.C., when her Clowns career was over. She divorced, remarried, and began a long nursing career at Sibley Hospital. Although her playing days had been brief, she called them "some of the most enjoyable years of my life," adding had there been a Mr. Rickey behind the women, "it might have been a different thing." She remembered the satisfaction of strikeouts and loved the constant motion and the allure of leaving some place behind. "It was a tremendous thing to wake up and look out the [bus] window," she remembered, "and be 500 miles from where you were before." Baseball "was my dream," she said. "I even thought of the major leagues, but when I got a littler older, I said, this will never happen." She had two strikes against her from the start, Johnson said. "I'm black and I'm a lady. So, there's no place for me to go."[25] After retiring from nursing, Johnson strolled in one day to a Negro Leagues Baseball Shop in nearby Maryland. She liked being among the old photographs, memorabilia, and replica team jerseys of the Clowns and the Monarchs. The store was more than a business—it also educated the public about the leagues and life during Jim Crow. She began working there. On some days, Johnson's old teammate Gordon "Hoppy" Hopkins joined her behind the counter and jumped to his former pitcher's defense when a customer wondered if she were mistaken saying she once pitched in the Negro League. "I say, 'look man,'" Hopkins said, "'the woman played on my team. I played with her and she did what she had to do.'"[26]

When Connie Morgan completed her business education, after her 1954 season with the Clowns, she began working for the AFL-CIO in Philadelphia and later was employed by a furrier, where long days in cold storage aggravated her arthritic hands. She ended her work life as a school bus driver and retired early, at age forty, when kidney disease set in. Morgan rarely talked about the Negro League. To many who saw her, she was just the lonely woman who sat for days by the window of her Federal Street row house with only the light of a flickering television set. The "sentinel," someone called her. When the recovery of black history took hold in the 1980s, a researcher with the Afro-American Museum in Philadelphia came across Morgan's name as a once notable local athlete. Donna DeVore was intrigued and spent months trying to find her, stopping into local barbershops and asking everyone she knew. She finally found her, and when the women first met, Morgan was not convinced she had an interesting story to tell. "I tried to give [Connie] her props," DeVore said. In 1995, the city's Afro-American Museum mounted a special exhibit on Connie Morgan and other women in Philadelphia sports, and the Pennsylvania Sports Hall of Fame inducted Morgan—only then did she begin to comprehend the significance of what she had accomplished. Sometimes Connie Morgan's niece, Leah, would look around her aunt's house and see a basketball, old sports equipment, or a scrapbook kept about Connie's playing days. But like most relatives who rarely imagine their elders as young people, Morgan's niece never thought to ask about her aunt's past. "Once I understood who she was," Leah admitted, "it was too late."[27]

Donna DeVore made frequent visits past Morgan's row house with the green awning. Somehow it made DeVore feel better to check, even if a stop meant only a quick glance at the window. Morgan's kidney problems had grown steadily worse, and she was on dialysis. In October 1996, after work one evening, DeVore drove past the Philadelphia Gas Works and the big Sunoco refineries to Morgan's Point Breeze neighborhood. She didn't see Connie at the window. A few days later, she read about Morgan's death in the *Philadelphia Tribune*: "Constance

Morgan, 61 Female Negro Leaguer." The late Oscar Charleston called Connie Morgan "one of the most sensational female players he had ever seen," the newspaper reported. Morgan's family prepared the printed program for the funeral. "She had a dream to play professional baseball and in 1954 that dream came true for her," the program read, adding that the highlight of her life was the July 1954 game at Connie Mack Stadium—the day her schoolmates crowded around the dugout to wish her well. On the final page of the funeral program, before a listing of pallbearers, was Connie's old photograph taken with Jackie Robinson on the day of her Clowns tryout in Baltimore.[28] Morgan was buried at Mount Lawn Cemetery in Sharon Hill, not far from the grave of Bessie Smith. Blues singer Janis Joplin thought it was a crime that Smith never had a headstone marking her grave. She arranged to have one set in a show of respect and gratitude for the singer. Morgan's grave remains unmarked.*

Toni had all but given up being recognized as a former professional baseball player. There had been one brief moment in the 1970s when the San Francisco Giants asked her to throw out the first pitch, but in the ensuing years she had grown resigned to people knowing few details about her baseball life. Her husband's care occupied most of Toni's days. Now that he was in a nursing home, she visited regularly. As usual, Alberga met her warmly—and always in a coat and tie. While acquaintances and even those close to Toni Stone and Aurelious Pescia Alberga continued to have their own theories about their marriage, the couple remained devoted to each other. If their marriage had been more of a business partnership than a romance, it was difficult to tell, given their years together. Some now called them "ahead of their time" in fashioning a marriage that allowed independence for each other, especially for Toni as a woman married in the Eisenhower era. She married an older man, Toni said, because "a younger one wouldn't let me play ball." Whatever sustained them

---

*Connie Morgan's grave is Block 1, Lot 138, Grave 2 in Mount Lawn Cemetery in Sharon Hill, Pennsylvania.

lasted until the end. When he turned one hundred years old in 1984, Alberga once again asked his wife to give up playing—sandlot baseball, that is. This time, Toni relented and stopped playing ball for good. She was sixty-five years old.[29] Few expected Alberga to live as long as he did. When he died in 1988 at 103, perhaps only Toni was not surprised at his longevity. Although he had never seen her play one game, Toni viewed Alberga as a worthy partner in her struggles with baseball, and she planned to acknowledge his contributions in a memoir she hoped to publish one day. "He goes with me in this book I'm writing," Toni said.[30]

If no one remembered her story, Toni figured she would tell it herself. She had not decided what to title the book. "So many names I want to use," she said. Toni pored through clippings that littered the floor of her home and reread the famous *Ebony* feature that now seemed to her more "jive" than true. Photographs also told the story. To visitors who stopped by Isabella Street, family pictures showed a strong and agile young woman—fearless, even. The work of remembering kept Toni up at night. Sometimes she would wake up and write notes, and she told anyone who asked that she wanted to "put it all on tape." Toni knew what she hoped to tell. "It didn't matter whether I was with the boys, the girls or anyone, it was just tough during that time trying to make a dream come true," she said. "I always had a dream. I had to find out who I was."[31]

One person from the old days could have helped her remember. When the Monarchs were sold to Ted Rasberry of Grand Rapids, Buck O'Neil took the Cubs up on their offer and joined the team, first as a scout, then as a coach—the first African American coach in major league baseball. No one doubted his instincts or his opinion: one of the first players he signed was an outfielder from Southern University in Baton Rouge, Lou Brock. After the Cubs, Buck moved back to Kansas City and took a job with the Royals. He joined others in establishing the Negro Leagues Baseball Museum, which opened in 1994 in the old 18th and Vine area of Kansas City. As Buck said, baseball was a powerful teacher and could "build a bridge across a chasm of prejudice."[32] One evening, not long after plans for the museum were announced, Toni met baseball historian Larry Lester for dinner at a restaurant. About the time the coleslaw arrived, talk turned to O'Neil. Lester knew Buck well, and Toni spoke with an interest that showed her former skipper remained on her mind. Over the years, her anger toward O'Neil had abated, as it does with most people who long forget what past arguments were about. More important, Toni's joy for the game had returned. It came back while coaching the Hard Heads, playing infield until her knees and hands could no longer bend. It came back while she sat in the stands at Oakland A's games—always alone and right behind the catcher's box, where "everything was moving."[33] The thrill she used to feel the first spring day in Saint Paul had not been lost forever on a garage floor in Kansas in 1954. Perhaps Toni realized that Buck O'Neil—more than just about anyone else—understood how much a person could love baseball. "I gave him your telephone number," Lester said. "He asked for it." Toni sounded surprised. Eating his meal slowly, Lester seemed already to suspect what had happened. "Did he ever call you?" he asked, tentatively. O'Neil had not. Toni waited a few moments before replying. "Time waits for no man," she said. "I think I've lost a lot of time."[34]

"There is no logical reason why girls shouldn't play baseball," Henry Aaron once said. "It's not that tough. . . . Some [women] can play better than a lot of guys who've been on the field. Baseball is not a game of strength."[35] Over twenty years after Toni fought to play professional baseball, the United States put into law the landmark Title IX legislation, opening the door to increased opportunities for female athletes in the nation's schools.* When the Negro Leagues Baseball

*The 1972 legislation brought more equitable treatment to women and girls in educational programs receiving federal assistance. The most well-known aspect of the Educational Amendments of 1972 was Title IX, which called for equal funding of girls' and women's sports programs in federally funded schools. Since Title IX became law, girls' participation in high school sports has increased 904 percent, 456 percent on the college level. Research also has shown that high school girls participating in sports are less likely to use drugs or become pregnant and are more likely to earn higher grades and graduate than their non-participating counterparts (data from Women's Sports Foundation).

Museum opened its doors in Kansas City, photographs of Toni Stone, Connie Morgan, and Peanut Johnson helped place baseball's women pioneers back before the public. Saint Paul also rediscovered its past and officially invited Toni home for "Toni Stone Day," where she met with schoolchildren, reconnected with old Rondo friends, and demonstrated how to move to the right to start a double play. A local professor who taught sports history confessed that he had never heard of her. "It speaks of my own ignorance," he admitted. "What makes her exceptional is that she had the fortitude and the guts to do what she did." The homecoming was so surreal, Toni felt disembodied. "It's like I'm floating," she gushed. "Just floating."[36] Already city leaders were talking about renaming the new baseball complex for her. The fields stood on the site where Toni had badgered Gabby Street into letting her play. Roger Nieboer, a local playwright, heard about her story and began research for a play, *Tomboy Stone*, to be performed at Great American History Theatre in Saint Paul.* In New York, producers of *This Week in Baseball* called. They wanted to do a special feature on Toni for Mother's Day. The attention on Toni kept building, and she thrilled with the recognition. When her hometown *Oakland Tribune* asked to do a story, Toni pedaled on her bike to the newspaper offices. She exploded "like a grenade," columnist Miki Turner remembered, arriving with jerseys and clippings and words cascading out of her mouth in a torrent. Later, when the Women's Sports Foundation elected her to its Hall of Fame, Toni bought a sequined evening gown with matching purse and shoes for the Waldorf-Astoria banquet. The woman who had put her baseball career on the line because she would not wear a skirt felt the time had come to be formal. There was urgency in all her actions, as though Toni worried that the time to tell what she had experienced—just like her playing career—would not last. She seized the moment and opened herself to the vulnerability it aroused. When she sat on the dais in New York along with women

---

*The baseball complex in Toni Stone's name is located at 1227 Marshall Avenue in Saint Paul's Dunning Field Complex. It was dedicated in 1997. Roger Nieboer's play *Tomboy Stone* premiered in Saint Paul in January 2007.

Olympians, Wimbledon stars, and NCAA champions, she had to concentrate on her breathing to keep from becoming overwhelmed. What made it so difficult? current athletes asked. Why were others threatened by you? Toni chose her words carefully. "People weren't ready for me. I wasn't classified," she said. "I was a menace to society."[37]

Former baseball commissioner A. Bartlett Giamatti once said, "Baseball is one of the few enduring institutions in America that has been continuous and adaptable and in touch with its origins. As a result, baseball is not simply an essential part of this country: it is a living memory of what American Culture at its best wishes to be."[38] Syd Pollock's son, Alan, who rambled on the Clowns bus in 1953 and watched Toni's lonely walks into the woods during rest stops, believed that as much as baseball tried Toni's spirit, it also brought out the best in her. "I suppose the number of women who could travel and play like that, discriminated on the basis of race and sex the whole time, would be few," he said. "And to do it with the energy and intensity of Toni Stone evidenced the power and beauty of the human spirit and made me proud to know her." No one loved the game more or sacrificed more to play it, said San Francisco sportswriter Ron Thomas.[39] If there were a scale to accurately weigh how much a baseball player loved the game, he wrote, few would top Toni Stone. Modern female athletes such Sheryl Swoopes and Venus and Serena Williams owe her a debt of gratitude for challenging stereotypes, umpire Bob Motley said.[40] They stand on her shoulders.

Ernie Banks, who went from the 1953 season with the Kansas City Monarchs to eighteen years with the Chicago Cubs and eventually to baseball's Hall of Fame, always wished he had known more about Toni Stone during their playing days. "I just wanted to know her and learn from her and her life. I missed that," he said. "I didn't see all of her struggle, but I saw some of it. She stood tall, didn't give up and was very determined. It was rugged for her, but she dealt with all her stuff." Banks credited Toni with helping him understand more about the inequity women face. "She kind of triggered my interest," he said. "Young people, especially women of all races could learn something from her, from her self-esteem and self-worth. From standing up for what you believed in and dealing with unfairness." Years after they had played together, Banks saw Toni at a San Francisco baseball game, but he didn't get a chance to speak to her. "She was so talented," he said.[41]

Of all the recognition Toni began receiving late in life, nothing meant more to her than the phone call from Cooperstown. There would be no induction, but Toni and other African American players were invited to the first official recognition of the Negro Leagues in the Hall of Fame's history. "For the Love of the Game: A Reunion of the Major League Players of the Negro Leagues" convened over a long weekend in August 1991. Seventy-five former Negro Leaguers from the Cleveland Buckeyes, the Chicago American Giants, the Birmingham Black Barons, and the Kansas City Monarchs made their way to Cooperstown with walkers and wheelchairs, on the arms of wives and grandchildren, for a gathering that many said was as much about healing as it was recognition. "As the eighth commissioner of baseball," Fay Vincent began, "I say to you with sorrow and regret, I apologize for the injustice you were subjected to. Every decent-thinking person in this country agrees. Your contribution to baseball was the finest kind because it was unselfish."[42] Old friends saw each other for the first time in decades. Henry Aaron met up with his old opponent Piper Davis from the Barons. Davis slapped the fifty-seven-year-old former rookie on the back. "Hey, the bat that used to whistle," he said to Aaron. "Whistle—just like mine," Davis joked. Players edged their way into the exhibit room, quietly and with reverence. "That's my glove!" one gasped and nudged an old pal next to him. *USA Today* sent sports reporter David Steele to cover the event. "Do you know we had a woman player?" he heard Aaron say. "It didn't cross my mind there could have been a woman," Steele said. "I was shocked and felt stupid." But when he saw the strong-looking woman with a thick head of dark hair and the carriage of an athlete, Steele admitted he "should have realized she was not one of the wives."[43] Stone exuded a powerful personality, Steele said, and was surrounded by well-wishers. Her good humor spilled over to mischievousness and playing tricks on old friends. Ralph "Big Cat" Johnson, an infielder with Toni with the Creoles and later the Monarchs, was eager to see her again. He walked around the room asking, "Has anyone seen Toni Stone?" People kept pointing him in different directions as he surveyed the crowd. "Ralph Johnson, you looking for me?" Toni asked, from right beside him. "Toni!" Johnson cried. She eyed him with amusement, saying, "'Yeah, you tried to kill me, didn't you?'" remembering the night in Iowa when Johnson's forceful throw to second ripped through her glove and knocked her unconscious.[44]

Later in the weekend, players gathered in a ballroom for presentations of medallions by Henry Aaron. Some questioned Cooperstown's commitment to inducting additional former Negro League players into the Hall of Fame. For the seventy-four men and one woman in the room, the unfinished work of equality was much on their minds, and they continued to prod. As the Hall of Fame representative concluded his official remarks, a small, high-pitched voice straining from the back of the room asked to be recognized. "Could I say something now, huh? I would like to thank those people who let me come to this deal," a woman began. As her words began to flow, it was as if Toni had found what she hoped to say in the book she never wrote. "This is Toni Stone Alberga. I had an opportunity to play with some of the finest guys in the whole country. I started out in New Orleans. . . . It was barnstorm. Hand hungry. Just like Hank said. Tighten your belts up. That was it. Now when you get on the old bus you was hungry after that two dollars, you know. They thought I would leave and not come back, 'cause things were tough. Nuh uh. Baseball is my game. And I have seen a lot of these old-timers that I have to thank. Sometimes they pat me on the back, next time they use the foot. But I'm thankful! I'm thankful! Because I learned when I was in school. They told me Babe Ruth was a great guy. He's a great guy, alright. But I had Josh Gibson. He's a great guy, too. So, I feel highly honored and thanks . . . to all of you guys for seeing I was here, OK?"[45]

Like many athletes who can't recall the date of an individual game from fifty years ago, but who can remember the exact arc of a single curveball, Toni could conjure up the happiest day of her life. It was a Sunday. She was barnstorming. Old Satchel Paige was on the mound playing a game for cash, then catching a train to pitch with his own team. As he often did, Satch would ask batters what pitch they wanted: fast or slow, inside or straight up the middle. So confident of his abilities, Paige would serve a player the ball just the way he liked it—then smile as the opponent swung wildly and missed. When Toni came up to bat, she knew Paige would give her the same treatment. "Hey, T.," he yelled. "How do you like it?" Toni was nervous, shaking even, but played along and yelled back, "It doesn't matter. Just don't hurt me." Satchel wound up. Would the pitch be Paige's famous hurry up ball, the bat dodger, the two-hump blooper, or the bee ball? All Toni could see was Satchel's big front shoe rearing high for the kick. He let loose. The pitch raced toward her, buzzing like a swarm of bees, and broke inside. She swung, connected, and the white ball sailed over second base for a hit. Toni was so surprised and happy with the single that she started laughing on her way to first base. When she turned around Satchel was laughing, too. "It was a lulu," Toni said. The first baseman, none too pleased that a woman had a hit off Satchel Paige, mumbled as she rounded the base. "You're a fool," he said. "The hell I am," Toni responded, and kept on running.[46]

Toni Stone Alberga died November 2, 1996, in Alameda, California. The cause of death was heart failure.

Acknowledgments

I have been the lucky recipient of much help in writing *Curveball* and would like to thank family, friends, colleagues, and fellow baseball researchers for their generosity in making this book possible. Their advice made this book better; any errors are my own. Members of the Society for American Baseball Research (SABR) showed me a zeal for the study of baseball that I found enormously fun and inspiring. I would like to recognize Jean Hastings Ardell, Tom Garrett, Leslie Heaphy, Kyle McNary, Wayne Stivers, and Stew Thornley for their assistance. Larry Lester deserves special recognition. His attention to detail, suggestions, and encouragement ("Go, Toni, Go!") meant the world to me.

Research for this book took me all over the country—into archives, bookstores, barbershops, libraries, newspaper offices, jazz halls, baseball parks, church basements, museums, and people's homes. It was a great way to spend a couple of years. For their help, I would like to thank Leah Aquillar, Ernie Banks, Maria Bartlow-Reed, Donna DeVore, Ray Doswell, Doug Grow, Brendan Henehan, Steve Hornbostel, Wendell Maxey, Roger Nieboer, Naja Palm, Andrew Salinas, David Sanford, Miki Turner, and Walt Wilson. I also would like to acknowledge Christopher Benfey, Constance H. Buchanan, Tara Fitzpatrick, Suzanne Juhasz, Donal O'Shea, and Susan Perry for paving the way for this book. The wonderful Research and Instructional Support (RIS) staff at Mount Holyoke College's Williston Memorial Library, particularly James Gehrt, Chrissa Godbout, and Leigh Mantle, cheerfully bailed me out and plugged me in. My 2008–2009 year at the Radcliffe Institute for Advanced Study was a dream come true and I am grateful for generative conversations with my "fellow fellows," especially Gail Mazur. Friends, of course, offer help of a more personal kind, and I am grateful for the support and good humor of Christina and Sara Barber-Just (who also suggested the book's title) as well as James Fitzpatrick, Donna Gaylord, Janet Schulte, Sherril Willis, and Kathy Dempsey Zimmerman.

Uncovering this forgotten story proved to be a prodigious challenge, and I was aided by exceptional research assistants. Mary McClintock has long been my go-to detective for locating difficult-to-find materials. At the Radcliffe Institute, Harvard students Rachael Goldberg '12 and Spencer Lenfield '12 brought both results and joy to the research process. Mount Holyoke College student assistants Betsy Johnson '11, Megan Mallory '04, Rachel Mallory '07, and Tsehay Shaw '06 were dedicated researchers, especially when it came to reading endless reels of microfilm. During her four years at Mount Holyoke, Becca Groveman '09 stayed with this project from start to finish and showed up at my office door always with a smile on her face and an important idea to share. I would be remiss if I did not recognize the help of my father, Florenze Ackmann, who offered a hand whenever I needed research back home in Missouri. My nephews, Christian Ackmann and Jonathan Ackmann, brought their keen eyes and impressive knowledge of baseball in helping me research the Kansas City Monarchs.

Over the years my literary agent, Ellen Geiger, has given me an endless supply of ideas and encouragement. I appreciate her potent combination of persistence and open-mindedness. Cynthia Sherry, Michelle Schoob, and Gerilee Hundt of Chicago Review Press have made this book tighter and sharper. I am lucky to have an editor like Cynthia Sherry who believes, as David Halberstam once observed, that every great sports story is also the story of a nation.

The gift of time is one of the most valuable beneficences a writer can receive. I would like to acknowledge several organizations that have afforded me that luxury. This work is supported by the John

Simon Guggenheim Foundation, Mount Holyoke College, the Radcliffe Institute for Advanced Study at Harvard University, the Society for the Study of American Baseball Research, and a Collaborative Gender and Women's Studies Research Grant awarded to Scripps College by the Andrew W. Mellon Foundation.

Ann Romberger encouraged me to return to an earlier passion and write about baseball again. We have attended Boston Red Sox games for three decades—through all the "almost" seasons and those two recent World Series wins. We both know how the sport can exhilarate and break your heart. In a way, Ann has been like the trusted coach Toni Stone always hoped to find—someone who stood on first and cheered you home. Her support has been incalculable. As usual, Yogi Berra may have stumbled upon the best way to put it—how to measure what defies quantifying. "You give 100 percent in the first half of the game," Yogi said, "and if that isn't enough in the second half, you give what's left."

Leverett, Massachusetts
August 17, 2009

Notes

Prologue

1. "He rubbed shoulders with greats of the game." [Norfolk] *Virginian-Pilot*, August 19, 1991.

2. Toni Stone interview with Kyle McNary, September 1993. McNary private archive.

3. *Chicago Defender*, May 16, 1953.

4. *Dare to Compete: The Struggle of Women in Sports* (HBO documentary, Ross Greenberg, executive producer), 1999.

5. Ernie Banks interview with the author, September 4, 2009.

6. Toni Stone interview with Bill Kruissink, March 27, 1996. National Baseball Hall of Fame and Museum, Inc. Cooperstown, NY.

7. My thanks to Kyle McNary, who generously shared the recording of his conversation with Toni Stone. McNary's telephone interview with Stone took place in September 1993. Unless otherwise indicated, all quotations in the prologue are taken from this interview. McNary is such an ardent scholar of Negro League baseball that he named his daughter Clare Double Duty Radcliffe McNary. Damon Runyon nicknamed Theodore Roosevelt Radcliffe "Double Duty" after Radcliffe played in two successive Negro Leagues World Series games—first as a catcher, then as a pitcher.

8. Maria Bartlow-Reed interview with the author, June 6, 2006.

9. Evelyn Fairbanks, *Days of Rondo* (Saint Paul: Minnesota Historical Society Press, 1990), 111.

10. *Minneapolis Spokesman*, June 4, 1943.

11. Ibid., August 30, 1937.

12. McNary recounting his interviews with former Negro League players; Toni Stone interview with McNary, September 1993. McNary private archive.

Chapter 1: A Question of Sin

1. Countee Cullen, "Two Who Crossed a Line," *Color* (New York: Harper & Brothers Company, 1925), 16.

2. Mike Weaver, "Female Player Was a Minority of One," *San Jose Mercury News*, August 11, 1991.

3. Bob Hayes, "To This Ms., Diamond Is Made of Dirt," *San Francisco Examiner*, May 4, 1976.

4. Ibid.

5. Toni Stone interview with Bill Kruissink, March 27, 1996. National Baseball Hall of Fame and Museum, Inc., Cooperstown, NY.

6. Melvin Carter Sr. interview with the author, May 20, 2008.

7. Toni Stone interview with Bill Krussink, March 27, 1996. National Baseball Hall of Fame and Museum, Inc., Cooperstown, NY.

8. Patti Schuck interview with the author, May 14, 2008.

9. Mark J. Moore, "Negro League First Female Player Recalls Life, Career in Pro Baseball," n.p., n.d. Lester private archive; Maria Bartlow-Reed interview with the author, March 10, 2008.

10. Hayes; Toni Stone interview with Kyle McNary, September 1993. McNary private archive.

11. Melvin Carter Sr. interview with the author, May 20, 2008.

12. Toni Stone interview with Miki Turner, August 1992. Turner interview notes shared with author July 10, 2009; Toni Stone interview with Jean Hastings Ardell, April 1992. Ardell interview notes shared with author June 22, 2009.

13. Stew Thornley, "Pay Days" (*Ramsay County History* vol. 23, no. 1, 1988), 22.

14. Brendan Henehan interview with the author, November 19, 2007.

15. E-mail from Lakeishia S. Richardson, June 10, 2008. I am indebted to Richardson for her research at Tuskegee in locating Boykin Stone among students listed in the *Tuskegee Institute Bulletin* for 1908–1909.

16. Melvin Carter Sr. interview with the author, May 20, 2008.

17. Maria Bartlow-Reed interview with the author, March 10, 2008.

18. Evelyn Fairbanks, *Days of Rondo* (Saint Paul: Minnesota Historical Society, 1990), 1.

19. Steven Hoffbeck, ed., *Swinging for the Fences: Black Baseball in Minnesota* (Saint Paul: Minnesota Historical Society, 2005), 55.

20. Fairbanks, 42; H. Janabelle Taylor Murphy interview with the author, November 18, 2007.

21. *Voices of Rondo: Oral Histories of Saint Paul's Historic Black Community as Told to Kateleen Jill Hope Cavett of Hand in Hand Productions* (Minneapolis: Syren Book Company, 2005), 87.

22. *Remembering Rondo: A Tradition of Excellence* (Saint Paul: Remembering Rondo Committee, 1995), 13.

23. Mark J. Moore, "Negro League First Female Player Recalls Life, Career in Pro Baseball," n.p. n.d. Lester private archive.

24. Jimmy Griffin with Kwame J. C. McDonald, *Jimmy Griffin, A Son of Rondo: A Memoir* (Saint Paul: Ramsay County Historical Society, 2001), 20.

25. Quincy Mills interview with the author, June 4, 2008. I am indebted to Professor Mills of Vassar College for his help in understanding the culture of "color-line barbers" in the 1930s.

26. Maria Bartlow-Reed interview with the author, December 14, 2008.

27. *Remembering Rondo: A Tradition of Excellence* (Saint Paul: Remembering Rondo Committee, 1995), 6.

28. David Taylor, *African Americans in Saint Paul* (Saint Paul, Minnesota, Historical Society Press, 2002), 42.

29. James Griffin. Voices of Minnesota Radio Series (Minnesota Historical Society, Minneapolis, MN).

30. Fairbanks, 73.

31. Maria Bartlow-Reed interview with the author, March 10, 2008.

32. Fairbanks, 85.

33. "The Duluth Tragedy," [Mankato, Minnesota] *Daily Free Press*, June 7, 1920.

34. Terry Kolb, "St. Peter Claver Member Recounts Struggles with Racism," *The Catholic Spirit*. http://extra.thecatholicspirit.com/heritage/st-peter-claver-member-recounts.html.

35. Fairbanks, 150.

36. Ibid., 150–160.

37. Ibid., 108. The rink was integrated by 1940.

38. *Voices of Rondo*, 21.

39. Fairbanks, 160.

40. Ibid., 31, 41, 75.

41. Toni Stone interview with Miki Turner, August 1992. Turner interview notes shared with author July 10, 2009.

42. H. Janabelle Murphy Taylor interview with the author, November 18, 2007.

43. *Voices of Rondo*, 53.

44. Ibid., 51.

45. Doug Grow, "Rondo Kids Were Tough, but 'Tomboy' Toughest," Minneapolis–Saint Paul *StarTribune*, January 3, 1991 (manuscript version from Grow personal archive).

46. Dorothy Snell Curtis, *Changing Edges* (1990), quoted in Minnesota Historical Society, "In Their Own Words: Minnesota's Greatest Generation" exhibit.

47. Hayes.

48. Norman Rollins interview with the author, May 21, 2008. Rollins said Rondo nicknames stuck so well that seventy years after their childhood people could not remember what a friend's legal name was. When Lester Howell died, Rollins said, no one knew who "Lester" was. Howell was forever "Rock Bottom" to all his childhood friends.

49. Hayes; Toni Stone interview with Bill Kruissink, March 27, 1996. National Baseball Hall of Fame and Museum, Inc., Cooperstown, NY.

50. Fairbanks, 98–99.

51. Hayes; Toni Stone interview with Kyle McNary, September 1993. McNary private archive.

52. Toni Stone interview with Kyle McNary, September 1993. McNary private archive.

Chapter 2: Miracle in Saint Paul

1. Florida Department of State, Bureau of Archives and Record Management, Bethune Index.

2. Holly Woolard, "It's Etched in Stone—She's a Women's Hall of Famer," *Marin Independent Journal*, October 3, 1993.

3. Miki Turner, "And Still She Rose," *Oakland Tribune*, August 28, 1992; Bob Hayes, "To This Ms., Diamond Is Made of Dirt," *San Francisco Examiner*, May 4, 1976.

4. Baltimore *Afro-American*. July 17, 1954.

5. "The Gal on Second Base," *Our World*, Vol. 8, No. 7, July 1953.

6. Armand Peterson e-mail to author, January 3, 2008.

7. Roger Nieboer interview with the author, November 19, 2007.

8. Bill Kruissink, "First Woman in Pro Baseball Remembers," *Alameda Journal*, April 2, 1996.

9. Evelyn Fairbanks, *Days of Rondo* (Saint Paul: Minnesota Historical Society, 1990), 142.

10. Toni Stone interview with Kyle McNary, September 1993. McNary private archive.

11. Norman Rollins interview with the author, June 11, 2008.

12. Toni Stone interview with Kyle McNary, September 1993. McNary private archive.

13. Ibid.

14. Diane DuBay, "I Just Wanted to Play Ball." *Minnesota Women's Press*, February 3–16, 1988, 5; Jady Yaeger Jones interview with the author, August 9, 2006.

15. Erin Egan, "Toni Stone Was One of the Only Women to Ever Play Pro Ball with Men," *Sports Illustrated for Kids*, April 1, 1994, 26.

16. "Honoring a Local Hero," *Minnesota Women's Press* vol. 5, no. 25, March 14–27, 1990, 11.

17. Toni Stone interview with Larry Lester, January 3, 1991. Lester private archive.

18. Ron Thomas, "She Made It a League of Her Own," *Emerge*, May 1986, 60.

19. Ibid.

20. Mark Moore, "Negro League's First Female Player Recalls Life, Career in Pro Baseball," n.p., n.d. Lester private archive.

21. www.chicagodefender.com/article-1369-about-us.html.

22. Toni Stone interview with Larry Lester, January 3, 1991. Lester private archive.

23. Toni Stone interview with Kyle McNary, September 1993. McNary private archive; Sandy Keenan, "Stone Had a Ball," *Newsday*, October 5, 1993.

24. Allen McMillan, "Four Clubs Battle for Top Baseball Honors in New York," *Chicago Defender*, September 28, 1935.

25. Hayes; Diane DuBay, "I Just Wanted to Play Ball," *Minnesota Women's Press*, February 3–16, 1988, 5.

26. Harry T. Brundidge, "Gabby Street, a Fighter All His Life, Spurns Title of Miracle Man, but Career Shows He Deserves It," *Sporting News*, October 2, 1930.

27. "Watermelon seed" comment was Ty Cobb's. Both the watermelon reference and Cobb's quotation are from www.cmgww.com/baseball/johnson.

28. Alan Gould, "Gabby Street: Ace of the Cards," n.p., n.d. National Baseball Hall of Fame and Museum, Inc., Cooperstown, NY. Gabby Street file.

29. Porter Wittich, n.p., n.d. National Baseball Hall of Fame, Inc., Cooperstown, NY. Gabby Street file.

30. Hayes.

31. Gabby Street, "It's Still Baseball," *American Legion Monthly* no. 70, April 1932, n.p.

32. Ibid.

33. *Minneapolis Spokesman*. June 5, 1936.

34. Toni Stone interview with Jean Hastings Ardell, April 1992. Ardell's interview notes shared with author June 22, 2009.

35. *Minnesota Spokesman*, June 5, 1936.

36. James M. Gould, "The Old Sarge Returns," n.p., February 1938. National Baseball Hall of Fame and Museum, Inc., Cooperstown, NY. Gabby Street file.

37. Gai Ingham Berlage, *The Forgotten Women in Baseball History* (Westport, CT: Praeger, 1994), 169; Hayes; Bill Kruissink, "First Woman in Pro Baseball Remembers," *Alameda Journal*, April 2, 1996.

38. Street, "It's Still Baseball."

39. "Old Sarge Inspects Saints' Muster Roll," *St. Paul Pioneer Press*, February 25, 1937.

40. George Minot, "Ball Stirs Old Memories of Street's Famed Catch," *Washington Post*, January 25, 1964.

41. J. G. Taylor Spink, "Looping the Loop," *Sporting News*, August 20, 1947; L. H. Addington, "Gabby Street Is Called 'Ball Player's Man,'" *Sporting News*, November 7, 1929; Bob Considine, "Big Time for Old Times' Gabby Street Tells of Monument Catch," *New York Daily Mirror*, October 12, 1944; Earle Marchres, "Famous Catch," *Ford Times*, March 1975.

42. Toni Stone interview with Kyle McNary, September 1993. McNary private archive.

43. Joe Williams, "Please, Kiddies, Mr. Street Could Catch, Too," n.p., n.d. National Baseball Hall of Fame and Museum, Inc., Cooperstown, NY. Gabby Street file; J. G. Taylor Spink, "Looping the Loop" *Sporting News*, August 20, 1947.

44. Fred Lieb, *Baseball as I Have Known It* (New York: Grosset & Dunlap, 1977), 54.

45. Ibid.

46. Alan Gould, "Gabby Street: Ace of the Cards," n.d., n.p. National Baseball Hall of Fame and Museum, Inc., Cooperstown, NY. Gabby Street file; Harry T. Brundridge, "Gabby Street, a Fighter All of His Life, Spurns Title of Miracle Man, but Career Shows He Deserves It," *Sporting News*, October 2, 1930.

47. Tim Brady, "Almost Perfect Equality," September 20, 2002. University of Minnesota Alumni Association. www.alumni.umn.edu/Almost_Perfect_Equality.html.

48. Nancy Vaillancourt interview with the author, June 16, 2008.

49. Jennifer Delton, *Making Minnesota Liberal: Civil Rights and the Transformation of the Democratic Party* (Minneapolis: University of Minnesota Press, 2002), 38.

50. "Lady Ball Player," *Ebony*, July 1953, 52.

51. "Lady Ball Player"; Maria Bartlow-Reed interview with the author, March 10, 2008.

52. Hayes; *Chicago Defender*, February 21, 1953.

53. James M. Gould, "The Old Sarge Returns," n.p., February 1938. National Baseball Hall of Fame and Museum, Inc., Cooperstown, NY. Gabby Street file.

Chapter 3: Barnstorming with the Colored Giants

1. Gwendolyn Brooks, "A Song in the Front Yard," *Selected Poems* (New York: Harper & Row, 1963), 6.

2. Brittan Fias (Saint Paul Schools Student Placement Center for Student Data Management), e-mail to author, August 12, 2008; Toni Stone interview with Kyle McNary, September 1993. McNary private archive; Maria Bartlow-Reed interview with the author , March 10, 2008; Toni Stone interview with Jean Hastings Ardell, April 1992. Ardell interview notes shared with author June 22, 2009; Robert L. Osgood, *The History of Special Education: A Struggle for Equality in American Public Schools* (Santa Barbara, CA: Praeger, 2007), 64–70.

3. "Girl Athlete," *Minneapolis Spokesman*, June 25, 1937.

4. Doug Grow, "League of Her Own: Tomboy Stone Dead at Age 75," Minneapolis–Saint Paul *StarTribune*, November 5, 1996.

5. Geraldine M. Williams, "Minnesota St. Paul," *Chicago Defender*, December 18, 1937.

6. Maria Bartlow-Reed interview with the author, March 10, 2008.

7. John Cotton interview with the author, June 25, 2008; Kyle McNary, "Maceo Breedlove: Big Fish in a Small Pond," *Swinging for the Fences: Black Baseball in Minnesota*, Steven R. Hoffbeck, ed. (Saint Paul: Minnesota Historical Society, 2005), 114; Toni Stone interview with Jean Hastings Ardell, April 1992. Ardell interview notes shared with author June 22, 2009; Mark J. Moore, n.p.. n.d. Lester private archive.

8. Steven R. Hoffbeck, ed. *Swinging for the Fences: Black Baseball in Minnesota* (Saint Paul: Minnesota Historical Society Press, 2005), 11–12, 58–83.

9. Leslie Heaphy e-mail to author, November 10, 2009.

10. *Chicago Daily News*, June 18, 1943, quoted at www.pitchblackbaseball.com/northdakotabaseball.

11. Ibid.

12. www.pitchblackbaseball.com/northdakotabaseball.

13. McNary, 112–119; Kyle McNary interview with the author, June 23, 2008; www.pitchblackbaseball.com/northdakotabaseball.

14. Sam Lacy, "First Woman in Pro Baseball," *Afro Magazine*, 1953, n.p. National Baseball Hall of Fame and Museum, Inc., Cooperstown, NY.

15. John Cotton interview with the author, June 25, 2008.

16. *Minneapolis Spokesman*, July 31, 1937.

17. Toni Stone interview with Kyle McNary, September 1993. McNary private archive.

18. John Cotton interview with the author, June 23, 2008.

19. McNary, 114.

20. McNary, 113–115; John Cotton interview with the author, June 25, 2008.

21. Kyle McNary interview with the author, January 7, 2008; Doug Grow, "Rondo Kids Were Tough, but 'Tomboy' Toughest," Minneapolis–Saint Paul *StarTribune* manuscript, January 3, 1991. Grow personal archive.

22. Toni Stone interview with Bill Kruissink, March 27, 1996. National Baseball Hall of Fame and Museum, Inc., Cooperstown, NY.

23. Roger Nieboer interview with the author, November 19, 2007.

24. Toni Stone interview with Kyle McNary, September 1993. McNary private archive.

25. Geraldine M. Williams, "Minnesota St. Paul," *Chicago Defender*, December 18, 1937.

26. Maria Bartlow-Reed interview with the author, March 10, 2008; Baltimore *Afro-American*, July 17, 1954.

27. Evelyn Fairbanks, *Days of Rondo* (Saint Paul: Minnesota Historical Society, 1990), 39.

28. James Stafford Griffin, *Voices of Rondo: Oral Histories of Saint Paul's Historic Black Community* (Minneapolis: Syren Book Company, 2005), 67–69; Roger Nieboer interview with the author, November 19, 2007.

29. Letter to author from Brittany Frias (Saint Paul Public Schools Placement Center for Student Data Management), August 12, 2008.

30. Toni Stone interview with Kyle McNary, September 1993. McNary private archive.

31. "Tom Boy Stone Kicked in Face by William Gillespie," *Minneapolis Spokesman*, March 19, 1943.

32. Merlene Davis, "Female Baseball Player Got the Ball Rolling," *Lexington Herald-Leader*, November 28, 1996.

33. Davis.

Chapter 4: Golden Gate

1. Lowell Fulson, lyrics to "San Francisco Blues," 1947, "Lowell Fulson 1946-1953," JSP Recordings, 2004.

2. John Dos Passos, "San Francisco Looks Back: The City in Wartime," *Harper's*, May 1944.

3. *Minneapolis Spokesman*, June 4, 1943.

4. Maria Bartlow-Reed interview with the author, March 10, 2008.

5. Rosie the Riveter World War II American Homefront Oral History Project: An Oral History with Willie Mae Cotright Conducted by Judith Dunning, 2002. Regional Oral History Office, Bancroft Library, University of California, Berkeley, 2007.

6. Toni Stone interview with Kyle McNary, September 1993. McNary private archive.

7. Maria Bartlow-Reed interviews with the author, March 10, 2008, and December 14, 2008; Diana DuBay, "From St. Paul Playgrounds to Big Leagues, Stone Always Loved Baseball," *Minnesota Women's Press*, February 13–16, 1988, 5; Miki Turner, "And Still She Rose," *Oakland Tribune*, August 28, 1992.

8. Toni Stone interview with Larry Lester January 3, 1991. Lester private archive.

9. Ibid.

10. Toni Stone interview with Jean Hastings Ardell, April 1992. Ardell interview notes shared with author June 22, 2009; Toni Stone interview with Larry Lester, January 3, 1991. Lester private archive.

11. www.nps.gov/historynr/travel/wwIIbayarea; Virtual Museum of the City of San Francisco; *San Francisco News*, January 15, 1954; *San Francisco News*, August 8, 1941.

12. Katherine Archibald, *Wartime Shipyard: A Study in Social Disunity* (San Francisco: University of California Press, 1947), 26, 36–39, 78.

13. www.sfmuseum.org/sunreporter/fleming.

14. Toni Stone interview with Jean Hastings Ardell, April 1992. Ardell interview notes shared with author June 22, 2009.

15. Elizabeth Pepin and Lewis Watts, *Harlem of the West: The San Francisco Fillmore Jazz Era* (San Francisco: Chronicle Books, 2006), 38.

16. Maya Angelou, *Singin' and Swingin' and Gettin' Merry Like Christmas* (New York: Random House, 1976), 3.

17. Pepin and Watts, 78.

18. Ibid., 38.

19. Jas Obrecht, *Rockin' and Tumblin': The Postwar Blues Guitarists* (San Francisco: Miller Freeman Books, 2000), 30.

20. Frank Jackson interview with the author, June 22, 2008.

21. Toni Stone interview with Kyle McNary, September 1993. McNary private archive.

22. Rosie the Riveter World War II American Homefront Oral History Project: An Oral History with Betty Reid Soskin conducted by Nadine Wilmot, 2002. Regional Oral History Office, Bancroft Library, University of California, Berkeley, 2007; Betty Reid Soskin e-mail with author, November 28, 2008.

23. Maria Bartlow-Reed interview with the author, March 10, 2008; "Oral History of Katherine Stewart Flippin," *Black Women Oral History Project* vol. 4, edited by Ruth Edmonds Hill and Patricia Miller King (Westport: CT: Meckler Publishing, 1991), 87. Copyright Radcliffe College.

24. Douglas Henry Daniels, *Pioneer Urbanites: A Social and Cultural History of Black San Francisco* (Philadelphia: Temple University Press, 1980), 78; Carol Brookman interview with the author, December 2, 2008; Maria Bartlow-Reed interview with the author, March 10, 2008; Oral history with Aurelious P. Alberga conducted by Albert S. Broussard, December 7, 1976, "Afro-Americans in San Francisco Prior to World War II," the Friends of the San Francisco Public Library and the San Francisco African-American Historical and Cultural Society, 36.

25. Mike Weaver, "Female Player Was a Minority of One," *San Jose Mercury News*, August 11, 1991

26. Jas Obrecht, editor. *Rockin' and Tumblin': The Postwar Blues Guitarists.* San Francisco: Miller Freeman Books, 2000, 29.

27. Obrecht, 30.

28. Toni Stone interview with Larry Lester, January 3, 1991. Lester private archive.

29. Daniels, 177.

30. Toni Stone interview with Miki Turner, August 1992. Tuner interview notes shared with author July 10, 2009.

31. Jim Quinlan interview with the author, December 8, 2008.

32. Bob Hayes, "To This Ms., Diamond Is Made of Dirt," *San Francisco Examiner;* David Hawley, "Toni Stone, a Baseball 'Tomboy,'" *Saint Paul Pioneer Press*, November 5, 1996; Merlene Davis, Lexington (Kentucky) *Herald-Leader*, November 28, 1996.

33. Jim Quinlan interview with the author, December 8, 2008.

34. Jim Brown interview with the author, August 16, 2008.

35. Barbara Gregorich, *Women at Play: The Story of Women in Baseball* (New York: Harcourt, Brace & Company, 1993), 171; Toni Stone interview with Larry Lester, January 3, 1991. Lester private archive.

36. *San Mateo Times*, August 9, 1947; *San Mateo Times*, August 19, 1947; Dave Lewis, "Once Over Lightly," *Long Beach Independent*, May 14, 1947; *Oakland Tribune*, July 14, 1947; *San Mateo Times*, June 21, 1948.

37. Toni Stone interview with Jean Hastings Ardell, April 1992. Ardell interview notes shared with author June 22, 2009.

38. William G. Swank and James D. Smith III, "This Was Paradise: Voices of the Pacific Coast League Padres: 1936–1958," *Journal of San Diego History* Winter 1995, vol. 41, no. 1. Interview with Pete Coscarart.

39. Michael Seidel, *Ted Williams: A Baseball Life* (Lincoln: University of Nebraska Press, 2003), 12–15.

40. Kevin Nelson, *The Golden Game: The Story of California Baseball* (Berkeley: California Historical Society Press, 2004), 218.

41. *Fresno Bee*, May 13, 1946.

42. Letter from Abe Saperstein to Byron "Speed" Reilly, June 13, 1946. Eddie Harris Manuscript Collection, African American Museum and Library Oakland, CA.

43. *Seattle Daily Times*, June 3, 1946.

44. Sammy J. Miller and Dick Clark, *Black Baseball in Detroit* (Mt. Pleasant, SC: Arcadia Publishing, 2000), 264.

45. Herald Gordon interview with the author, July 18, 2008.

46. Brent Kelley, *I Will Never Forget: Interviews with 39 Former Negro League Players* (Jefferson, NC: McFarland & Company, 2003), 60–61.

47. Kelley, 61.

48. Joseph A. Reaves, *Taking in a Game: A History of Baseball in Asia* (Lincoln: University of Nebraska Press, 2004), 106–107.

49. Baltimore *Afro-American*. July 17, 1954.

50. Ibid.; Toni Stone interview with Jean Hastings Ardell, April 1992. Ardell interview notes shared with author June 22, 2009.

51. Jonathan Eig, *Opening Day: The Story of Jackie Robinson's First Season* (New York: Simon & Schuster, 2007), 18.

52. Ibid., 70.

53. Ibid., 4.

54. Jackie Robinson as told to Alfred Duckett, *I Never Had It Made: An Autobiography of Jackie Robinson* (New York: Harper Collins, 1972), xvii.

55. Eig, 161. The rhyme is attributed to sportswriter Wendell Smith.

56. Toni Stone interview with Miki Turner, August 1992. Turner interview notes shared with author July 10, 2009.

57. Ibid.; "Baseball Pioneer Tells Students to Follow Dreams," Saint Paul *Pioneer Press*, March 7, 1990.

58. George Nathan, *Maryville Daily Forum*, June 24, 1953.

59. "Girls of Summer," San Francisco Exploratorium exhibit.

60. Ron Thomas, "She Made It a League of Her Own," *Emerge*, May 1996.

61. Letter from Eddie Harris to Clifford Allen, postmarked January 31, 1949. Eddie Harris Collection. African-American Museum and Library, Oakland, California.

62. Alan Ward, "On Second Thought," *Oakland Tribune*, May 25, 1953.

Chapter 5: Finding the Heart of the Game

1. Afrohistory.about.com.

2. Almanac.com/weatherhistory.

3. Adam Fairclough, *Race & Democracy: The Civil Rights Struggle in Louisiana, 1915–1972* (Athens: University of Georgia Press, 1995), 111.

4. Fairclough, 84.

5. Ibid., xvii.

6. Ted Lewis, "Negro Leagues Had Local Flavor," New Orleans *Times-Picayune*, July 4, 1994.

7. Mike Mulhern, "Barnstorming Days Put Clark in Contact with Game's Best," Baton Rouge *State-Times*, August 4, 1987.

8. *Louisiana Weekly*, May 15, 1948.

9. www.attheplate.com.

10. Marty Mule, "Walter Wright Savors Black Pels' Glory Days," New Orleans *Times-Picayune*, May 5, 1983.

11. *Louisiana Weekly*, April 17, 1948.

12. Ibid., February 19, 1949.

13. Ibid., May 10, 1950.

14. S. Derby Gisclair. *Baseball in New Orleans* (Portsmouth, NH: Arcadia Publishing, 2004), 36, 75, 89.

15. Bob Hayes, "To This Ms., Diamond Is Made of Dirt," *San Francisco Examiner*, May 4, 1976.

16. Lenny Yochim interview with the author, October 4, 2008.

17. Willie Mays with Lou Sahadi, *Say, Hey: The Autobiography of Willie Mays* (New York: Simon and Schuster, 1988), 70.

18. Rick Swaine, *The Black Stars Who Made Baseball Whole: The Jackie Robinson Generation in the Major Leagues, 1947–1959* (Jefferson, NC: McFarland & Company, 2006), 114.

19. D. L. Cummings, "The Genuine Article Sam Lacy, 93, and Going Strong in Black Journalism," *New York Daily News*, February 2, 1997.

20. Bruce Adelson, *Brushing Back Jim Crow: The Integration of Minor-League Baseball in the American South* (Charlottesville: University Press of Virginia, 1999), 78, 89, 94.

21. Jeffrey Flanagan, "A Stop in Kansas City," *Kansas City Star*, April 15, 1997.

22. http://explorepahistory.com/odocument.php?docId=224; Ted Lewis, "Negro Leagues Had Local Flavor," New Orleans *Times-Picayune*, July 4, 1994; Wilmer Fields, *My Life in the Negro Leagues: An Autobiography of Wilmer Fields* (Westport, CT: Meckler, 1992), 3.

23. Lewis.

24. *Louisiana Weekly*, June 5, 1948.

25. Hayes.

26. Adelson, 92, 70.

27. Chuck Harmon, quoted in Adelson, 80.

28. Herald Gordon interview with the author, July 22, 2008.

29. Russell Stockard interview with the author, October 16, 2008.

30. *Louisiana Weekly*, May 7, 1949.

31. Jim Reisler, *Black Writers/Black Baseball: An Anthology of Articles from Black Sportswriters Who Covered the Negro Leagues* (Jefferson, NC: McFarland & Company, 2007), 7.

32. Reisler, 148–149.

33. Herald Gordon interview with the author, July 22, 2008.

34. Leslie Heaphy, *The Negro Leagues, 1869–1960* (Jefferson, NC: McFarland & Company), 127.

35. Heaphy, 128.

36. Willie Mays with Lou Sahadi, *Say Hey: The Autobiography of Willie Mays* (New York: Simon and Schuster, 1988), 36.

37. Wilmer Fields, *My Life in the Negro Leagues: An Autobiography of Wilmer Fields* (Westport, CT: Meckler, 1992), 18.

38. Adam Fairclough, *Race & Democracy: The Civil Rights Struggle in Louisiana, 1915–1972* (Athens: University of Georgia Press, 1995), xvii.

39. Russell Stockard interview with the author, October 16, 2008. Stockard succeeded Jim Hall at the *Louisiana Weekly.*

40. Paul Dickson, *Fiftieth Anniversary Hall of Fame Yearbook*, 1989, 38. National Baseball Hall of Fame and Museum, Inc., Cooperstown, NY.

41. *Louisiana Weekly*, December 18, 1948.

42. Ibid., March 5, 1949.

43. Ibid., February 9, 1952.

44. Ibid., June 17, 1950.

45. Lucille Bland interviews with the author, October 1, 2008, and October 7, 2008.

46. Ibid.; *Louisiana Weekly*, July 17, 1948, June 17, 1950.

47. Fields, 14.

48. Herald Gordon interview with the author, July 22, 2008.

49. Ibid.

50. *New York Times*, June 30, 1949.

51. Herald Gordon interview with the author, July 22, 2008; *Louisiana Weekly*, April 9, 1949.

52. Hayes.

53. *Louisiana Weekly*, January 22, 1949.

54. Ibid., April 9, 1949.

55. Adelson, 7–8.

56. Adam Fairclough, *Race & Democracy: The Civil Rights Struggle in Louisiana, 1915–1972* (Athens: University of Georgia Press, 1995), introductory epigraph.

57. Ibid.

58. *Louisiana Weekly*, March 29, 1948.

59. Elec Njaker, *Louisiana Weekly*, April 2, 1949, 10.

60. *Louisiana Weekly*, March 5, 1949, and May 10, 1952.

61. *Louisiana Weekly*, March 5, 1949.

62. *Louisiana Weekly*, February 19, 1949, February 26, 1949, March 5, 1949, March 12, 1949; *Time*, February 21, 1949, March 14, 1949; Arthur Hardy, *Mardi Gras in New Orleans* (Metairie, LA: Alan Hardy Enterprises, 2001).

63. Ted Lewis, "Negro Leagues Had Local Flavor," New Orleans *Times-Picayune*, July 4, 1994.

64. John Holway, *Black Diamonds: Life in the Negro Leagues from the Men Who Loved It* (Westport, CT: Meckler Publishing, 1989), 139–140; Raymond Mohl, "Clowning Around: The Miami Ethiopian Clowns and Cultural Conflict in Black Baseball," *Tequesta: The Journal of the Historical Association of Southern Florida* no. LXII, 2002, 40–68.

65. Hayes.

66. *Louisiana Weekly*, July 23, 1949.

67. *Chicago Defender*, July 9, 1949.

68. "Lady Ball Player," *Ebony*, July 1953, 48–53.

69. Toni Stone interview with Jean Hastings Ardell, April 1992. Ardell's interview notes shared with author June 22, 2009.

70. *The Black List: Volume One* (HBO documentary, Timothy Greenfield-Sanders, Elvis Mitchell, Michael Slap Sloane, producers), 2008; Thom Loverro, *The Encyclopedia of Negro League Baseball* (New York: Checkmark Books, 2003), 83.

71. *Louisiana Weekly*, July 23, 1949.

72. Ibid., May 20, 1950.

73. Greenville (Mississippi) *Democrat-Times*, April 6, 1950.

74. Maria Bartlow-Reed interview with the author, March 10, 2008.

75. Ibid.

76. *Chicago Defender*, May 27, 1950.

77. "Monte Irvin 'Hard Luck Giant,'" *Louisiana Weekly*, September 6, 1952.

78. "Lady Ball Player," *Ebony*, July 1953, 52.

79. [Council Bluffs, Iowa] *Daily Nonpareil*, July 10, 1950; Benton Harbor *News-Palladium*, August 25, 1950.

80. Toni Stone interview with Jean Hastings Ardell, April 1992. Ardell's interview notes shared with author June 22, 2009.

81. [Council Bluffs, Iowa] *Daily Nonpareil*, July 12, 1950.

82. Kelley Brent, *The Negro Leagues Revisited: Conversations with 66 More Baseball Heroes* (Jefferson, NC: McFarland & Company, 2000), 161.

83. Miki Turner, "And Still She Rose," *Oakland Tribune*, August 28, 1992. Stone indicated that she believed the incident with the older woman who praised her took place in 1952, but newspaper records from the *Delta Democrat-Times* of April 9, 1950, suggest it was more likely to have taken place in 1950.

84. Toni Stone interview with Miki Turner, August 1992. Turner shared interview notes with author July 10, 2009.

85. [Council Bluffs, Iowa] *Daily Nonpareil*, July 23, 1950.

86. Mark J. Moore, "Negro League's First Female Player Recalls Life, Career in Pro Baseball," n.p., n.d. Lester personal archive.

87. "Lady Ball Player," *Ebony*, July 1953, 53.

88. Erin Egan, "Toni Stone Was One of the Only Women Ever to Play Pro Baseball with Men," *Sports Illustrated for Kids*, April 1994, 26.

89. Toni Stone interview with Jean Hastings Ardell, April 1992. Ardell's interview notes shared with author June 22, 2009.

Chapter 6: On Deck

1. James Baldwin, "The Devil Finds Work," *The Price of the Ticket: Collected Nonfiction, 1948–1985* (New York: St. Martin's Press, 1985), 576.

2. Mike Weaver, "Female Player Was a Minority of One," *San Jose Mercury News*, August 11, 1991.

3. Toni Stone interview with Bill Kruissink, March 27, 1996. National Baseball Hall of Fame and Museum, Inc., Cooperstown, NY.

4. Jim Brown interview with the author, August 16, 2008.

5. *Chicago Defender*, May 27, 1950.

6. Maria Bartlow-Reed interview with the author, March 10, 2008.

7. Nan Alamilla Boyd, "Oral History of Reba Hudson," *Wide Open Town: A History of Queer San Francisco to 1965* (Berkeley: University of California Press, 2003).

8. Vern L. Bullough, ed., *Before Stonewall: Activists for Gay and Lesbian Rights in Historical Context* (New York: Routledge, 2002), 377.

9. Toni Stone interview with Bill Kruissink, March 27, 1996. National Baseball Hall of Fame and Museum, Inc., Cooperstown, NY.

10. Unpublished letter from Aurelious Alberga to Toni Stone, April 13, 1953. Bartow-Reed private archive.

11. Doug Grow, "Baseball Pioneer Never Listened to Naysayers," Minneapolis–Saint Paul *StarTribune*, January 31, 1997.

12. Toni Stone interview with Kyle McNary, September 1993. McNary private archive.

13. *Louisiana Weekly*, January 20, 1951.

14. Douglas Flamming, *Bound for Freedom: Black Los Angeles in Jim Crow America* (Berkeley: University of California Press, 2006), 206.

15. Aurelious P. Alberga, Oral History Project: Afro-Americans in San Francisco Prior to World War II, Cosponsored by the San Francisco Public Library and the San Francisco African-American Historical and Cultural Society. Interviewer Albert S. Broussard, December 7, 1976, 14.

16. Maria Bartlow-Reed interview with the author, March 10, 2008.

17. Jim Hall, "Time Out," *Louisiana Weekly*, May 26, 1951.

18. Jean Hastings Ardell, *Breaking into Baseball: Women and the National Pastime* (Carbondale: Southern Illinois University Press, 2005), 113.

19. George Rugg e-mail to author, November 13, 2009, citing November 14, 1951, AAGPBL Board of Directors minutes. Harold Daily Notebooks vol. 9, f 108v. Department of Special Collections. Hesburgh Libraries of Notre Dame.

20. Mame Redman interview with the author, September 27, 2009.

21. Leslie Heaphy and Mel Anthony May, *Encyclopedia of Women in Baseball* (Jefferson, NC: McFarland & Company, 2006), 28, 31; Kevin Czerwinski, "Media Tarnishes Engle's Historic Moment," www.mlb.com.

22. "A Stop in Kansas City," *Kansas City Star*, April 15, 1997. National Baseball Hall of Fame and Museum, Inc., Cooperstown, NY.

23. *Louisiana Weekly*, May 19, 1951.

24. Letter from Tom Baird to Lee MacPhail, January 17, 1949, Negro Leagues Ashland Collection, National Baseball Hall of Fame and Museum, Inc., Cooperstown, NY.

25. *Louisiana Weekly*, July 1, 1950.

26. Leslie Heaphy e-mail to author, November 12, 2009.

27. Austin Wilson, "Black Pioneer Hangs to Threads of Hope," *Vicksburg* (Mississippi) *Sunday Post*, August 7, 1977.

28. Jim Banks, *The Pittsburgh Crawfords* (Jefferson, NC: McFarland & Company, 2001), 84.

29. Larry Moffi, *The Conscience of the Game: Baseball's Commissioners from Landis to Selig* (Lincoln: University of Nebraska Press/Bison Books, 2006), 127–128.

30. Alan J. Pollock with James A. Riley, editor, *Barnstorming to Heaven: Syd Pollock and His Great Black Teams* (Tuscaloosa: University of Alabama Press, 2006), 225.

31. Hank Aaron with Lonnie Wheeler, *I Had a Hammer: The Hank Aaron Story* (New York: Harper Torch, 1991), 12.

32. Pollock, 228.

33. Charlie Vascellaro, *Hank Aaron: A Biography* (Santa Barbara, CA: Greenwood Press, 2005), 10.

34. Pollock, 228.

35. Aaron, 47.

36. Ibid., 46.

37. Ibid., 39.

38. *Louisiana Weekly*, February 23, 1952.

39. Pollock, 233.

40. Hall, Jim, "Time Out," *Louisiana Weekly*, May 26, 1951.

41. Pollock, 240.

42. Sam Lacy, "First Women in Pro Baseball," *Afro Magazine*, 1953. n.p.

43. Melvin Carter Sr. interview with the author, May 20, 2008.

44. John Cotton interview with the author, August 10, 2008.

45. Mike Hudson, "She Was a Relentless Spirit," *Roanoke* (Virginia) *Times and World-News*, May 4, 1997.

Chapter 7: Number 29

1. Maya Angelou, "They Went Home," in *Just Give Me a Cool Drink of Water 'fore I Diiie* (New York, Random House, 1971), 4.

2. Alan Pollock with James A. Riley, ed., *Barnstorming to Heaven: Syd Pollock and His Great Black Teams* (Tuscaloosa: University of Alabama Press, 2006), 46.

3. *Los Angeles Weekly*, February 28, 1953.

4. Toni Stone interview with Bill Kruissink, March 27, 1996. National Baseball Hall of Fame and Museum, Inc., Cooperstown, NY.

5. Maria Bartlow-Reed interview with the author, March 10, 2008.

6. Toni Stone interview with Bill Kruissink.

7. Pollock, 138.

8. Ibid., 153–154.

9. D. L. Stanley, "Women in Negro Baseball League," *Atlanta Inquirer*, April 28, 2001.

10. Pollock, 222.

11. *Pittsburgh Courier*, April 25, 1953.

12. "Lady Ball Player," *Ebony*, July 1953, 51.

13. *Chicago Defender*, February 21, 1953.

14. Mark Ribowsky, *Josh Gibson: The Power and the Darkness* (Urbana: University of Illinois Press, 2004), 283.

15. Toni Stone interview with Bill Kruissink; Baltimore *Afro-American*, July 17, 1954.

16. "The Gal on Second Base," *Our World*, Vol. 8, No. 7, July 1953.

17. "Lady Ball Player," 50.

18. Ibid., 48.

19. Ibid., 51.

20. Letter from Aurelious Alberga to Toni Stone, April 13, 1953. Bartlow-Reed private archive.

21. Pollock, 53.

22. Pollock, 244; *Chicago Defender*, April 18, 1953.

23. *Kansas City Call*, May 29, 1953; Greenville (Mississippi) *Delta Democrat Times*, May 4, 1953.

24. Norfolk (Virginia) *Journal and Guide*, May 18, 1953.

25. Pollock, 110, 114; *Chicago Defender*, April 15, 1953.

26. Ernie Banks file, the Ashland Collection, National Baseball Hall of Fame and Museum, Inc., Cooperstown, NY.

27. Ibid.

28. Ibid.

29. Toni Stone interview with Larry Lester, January 3, 1991. Lester private archive.

30. Ernie Banks interview with the author, September 4, 2009.

31. *Kansas City Call*, May 22, 1953.

32. Pollock, 244.

33. Toni Stone interview with Bill Kruissink.

34. Pollock, 137.

35. Ibid., 305.

36. Ibid., 141–142.

37. Ibid., 137.

38. Indianapolis Clowns file, National Baseball Hall of Fame and Museum, Inc., Cooperstown, NY.

39. *Chicago Defender*, May 28, 1953.

40. Ibid., May 25, 1953.

41. Toni Stone interview with Bill Kruissink.

42. Opening Day coverage from *Kansas City Call*, May 22, 1953; *Kansas City Call*, May 24; *Kansas City Call*, May 29, 1953; Chicago *Defender*, May 16, 1953; *Chicago Defender*, May 28, 1953; *Pittsburgh Courier*, June 6, 1953; Norfolk (Virginia) *Journal and Guide*, May 29, 1953.

43. *Chicago Defender*, May 28, 1953; *Pittsburgh Courier*, May 30, 1953.

44. Pollock, 63.

45. *Pittsburgh Courier*, June 20, 1953.

46. *Kansas City Call*, May 5, 1953.

47. Doug Grow, "League of Her Own: Tomboy Stone Dead at Age 75," Minneapolis–Saint Paul *StarTribune*, November 5, 1996.

48. "Lady Ball Player," 52.

49. *Pittsburgh Courier*, June 20, 1953.

50. Norfolk (Virginia) *Journal and Guide*, June 20, 1953.

51. Dr. J. B. Martin, "Negro League President Comments," *Los Angeles Sentinel*, June 11, 1953.

52. *Chicago Defender*, June 25, 1953.

53. *Dallas Morning News*, February 17, 1999.

54. *Washington Post*, July 13, 1953.

55. *Atlanta Daily World*, August 24, 1953.

56. Letter from Aurelious Alberga to Toni Stone, July 30, 1953. Bartlow-Reed private archive.

57. Bob Hayes, "To This Ms., Diamond Is Made of Dirt," *San Francisco Examiner*, May 4, 1976.

58. Pollock, 244.

59. *Kansas City Call*, July 10, 1953; *Chicago Defender*, July 2, 1953.

60. Doug Grow, "She Wasn't Afraid to Swing for the Fences," Minneapolis *Star Tribune*, March 6, 1990.

61. Toni Stone interview with Jean Hastings Ardell, April 1992. Ardell shared interview notes with author June 22, 2009.

62. Bob Motley with Byron Motley, *Ruling Over Monarchs, Giants & Stars* (Champaign, IL: Sports Publishing, 2007), 112.

63. *Kansas City Call*, July 31, 1953; *Kansas City Call*, August 7, 1953; *Chicago Defender*, July 16, 1953; *Chicago Defender*, July 30, 1953.

64. "Lady Ball Player," 52.

65. Pollock, 245–246.

66. Toni Stone interview with Kyle McNary, September 1993. McNary private archive.

67. Belva T. Simmons, *Saint Louis Argus*, July 31, 1953.

68. Pollock, 255.

69. Belva T. Simmons, *Saint Louis Argus*, July 31, 1953.

70. *St. Louis Globe Democrat*, August 8, 1953.

71. *Kansas City Call*, August 7, 1953.

72. Jefferson City (Missouri) *Daily Capitol News*, August 9, 1953.

Chapter 8: Keep on at It

1. Langston Hughes, Arnold Rampersad, ed., "Evil," *The Poems: 1941–1950 (Collected Poems of Langston Hughes, vol. 2)* (Columbia: University of Missouri Press, 2001), 29.

2. Jefferson City (Missouri) *Daily Capital News*, August 9, 1953; *Kansas City Call*, August 14, 1953; Norfolk (Virginia) *Journal and Guide*, August 22, 1953; *Atlanta Daily World*, August 15, 1953; Baltimore *Afro-American*, August 18, 1953.

3. Sam Lacy, "A to Z" Baltimore *Afro-American*, July 21, 1953.

4. *Kansas City Call*, August 14, 1953; *Chicago Defender*, August 13, 1953; Alan Pollock with James A. Riley, ed., *Barnstorming to Heaven: Syd Pollock and His Great Black Teams* (Tuscaloosa: University of Alabama Press, 2006), 150.

5. *Kansas City Call*, September 11, 1953; *Chicago Defender*, September 3, 1953.

6. Cal Jacox, "Press Box," Norfolk (Virginia) *Journal and Guide*, August 8, 1953; Pollock, 248.

7. Toni Stone interview with Larry Lester, January 3, 1991. Lester private archive.

8. *Kansas City Call*, July 10, 1953.

9. Bill Kruissink, "First Woman in Pro Baseball Remembers," *Alameda Journal*, April 2, 1996.

10. Toni Stone interview with Bill Kruissink, March 27, 1996. National Baseball Hall of Fame and Museum, Inc., Cooperstown, NY.

11. Pollock, 256.

12. Ibid., 239.

13. Toni Stone interview with Larry Lester.

14. Toni Stone interview with Kyle McNary, September 1993. McNary private archive.

15. Pollock, 307, 351.

16. Ibid., 148.

17. Ibid., 144.

18. Toni Stone interview with Larry Lester.

19. Brent Kelley, *Voices from the Negro Leagues: Conversations with 52 Black Standouts* (Jefferson, NC: McFarland & Company, 1998), 160.

20. Pollock, 307.

21. National Visionary Leadership Project, Oral history with Ernie Banks. http://visionaryproject.org/banksernie.

22. Toni Stone interview with Kyle McNary.

23. Ibid.

24. "Lady Ball Player," *Ebony*, July 1953, 52.

25. Toni Stone interview with Jean Hastings Ardell. Ardell interview notes shared with author June 22, 2009.

26. Maria Bartlow-Reed interviews with the author, July 3, 2006, and March 10, 2008.

27. Ron Thomas, "Baseball Pioneer Looks Back: Woman Played in Negro Leagues," *San Francisco Chronicle*, August 23, 1991.

28. Joseph White, "Female Pitcher in Negro Leagues Enjoyed String 'Em Out," *Seattle Times*, May 10, 1998; Eugene Meyer, "For Love of the Game," *Washington Post*, February 24, 1999; *Contemporary Black Biography* vol 40, Ashyia Henderson, ed. (Florence, Kentucky: Gale Group Publishing, 2003); *Sports Connection Digest*, October 22, 1999; Mamie Belton Johnson Goodman interview with the author, April 18, 2005; Tom Mashberg, "'Peanut' a Big Deal: Was Negro League Pioneer," *Boston Herald*, July 23, 2000; Jean Hastings Ardell, "Oral History Mamie 'Peanut' Johnson: The Last Female Voice of the Negro League," *Nine*, vol. 10. 1, 185; Charles Rowe, "Pitcher Johnson a Distinct Figure in Baseball History" Charleston (South Carolina) *Post and Courier*, February 12, 2000; Brent Kelley, "Peanut Johnson: First Woman to Win a Pro Ballgame," *Sports Collectors Digest*, October 22, 1999.

29. Mamie Belton Johnson Goodman interview with the author, April 18, 2005; Michele Y. Green, *A Strong Right Arm: The Story of Mamie "Peanut" Johnson* (New York: Dial Books, 2002), 37; Eugene Meyer, "For Love of the Game," *Washington Post*, February 24, 1999; Mamie Johnson, Mount Holyoke College Public Lecture, April 18, 2005; Kevin Kernan, "Li'l Lady Dazzled Negro League Hit Men," *New York Post*, June 3, 2001; Steven Goode, "She Was a Pioneer, Playing Pro Baseball with the Great Ones," *Hartford Courant*, September 30, 1999; www.visionaryproject.org/johnsonmamie.

30. Green, 49; Norfolk (Virginia) *Journal and Guide*, September 24, 1953; Mamie Belton Johnson Goodman interview with the author, April 18, 2005; "Morning Edition," National Public Radio, February 18, 2003; Ardell, 189; Norfolk (Virginia) *Journal and Guide*, March 13, 1954.

31. Donna DeVore interview with Connie Morgan, approximately 1993. Archives of the Afro-American Historical and Cultural Museum of Philadelphia.

32. Horace Johnson interview with the author, April 14, 2008; Yvonne Morgan Vinson interview with the author, February 25, 2008.

33. "Constance Morgan, 61 Female National Negro Leaguer," *Philadelphia Tribune*, October 25, 1996.

34. Donna DeVore interview with Connie Morgan.

35. Pollock, 256.

36. Bill Dunhurt, "Afro Americans Honor Connie Morgan," *Philadelphia Tribune*, October 19, 1993.

37. Donna DeVore interview with Connie Morgan.

38. Toni Stone interview with Larry Lester, January 3, 1991. Lester private archive.

39. Ibid.

40. Pollock, 268–270; Luix Virgil Overbrea, *Chicago Defender*, January 2, 1954.

41. Letter from Aurelious Alberga to Toni Stone, July 20, 1953. Bartlow-Reed private archive.

42. *Chicago Defender*, September 24, 1953.

43. Letter from Syd Pollock to Toni Stone, January 2, 1954. Bartlow-Reed private archive.

44. Baltimore *Afro-American*, February 20, 1954.

45. Pollock, 112.

46. Thom Loverro, *The Encyclopedia of Negro League Baseball* (New York: Checkmate Books, 2003), 52.

47. Letter from Syd Pollock to Toni Stone, January 2, 1954. Bartlow-Reed private archive.

48. Letter from Bunny Downs to Toni Stone, January 20, 1954. Bartlow-Reed private archive.

49. "Lady Ball Player," 52.

50. *Charleston* (West Virginia) *Daily Mail*, October 8, 1953; Letter from Bunny Downs to Toni Stone, January 20, 1954. Bartlow-Reed private archive.

Chapter 9: A Baseball Has 108 Stitches

1. Bessie Smith, "Long Road" 1931.

2. Letter from Syd Pollock to Toni Stone, January 19, 1954; letter from Bunny Downs to Toni Stone, January 20, 1954. Bartlow-Reed private archive.

3. Letter from Toni Stone to Syd Pollock, January 26, 1954. Bartlow-Reed private archive.

4. Letter from Toni Stone to T. Y. Baird, February 15, 1954; letter from Toni Stone to T. Y. Baird, February 2, 1954. Bartlow-Reed private archive.

5. Letter from Toni Stone to Bunny Downs, January 26, 1954. Bartlow-Reed private archive.

6. Letter from T. Y. Baird to Toni Stone, March 31, 1954. Bartlow-Reed private archive.

7. Larry Lester, "Only the Stars Come Out at Night," *Satchel Paige and Company: Essays on the Kansas City Monarchs, Their Greatest Star and the Negro Leagues*, edited by Leslie A. Heaphy (Jefferson, NC: McFarland & Company, 2007), 113.

8. Thom Loverro, *The Encyclopedia of Negro League Baseball* (New York: Checkmate Books, 2003), 310.

9. Lester, 120; Michael Harkness-Roberto and Leslie A. Heaphy, "The Monarchs: A Brief History of the Franchise," *Satchel Paige and Company: Essays on the Kansas City Monarchs, Their Greatest Star and the Negro Leagues*, edited by Leslie A. Heaphy (Jefferson, NC: McFarland & Company, 2007), 99–100; Phil Dixon with Patrick J. Hannigan, *The Negro Baseball Leagues: A Photographic History* (Mattituck, NJ: Amereon, Ltd., 1992), 149, 151; Loverro, 310.

10. Lester, 130.

11. Tim Rives e-mail to author, August 20, 2009.

12. I am indebted to Tim Rives's excellent essay "Tom Baird: A Challenge to the Modern Memory of the Kansas City Monarchs" for his analysis of Baird's KKK associations. Tim Rives, "Tom Baird: A Challenge to the Modern Memory of the Kansas City Monarchs" *Satchel Paige and Company: Essays on the Kansas City Monarchs, Their Greatest Star and the Negro Leagues*, edited by Leslie A. Heaphy (Jefferson, NC: McFarland & Company, 2007), 147, 149–152.

13. Bob Motley interview with the author, June 21, 2009.

14. Letter from Syd Pollock to Toni Stone, April 1, 1954. Bartlow-Reed private archive.

15. Buck O'Neil with Steve Wulf and David Conrads, *I Was Right on Time: My Journey from the Negro Leagues to the Majors* (New York: Fireside Books, 1997), 76.

16. O'Neil, 24, 27, 34, 155; Frank Driggs and Chuck Haddix, "Carrie's Gone to Kansas City," *Kansas City Jazz: From Ragtime to Bebop, A History* (Oxford University Press, 2006), 28; Roger Niebohr interview with the author, November 19, 2007.

17. O'Neil, 76; Lew Freedman, *African American Pioneers of Baseball.* (Santa Barbara, CA: Greenwood Press, 2007), 7.

18. Bob Motley interview with the author, June 22, 2009.

19. James Bankes, *The Pittsburgh Crawfords* (Jefferson, NC: McFarland & Company, 2001), 53.

20. Bob Motley with Byron Motley, *Ruling Over Monarchs, Giants & Stars* (Champaign, IL: Sports Publishing, 2007), 109.

21. Donna DeVore interview with Connie Morgan, approximately 1993. Archives of the Afro-American Historical and Cultural Museum of Philadelphia; Pollock, 252.

22. *Chicago Defender*, May 1, 1954; *Pittsburgh Courier*, May 4, 1954; *Chicago Defender*, May 8, 1954.

23. Baltimore *Afro-American*, July 31, 1954.

24. *Atlanta Daily World*, March 25, 1954.

25. Wilmer Fields, *My Life in the Negro Leagues: An Autobiography of Wilmer Fields* (Westport, CT: Meckler, 1992), 13, 22.

26. Bob Motley interview with the author, June 23, 2009; Motley, 142–143; *Kansas City Call*, May 7, 1954; *Atlanta Daily World*, May 7, 1954.

27. *Kansas City Call*, May 21, 1954.

28. *Kansas City Call*, May 21, 1954; *Kansas City Call*, May 28, 1954; *Kansas City Call*, June 4, 1954; *Chicago Defender*, June 5, 1954; *Chicago Defender*, June 12, 1954; Charles Sandy, "Blues Stadium," *The Best of Remember When: 100 Warm Tales of Life As We Knew It* (Kansas City: Kansas City Star Books, 2001), 17.

29. Michael Carlson, "Buck O'Neil," *The Guardian*, October 8, 2006.

30. Toni Stone interview with Kyle McNary, September 1993. McNary private archive.

31. Paul Dickson, *Baseball's Greatest Quotations* (New York: Harper Perennial, 1992), 198.

32. Steve Jacobson, *Carrying Jackie's Torch: The Players Who Integrated Baseball and America* (Chicago: Chicago Review Press, 2007), 69, 71.

33. Tracy Ringolsby, "Will a Woman Ever Make It to the Major Leagues? Stone Rock Solid in Negro League," *Rocky Mountain News*, May 11, 1995.

34. Baltimore *Afro-American*, July 17, 1954.

35. Toni Stone interview with Kyle McNary, September 1993. McNary private archive.

36. *Kansas City Call*, May 14, 1954.

37. Bob Hayes, "To This Ms., Diamond Is Made of Dirt," *San Francisco Examiner*, May 4, 1976.

38. Wendell Smith, *Pittsburgh Courier*, August 22, 1953; Larry Lester, *Black Baseball's National Showcase: The East-West All-Star Game, 1933–1953* (Lincoln: University of Nebraska Press, 2001), 389.

39. *Kansas City Call*, March 12, 1954.

40. Bob Gibson and Phil Pepe, ed., *From Ghetto to Glory: The Story of Bob Gibson* (Englewood Cliffs, NJ: Prentice Hall, 1968), 21–22.

41. [Norfolk, Virginia] *Journal and Guide*, July 3, 1954.

42. *Kansas City Call*, May 21, 1954.

43. Connie Morgan interview with Donna DeVore, approximately 1993. Archives of the Afro-American Historical and Cultural Museum of Philadelphia.

44. Toni Stone interview with Larry Lester, January 3, 1991. Lester private archive.

45. *New York Times*, July 12, 1954; *New York Amsterdam News*, July 17, 1954.

46. *Kansas City Call*, July 23, 1954.

47. Toni Stone interview with Larry Lester; Doug Grow's notes on Toni Stone interview and 1990 visit shared with author December 3, 2007. Grow private archive.

48. Hayes.

49. Letter from Toni Stone to Aurelious Alberga, August 11, 1954. Bartlow-Reed private archive.

50. [Jefferson City, Missouri] *Post-Tribune*, August 5, 1954; *Kansas City Call*, September 18, 1954; *Kansas City Call*, August 7, 1954.

51. Motley, 113.

52. O'Neil, 154.

53. Motley, 111.

54. Ibid., 2–4.

55. Larry Lester e-mails to author, August 31, 2009, and November 9. 2009; Ray Doswell e-mail to author, November 15, 2009.

56. Doc Young, "Toss 'Em Out: Should Girls Play Ball; No, Says Doc," *Chicago Defender*, August 28, 1954.

57. Toni Stone interview with Larry Lester, January 3, 1991. Lester private archive.

58. [Norfolk, Virginia] *Journal and Guide*, October 30, 1954.

59. Toni Stone interview with Larry Lester; Maria Barlow-Reed interview with the author, March 10, 2008; Pollock, 276.

Chapter 10: Happiest Day of My Life

1. *Brooklyn Eagle*, August 17, 1949, quoted in Leslie A. Heaphy, *The Negro Leagues, 1869–1960* (Jefferson, NC: McFarland & Company, 2002), 225.

2. Brent Kelley, *Negro Leagues Revisited: Conversations with 66 More Baseball Heroes* (Jefferson, NC: McFarland & Company, 2000), 299.

3. Alan J. Pollock, ed. by James A. Riley, *Barnstorming to Heaven: Syd Pollock and His Great Black Teams* (Tuscaloosa: University of Alabama Press, 2006), 174.

4. Jackie Robinson, *I Never Had It Made: An Autobiography* (New York: Ecco/Harper Collins, 1998), 118–119.

5. Diane DuBay, "If You Think No Woman Has Ever Said It Before, You Haven't Checked History," *Minnesota Women's Press*, February 3–16, 1988, 5.

6. Ron Thomas, "Baseball's 'Intruder' Loved Game," *San Francisco Chronicle*, August 23, 1991.

7. Ernest C. Withers, essay by Daniel Wolfe, ed. by Anthony Decaneas, *Negro League Baseball* (New York: Harry N. Abrams Inc., 2005), 11.

8. Carolyn Kleiner Butler, "The Old Ballgames," *Smithsonian*, April 2005; Henry Louis Gates Jr. e-mail to author, October 17, 2007; Martin Luther King Jr., *Why We Can't Wait* (New York: Signet, 1964), 25.

9. Donnie Williams and Wayne Greenhaw, *The Thunder of Angels: The Montgomery Bus Boycott and the People Who Broke the Back of Jim Crow* (Chicago: Lawrence Hill/Chicago Review Press, 2005), 48.

10. Toni Stone interview with Bill Kruissink, March 27, 1996. National Baseball Hall of Fame and Museum, Inc., Cooperstown, NY.

11. Doug Grow, "Baseball Pioneer Never Listened to Naysayers," Minneapolis–Saint Paul *StarTribune*, January 31, 1997; Maria Bartlow-Reed interview with the author, March 10, 2008. While Toni admitted a vague memory of the event and some details changed with the telling, Stone family members corroborate that the story was typical of her lifelong interaction with and reliance on the church.

12. Toni Stone interview with Jean Hasting Ardell, April 1992. Ardell interview notes shared with author June 22, 2009.

13. Toni Stone interview with Jean Hasting Ardell; Maria Bartlow-Reed interview with the author.

14. Motley, 90.

15. Bruce Markusen, *Ted Williams: A Biography* (Santa Barbara, CA: Greenwood Press, 2004), 98.

16. James F. Vail, *The Road to Cooperstown: A Critical History of Baseball's Hall of Fame Selection Process* (Jefferson, NC: McFarland & Company, 2001), 245.

17. Arthur M. Schlesinger, *Robert Kennedy and His Times* (New York: Mariner Books/Houghton Mifflin Harcourt, 2002), 745.

18. Robert Peterson, *Only the Ball Was White: A History of Legendary Black Players and All-Black Professional Teams* (New York: Oxford University Press, 1970), preface, 15, 204.

19. Buck O'Neil with Steve Wulf and David Conrads, *I Was Right on Time: My Journey from the Negro Leagues to the Majors* (New York: Fireside Books, 1997), 197.

20. Lawrence D. Hogan, *Shades of Glory: The Negro Leagues and the Story of African-American Baseball* (Washington, DC: National Geographic, 2006), 352.

21. Toni Stone interview with Jean Hastings Ardell, April 1992. Ardell interview notes shared with author June 22, 2009.

22. Ernie Banks oral history. Visionaryproject.org/banksernie; Willie Mays and Lou Sahadi, *Say Hey: The Autobiography of Willie Mays* (New York: Simon & Schuster, 1988), 14.

23. Baltimore *Afro-American*, July 17, 1954.

24. Jay Jennings, "A League of His Own," *New York Times*, June 3, 2007; Michael Schwarz, "Honoring the Pioneers of the Negro Leagues," *Atlanta Journal-Constitution*, August 11, 1991; "For Love of the Game," 1991 Negro Leagues Reunion file. Archive of the Baseball Hall of Fame and Museum, Inc., Cooperstown, NY.

25. *Dare to Compete: The Struggle of Women in Sports* (HBO documentary, Ross Greenburg, executive producer), 1999.

26. Joseph White, "Female Pitcher in Negro Leagues Enjoyed Striking 'Em Out," *Seattle Times*, May 10, 1998; *Los Angeles Sentinel*, May 28, 1998; Eugene Meyer, "For Love of the Game," *Washington Post*, February 24, 1999.

27. Donna DeVore interview with the author, March 1, 2008; Horace Johnson interview with the author, April 10, 2008; Leah Aguillar interview with the author, February 17, 2008.

28. Donna DeVore interview with the author.; Kendall Wilson, *Philadelphia Tribune*, October 25, 1996; "Homecoming and Victory Service for Constance Enola Morgan," October 22, 1996. James L. Hawkins Funeral Home, Inc., Philadelphia, Pennsylvania. Horace Johnson private archive.

29. Doug Grow interview with the author, December 7, 2007; Roger Nieboer interview with the author, November 19, 2007.

30. Toni Stone interview with Miki Turner, August 1992. Turner interview notes shared with author July 10, 2009; Toni Stone interview with Larry Lester, January 3, 1991. Lester private archive.

31. Toni Stone interview with Miki Turner, August 1992. Turner interview notes shared with author July 10, 2009; Ross Furman, "Marcenia 'Toni' Stone: Veteran of the Negro Leagues," n.d., n.p. Lester private archive.

32. Buck O'Neil, opening remarks, Baseball Hall of Fame induction ceremonies, July 29, 2006, Cooperstown, NY.

33. Toni Stone interview with Jean Hasting Ardell, April 1992. Ardell interview notes shared with author June 22, 2009.

34. Toni Stone interview with Larry Lester.

35. Dorothy Uris, *Say It Again: Dorothy Uris' Personal Collection of Quotes, Comments, & Anecdotes* (New York: E. P. Dutton, 1979), 214.

36. Doug Grow, "She Wasn't Afraid to Swing for the Fences," Minneapolis–Saint Paul *StarTribune*, March 6, 1990; *Saint Paul Pioneer Press*, March 6, 1990, and March 7, 1990.

37. Merlene Davis, *Lexington Herald-Leader*, November 28, 1996; Sandy Keenan, "Stone Had a Ball," *Newsday*, October 5, 1993.

38. Joseph L. Price, *Rounding the Bases: Baseball and Religion in America* (Macon, GA: Mercer University Press, 2006), 125–126.

39. Ron Thomas, "Baseball's 'Intruder' Loved Game," *San Francisco Chronicle*, August 23, 1991.

40. Bob Motley with Byron Motley, *Ruling Over Monarchs, Giants & Stars*, Champaign, IL: Sports Publishing, 2007), 123–124.

41. Ernie Banks interview with author, September 4, 2009.

42. Claire Smith, "Belated Tribute to Baseball's Negro Leagues," *New York Times*, August 13, 1991.

43. David Steele interview with the author, March 14, 2007.

44. Brent Kelley, *Negro Leagues Revisited: Conversations with 66 More Baseball Heroes* (Jefferson, NC: McFarland & Company, 2000), 161.

45. Recording of proceedings from "For the Love of the Game: A Reunion of the Major League Players of the Negro Leagues," August 1991. Archives of the Baseball Hall of Fame and Museum, Inc., Cooperstown, NY.

46. Doug Grow, "She Wasn't Afraid to Swing for the Fences," Minneapolis–Saint Paul *StarTribune*, March 6, 1990; Ron Thomas, *Emerge*, May 1996, 60; Sandy Keenan, "Stone Had a Ball," *Newsday*, October 5, 1993; Bill Kruissink, "First Woman in Pro Baseball Remembers," *Alameda Journal*, April 2, 1996; Maria Bartlow-Reed interview with the author, March 10, 2008; Bob Motley with Bryon Motley, *Ruling Over Monarchs, Giants & Stars* (Champaign, IL: Sports Publishing, 2007), 85.

Selected Bibliography

Aaron, Hank, with Lonnie Wheeler. *I Had a Hammer: The Hank Aaron Story*. New York: Harper Torch, 1991.

Addington, L. H. "Gabby Street Is Called 'Ball Player's Man.'" *The Sporting News*, November 7, 1929.

Adelson, Bruce. *Brushing Back Jim Crow: The Integration of Minor-League Baseball in the American South*. Charlottesville: University Press of Virginia, 1999.

Archibald, Katherine. *Wartime Shipyard: A Study in Social Disunity*. San Francisco: University of California Press, 1947.

Ardell, Jean Hastings. *Breaking into Baseball: Women and the National Pastime*. Carbondale: Southern Illinois University Press, 2005.

———. "Oral History Mamie 'Peanut' Johnson: The Last Female Voice of the Negro League." *Nine*, Vol. 10, no. 1, Fall 2001.

Baldwin, James. "The Devil Finds Work." *The Price of the Ticket: Collected Nonfiction, 1948–1985*. New York: St. Martin's Press, 1985.

Bankes, James. *The Pittsburgh Crawfords*. Jefferson, NC: McFarland & Company, 2001.

Banks, Ernie, and Jim Enright. *"Mr. Cub."* Chicago: Follett Publishing Company, 1971.

Banks, Ernie, file. Ashland Collection. National Baseball Hall of Fame and Museum, Inc., Cooperstown, NY.

"Baseball Pioneer Tells Students to Follow Dreams." *Saint Paul Pioneer-Press*, March 7, 1990.

Beasley, Delilah Leontium. *Negro Trailblazers of California, 1910–1940*. Whitefish, MT: Kessinger Publishing, 2005.

Berlage, Gai Ingham. *The Forgotten Women in Baseball History*. Westport, CT: Praeger, 1994.

———. "Robinson's Legacy: Black Women and Negro Baseball." *The Cooperstown Symposium on Baseball and American Culture, 1997 (Jackie Robinson)*. Peter M. Rutkoff, ed. Alvin Hall, series editor. Jefferson, NC: McFarland & Company, 2000.

The Black List: Volume One. Timothy Greenfield-Sanders, Elvis Mitchell, Michael Slap Sloane, producers. HBO documentary, 2008.

Boyd, Nan Alamilla. "Oral History of Reba Hudson." *Wide Open Town: A History of Queer San Francisco to 1965*. Berkeley: University of California Press, 2003.

Brady, Tim. "Almost Perfect Equality." September 20, 2002. University of Minnesota Alumni Association. www.alumni.umn.edu/Almost_Perfect_Equality.html.

Branch, Taylor. *Parting the Waters: America in the King Years, 1954–1963*. New York: Simon & Schuster, 1988.

Bristol, David, Jr. "From Outposts to Enclaves: A Social History of Black Barbers from 1750–1915." *Enterprise & Society*. Vol. 5, no. 4. Business History Conference, 2004.

Broussard, Albert S. "The Politics of Despair: Black San Franciscans and the Political Process." *Journal of Negro History*. Vol. 69, no. 1, Winter 1984.

Bruce, Janet. *The Kansas City Monarchs: Champions of Black Baseball*. Lawrence: University of Kansas Press, 1985.

Brundidge, Harry T. "Gabby Street, a Fighter All His Life, Spurns Title of Miracle Man, but Career Shows He Deserves It." *The Sporting News*, October 2, 1930.

Bullough, Vern L., ed. *Before Stonewall: Activists for Gay and Lesbian Rights in Historical Context.* New York: Routledge, 2002.

Butler, Carolyn Kleiner. "The Old Ballgames," *Smithsonian.* April 2005.

Carlson, Michael. "Buck O'Neil." *The Guardian*, October 8, 2006.

Chasteen, Edgar R. "Public Accommodations: Social Movements in Conflict." Dissertation. University of Missouri, 1966.

Cohen, Marilyn. *No Women in the Clubhouse: The Exclusion of Women from Baseball.* Jefferson, NC: McFarland & Company, 2009.

Conrads, David. "Biography of Thomas Y. Baird." Kansas City Public Library. Missouri Valley Special Collections, 1999.

Considine, Bob. "Big Time for Old Times Gabby Street Tells of Monument Catch." *New York Daily Mirror*, October 12, 1944.

"Constance Morgan, 61 Female National Negro Leaguer." *Philadelphia Tribune*, October 25, 1996.

Crowe, Daniel. *Prophets of Rage: The Black Freedom Struggle in San Francisco, 1945–1969.* New York: Garland, 2000.

Cummings, D. L. "The Genuine Article Sam Lacy, 93, and Going Strong in Black Journalism." *New York Daily News*, February 2, 1997.

Curtis, Dorothy Snell. *Changing Edges*, 1990. Quoted in Minnesota Historical Society. "In Their Own Words: Minnesota's Greatest Generation" exhibit.

Czerwinski, Kevin. "Media Tarnishes Engle's Historic Moment." mlb.com.

Daniels, Douglas Henry. *Pioneer Urbanites: A Social and Cultural History of Black San Francisco.* Philadelphia: Temple University Press, 1980.

Dare to Compete: The Struggle of Women in Sports. HBO Documentary. Ross Greenberg, executive producer. 1999.

Davis, Merlene. "Female Baseball Player Got the Ball Rolling." *Lexington Herald-Leader*, November 28, 1996.

Delton, Jennifer. "Labor, Politics and Afro-American Identity in Minneapolis, 1930–1950." *Minnesota History*, Vol. 57, no. 8, Winter 2001.

———. *Making Minnesota Liberal: Civil Rights and the Transformation of the Democratic Party*. Minneapolis: University of Minnesota Press, 2002.

Dickson, Paul. *Baseball's Greatest Quotations*. New York: Harper Perennial, 1991.

Dickson, Paul. *Fiftieth Anniversary Hall of Fame Yearbook*. National Baseball Hall of Fame and Museum, Inc., 1989.

Dixon, Johnny. "Johnny on the Spot." *Long Beach Independent*, August 19, 1947.

Dixon, Phil, with Patrick J. Hannigan. *The Negro Baseball Leagues: A Photographic History*. Mattituck, NJ: Amereon, Ltd., 1992.

Dos Passos, John. "San Francisco Looks Back: The City in Wartime." *Harper's*, May 1944.

Driggs, Frank, and Chuck Haddix. "Carrie's Gone to Kansas City." *Kansas City Jazz: From Ragtime to Bebop, A History*. Oxford University Press, 2006.

DuBay, Diana. "From St. Paul Playgrounds to Big Leagues, Stone Always Loved Baseball." *Minnesota Women's Press*, February 13–16, 1988.

———. "I Just Wanted to Play Ball." *Minnesota Women's Press*, February 3–16, 1988.

———. "If You Think No Woman Has Ever Said It Before, You Haven't Checked History." *Minnesota Women's Press*, February 3–16, 1988.

"The Duluth Tragedy." *Daily Free Press*, June 7, 1920.

Dunhurt, Bill. "Afro Americans Honor Connie Morgan." *Philadelphia Tribune*, October 19, 1993.

Egan, Erin. "Toni Stone Was One of the Only Women to Ever Play Pro Ball with Men." *Sports Illustrated for Kids*, April 1, 1994.

Eig, Jonathan. *Opening Day: The Story of Jackie Robinson's First Season.* New York: Simon & Schuster, 2007.

Enk, Anne. "Pioneers, Players and Politicos: Women's Softball in Minnesota." *Minnesota History*, Vol. 58, no. 4, 2002.

Everbach, Tracy. "Breaking Baseball Barriers: The 1953–1954 Negro League and Expansion of Women's Public Roles." *American Journalism*, Vol. 22, no. 1, Winter 2005.

Fairbanks, Evelyn. *Days of Rondo*. Saint Paul: Minnesota Historical Society Press, 1990.

Fairclough, Adam. *Race & Democracy: The Civil Rights Struggle in Louisiana, 1915–1972*. Athens: University of Georgia Press, 1995.

Fields, Wilmer. *My Life in the Negro Leagues: An Autobiography of Wilmer Fields.* Westport, CT: Meckler, 1992.

"Fillmo," documentary by Nijla Mumin, www.youTube.com. November 2007.

Fischer, Bernice. "Growing Up in St. Paul: Mechanics Arts, an Imposing Melting Pot High School That Drew Minorities Together." *Ramsey County History*, Vol. 39, no. 1, 2004.

Flamming, Douglas. *Bound for Freedom: Black Los Angeles in Jim Crow America*. Berkeley: University of California Press, 2006.

Flanagan, Jeffrey. "A Stop in Kansas City." *Kansas City Star*, April 15, 1997.

Fleming, Thomas. "Reflections on Black History: The Klan Marches in California." *San Francisco Sun-Reporter*, December 31, 1997.

Florida Department of State. Bureau of Archives and Record Management. Bethune Index.

"For the Love of the Game." 1991 Negro Leagues Reunion file. Archive of the Baseball Hall of Fame and Museum, Inc., Cooperstown, NY.

Freedman, Lew. *African American Pioneers of Baseball.* Santa Barbara, CA: Greenwood Press, 2007.

Furman, Ross. "Marcenia 'Toni' Stone: Veteran of the Negro Leagues." n.d., n.p. Lester private archive.

"The Gal on Second Base." *Our World,* Vol. 8, no. 7, July 1953.

Gibson, Bob, and Phil Pepe, ed. *From Ghetto to Glory: The Story of Bob Gibson.* Englewood Cliffs, NJ: Prentice Hall, 1968.

"Girl Athlete." *Minneapolis Spokesman,* June 25, 1937.

"Girls of Summer." San Francisco Exploratorium exhibit.

Gisclair, S. Derby. *Baseball in New Orleans.* Portsmouth, NH: Arcadia Publishing, 2004.

Goode, Steven. "She Was a Pioneer, Playing Pro Baseball with the Great Ones." *Hartford Courant,* September 30, 1999.

Gould, Alan. "Gabby Street: Ace of the Cards." n.p., n.d. Gabby Street file. National Baseball Hall of Fame and Museum, Inc., Cooperstown, NY.

Gould, James M. "The Old Sarge Returns." n.p. February 1938. Gabby Street file. National Baseball Hall of Fame and Museum, Inc., Cooperstown, NY.

Graham, Frank. "Setting the Pace." n.d., n.p. Gabby Street file, National Baseball Hall of Fame and Museum, Inc., Cooperstown, NY.

Green, Michelle Y. *A Strong Right Arm: The Story of Mamie "Peanut" Johnson.* New York: Dial Books, 2002.

Gregorich, Barbara. *Women at Play: The Story of Women in Baseball.* New York: Harcourt, Brace & Company, 1993.

Griffin, James. Voices of Minnesota Radio Series. Minnesota Historical Society, Minneapolis, MN.

Griffin, Jimmy, with Kwame J. C. McDonald. *Jimmy Griffin, A Son of Rondo: A Memoir.* Saint Paul: Ramsay County Historical Society, 2001.

Grow, Doug. "Baseball Pioneer Never Listened to Naysayers." Minneapolis–Saint Paul *StarTribune.* January 31, 1997.

———. "League of Her Own: Tomboy Stone Dead at Age 75." Minneapolis–Saint Paul *StarTribune.* November 5, 1996.

———. "Rondo kids Were Tough, but 'Tomboy' Toughest." Minneapolis–Saint Paul *StarTribune.* January 3, 1991, manuscript version from Grow personal archive.

———. "She Wasn't Afraid to Swing for the Fences." Minneapolis–Saint Paul *StarTribune.* March 6, 1990.

Hall, Jim. "Time Out." *Louisiana Weekly*, May 26, 1951.

Hardy, Arthur. *Mardi Gras in New Orleans.* Metarie, LA: Alan Hardy Enterprises, 2001.

Harkness-Roberto, Michael, and Leslie A. Heaphy. "The Monarchs: A Brief History of the Franchise." *Satchel Paige and Company: Essays on the Kansas City Monarchs, Their Greatest Star and the Negro Leagues.* Edited by Leslie A. Heaphy. Jefferson, NC: McFarland & Company, 2007.

Hawley, David. "Toni Stone, a Baseball 'Tomboy.'" Saint Paul *Pioneer Press*, November 5, 1996.

Hayes, Bob. "To This Ms., Diamond Is Made of Dirt." *San Francisco Examiner*, May 4, 1976.

Heaphy, Leslie. *The Negro Leagues, 1869–1960.* Jefferson, NC: McFarland & Company, 2002.

Heaphy, Leslie, ed. *Satchel Paige and Company: Essays on the Kansas City Monarchs, Their Greatest Star and the Negro Leagues.* Jefferson, NC: McFarland & Company, 2007.

Heaphy, Leslie, and Mel Anthony May. *Encyclopedia of Women in Baseball.* Jefferson, NC: McFarland & Company, 2006.

Henderson, Ashyia, ed. *Contemporary Black Biography*. Volume 40. Independence, KY: Gale Publishing Group, 2003.

"He Rubbed Shoulders with Greats of the Game." *Virginian Pilot*, August 19, 1991.

Hoffbeck, Steven, ed. *Swinging for the Fences: Black Baseball in Minnesota*. Saint Paul: Minnesota Historical Society, 2005.

Hogan, Lawrence D. *Shades of Glory: The Negro Leagues and the Story of African-American Baseball.* Washington, DC: National Geographic, 2006.

Holway, John. *Black Diamonds: Life in the Negro Leagues from the Men Who Loved It*. Westport, CT: Meckler Publishing, 1989.

"Homecoming and Victory Service for Constance Enola Morgan," October 22, 1996. James L. Hawkins Funeral Home, Inc. Philadelphia, PA. Horace Johnson private archive.

"Honoring a Local Hero." *Minnesota Women's Press*, Vol. 5, no. 25, March 14–27, 1990.

Hudson, Mike. "She Was a Relentless Spirit." *Roanoke Times and World-News*, May 4, 1997.

Indianapolis Clowns file. National Baseball Hall of Fame and Museum, Inc., Cooperstown, NY.

"Is Negro Baseball Through?" *Our Sports*, Vol. 1, no. 1, May 1953.

Jacobson, Steve. *Carrying Jackie's Torch: The Players Who Integrated Baseball and America.* Chicago: Chicago Review Press, 2007.

Jacox, Cal. "Press Box." *Norfolk Journal and Guide*, August 8, 1953.

James, Joy. *Shadowboxing: Representation of Black Feminist Politics.* New York: Palgrave, 1999.

Jennings, Jay. "A League of His Own." *New York Times*, June 3, 2007.

Keenan, Sandy. "Stone Had a Ball." *Newsday*, October 5, 1993.

Kelley, Brent. *I Will Never Forget: Interview with 39 Former Negro League Players.* Jefferson, NC: McFarland & Company, 2003.

———. *The Negro Leagues Revisited: Conversations with 66 More Baseball Heroes.* Jefferson, NC: McFarland & Company, 2000.

———. "Peanut Johnson: First Woman to Win a Pro Ballgame. *Sports Collectors Digest*, October 22, 1999.

———. *Voices from the Negro Leagues: Conversations with 52 Black Standouts.* Jefferson, NC: McFarland & Company, 1998.

Kernan, Kevin. "Li'l Lady Dazzled Negro League Hit Men." *New York Post*, June 3, 2001.

Kimball, Richard Ian. "Beyond the 'Great Experiment': Integrated Baseball Comes to Indianapolis." *Journal of Sports History*, Vol. 26, no. 1, Spring 1999.

King, Martin Luther Jr. *Why We Can't Wait.* New York: Signet, 1964.

Kolb, Terry. "St. Peter Claver Member Recounts Struggles with Racism." *The Catholic Spirit.* http://extra.thecatholicspirit.com/heritage/st-peter-claver-member-recounts.html.

Kruissink, Bill. "First Woman in Pro Baseball Remembers." *Alameda Journal*, April 2, 1996.

Lacy, Sam. "A to Z." Baltimore *Afro-American*, July 21, 1953.

Lacy, Sam. "First Woman in Pro Baseball." *Afro Magazine* 1953, n.p. National Baseball Hall of Fame and Museum, Inc., Cooperstown, NY.

"Lady Ball Player." *Ebony*, July 1953.

Lanctot, Neil. *Negro League Baseball: The Rise and Ruin of a Black Institution.* Philadelphia: University of Pennsylvania Press, 2004.

Lester, Larry. "Only the Stars Come Out at Night." *Satchel Paige and Company: Essays on the Kansas City Monarchs, Their Greatest Star and the Negro Leagues.* Edited by Leslie A. Heaphy. Jefferson, NC: McFarland & Company, 2007.

———. *Black Baseball's National Showcase: The East-West All-Star Game, 1933–1953.* Lincoln: University of Nebraska Press, 2001.

Lewis, Dave. "Once Over Lightly." *Long Beach Independent*, May 14, 1947.

Lewis, Ted. "Negro Leagues Had Local Flavor." New Orleans *Times-Picayune*, July 4, 1994.

Lieb, Fred. *Baseball As I Have Known It.* New York: Grosset & Dunlap, 1977.

Loverro, Thom. *The Encyclopedia of Negro League Baseball.* New York: Checkmark Books, 2003.

Madden, W. C. *Baseball in Indianapolis.* Charleston, SC: Arcadia Publishing, 2003.

Marchres, Earle. "Famous Catch." *Ford Times*, March 1975.

Markusen, Bruce. *Ted Williams: A Biography.* Santa Barbara, CA: Greenwood Press, 2004.

Martin, Dr. J. B. "Negro League President Comments." *Los Angeles Sentinel*, June 11, 1953.

Mashberg, Tom. "'Peanut' a Big Deal: Was Negro League Pioneer." *Boston Herald*, July 23, 2000.

Mays, Willie, with Lou Sahadi. *Say Hey: The Autobiography of Willie Mays.* New York: Simon and Schuster, 1988.

McMillan, Allen. "Four Clubs Battle for Top Baseball Honors in New York." *Chicago Defender*, September 28, 1935.

McNary, Kyle. "Maceo Breedlove: Big Fish in a Small Pond." *Swinging for the Fences: Black Baseball in Minnesota*, Steven R. Hoffbeck, ed., Saint Paul: Minnesota Historical Society, 2005.

McWatt, Arthur C. "'Small and Cohesive': St. Paul's Resourceful African-American Community." *Ramsey County History*, Vol. 26, no. 1, Spring 1991.

Meyer, Eugene. "For Love of the Game." *Washington Post*, February 24, 1999.

Miller, Sammy J., and Dick Clark. *Black Baseball in Detroit*. Mt. Pleasant, SC: Arcadia Publishing, 2000.

Mills, Quincy T. "'Color-Line' Barbers and the Emergence of Black Public Space: A Social and Political History of Black Barbers and Barber Shops, 1830–1970." Dissertation, University of Chicago, 2006.

Minot, George. "Ball Stirs Old Memories of Street's Famed Catch." *Washington Post*, January 25, 1964.

Moffi, Larry. *The Conscience of the Game: Baseball's Commissioners from Landis to Selig*. Lincoln: University of Nebraska Press/Bison Books, 2006.

Mohl, Raymond. "Clowning Around: The Miami Ethiopian Clowns and Cultural Conflict in Black Baseball." *Tequesta: The Journal of the Historical Association of Southern Florida*, No. LXII, 2002, 40–68.

"Monte Irvin 'Hard Luck Giant.'" *Louisiana Weekly*, September 6, 1952.

Moore, Mark J. "Negro League First Female Player Recalls Life, Career in Pro Baseball." n.p., n.d. Lester private archive.

Morgan, Connie. Interview with Donna DeVore. Approximately 1993. Archives of the Afro-American Historical and Cultural Museum of Philadelphia.

Motley, Bob, with Byron Motley. *Ruling Over Monarchs, Giants & Stars: Umpiring in the Negro Leagues & Beyond.* Champaign, IL: Sports Publishing, 2007.

Mule, Marty. "Walter Wright Savors Black Pels' Glory Days." New Orleans *Times-Picayune*, May 5, 1983.

Mulhen, Mike. "Barnstorming Days Put Clark in Contact with Game's Best." Baton Rouge *State-Times*, August 4, 1987.

National Visionary Leadership Project. Oral History with Ernie Banks. http://visionaryproject.org/banksernie.

Nelson, Kevin. *The Golden Game: The Story of California Baseball.* Berkeley: California Historical Society Press, 2004.

Nieboer, Roger. *Tomboy Stone*. Script for play produced by Great North American History Theatre, 2007.

North Star: Minnesota's Black Pioneers. Twin Cities Public Television. Brendan Henehan, executive producer, 2004.

Obrecht, Jas. *Rockin' and Tumblin': The Postwar Blues Guitarists.* San Francisco: Miller Freeman Books, 2000.

"Old Sarge Inspects Saints' Muster Roll." *Saint Paul Pioneer Press*, February 25, 1937.

O'Neil, Buck, with Steve Wulf and David Conrads. *I Was Right on Time: My Journey from the Negro Leagues to the Majors.* New York: Fireside Books, 1997.

O'Neil, Buck. Opening Remarks. Baseball Hall of Fame Induction Ceremonies. Cooperstown, NY. July 29, 2006.

"Oral History of Katherine Stewart Flippin." *The Black Women Oral History Project*, Vol. 4. Edited by Ruth Edmonds Hill and Patricia Miller King. Westport: CT: Meckler Publishing, 1991.Copyright Radcliffe College.

"Oral History with Aurelious P. Alberga Conducted by Albert S. Broussard, December 7, 1976. "Afro Americans in San Francisco Prior to World War II." Friends of the San Francisco Public Library and the San Francisco African-American Historical and Cultural Society.

Osgood, Robert L. *The History of Special Education: A Struggle for Equality in American Public Schools.* Santa Barbara, CA: Praeger, 2007.

Pepin, Elizabeth, and Lewis Watts. *Harlem of the West: The San Francisco Fillmore Jazz Era.* San Francisco: Chronicle Books, 2006.

Peterson, Armand, and Tom Tomashek. *Town Ball: The Glory Days of Minnesota Amateur Baseball.* Minneapolis: University of Minnesota Press, 2006.

Peterson, Robert. *Only the Ball Was White: A History of Legendary Black Players and All-Black Professional Teams.* New York: Oxford University Press, 1970.

Pollock, Alan J., with James A. Riley, ed. *Barnstorming to Heaven: Syd Pollock and His Great Black Teams.* Tuscaloosa: University of Alabama Press, 2006.

Price, Joseph. L. *Rounding the Bases: Baseball and Religion in America.* Macon, GA: Mercer University Press, 2006.

Reaves, Joseph A. *Taking in a Game: A History of Baseball in Asia.* Lincoln: University of Nebraska Press, 2004.

Reisler, Jim. *Black Writers/Black Baseball: An Anthology of Articles from Black Sportswriters Who Covered the Negro Leagues.* Jefferson, NC: McFarland & Company, 2007.

Remembering Rondo: A Tradition of Excellence. Saint Paul: Remembering Rondo Committee, 1995.

Ribowsky, Mark. *Josh Gibson: The Power and the Darkness.* Urbana: University of Illinois Press, 2004.

Riley, James A. *The Biographical Encyclopedia of the Negro Baseball Leagues.* New York: Carroll & Graf Publishers, 1994.

Ring, Jennifer. *Stolen Bases: Why American Girls Don't Play Baseball.* Urbana: University of Illinois Press, 2009.

Ringolsby, Tracy. "Will a Woman Ever Make It to the Major Leagues? Stone Rock Solid in Negro League." *Rocky Mountain News,* May 11, 1995.

Rives, Tim. "Tom Baird: A Challenge to the Modern Memory of the Kansas City Monarchs." *Satchel Paige and Company: Essays on the Kansas City Monarchs, Their Greatest Star and the Negro Leagues.* Edited by Leslie A. Heaphy. Jefferson, NC: McFarland & Company, 2007.

Roberts, Robin. *From the Heart: Seven Rules to Live By.* New York: Hyperion, 2007.

Robinson, Frazier, with Paul Bauer. *Catching Dreams: My Life in the Negro Baseball Leagues.* Syracuse, NY: Syracuse University Press, 1999.

Robinson, Jackie, as told to Alfred Duckett. *I Never Had It Made: An Autobiography of Jackie Robinson.* New York: Harper Collins, 1972.

Rosie the Riveter World War II American Homefront Oral History Project: An Oral History with Betty Reid Soskin Conducted by Nadine Wilmot, 2002. Regional Oral History Office, the Bancroft Library, University of California, Berkeley, 2007.

Rosie the Riveter World War II American Homefront Oral History Project: An Oral History with Frank Stevenson Conducted by Esther Ehrlich 2003. Regional Oral History Office, the Bancroft Library, University of California, Berkeley, 2007.

Rosie the Riveter World War II American Homefront Oral History Project: An Oral History with Matilda Foster Conducted by David Washburn and Tiffany Lok 2005. Regional Oral History Office, the Bancroft Library, University of California, Berkeley, 2007.

Rosie the Riveter World War II American Homefront Oral History Project: An Oral History with Willie Mae Cotright Conducted by Judith Dunning, 2002. Regional Oral History Office, the Bancroft Library, University of California, Berkeley, 2007.

Rowe, Charles. "Pitcher Johnson a Distinct Figure in Baseball History." *Post and Courier*, February 12, 2000.

Sandy, Charles. "Blues Stadium." *The Best of Remember When: 100 Warm Tales of Life As We Knew It.* Kansas City: Kansas City Star Books, 2001.

Schlesinger, Arthur M. *Robert Kennedy and His Times.* New York: Mariner Books/Houghton Mifflin, 2002.

Schwarz, Michael. "Honoring the Pioneers of the Negro Leagues." *Atlanta Journal-Constitution*, August 11, 1991.

Scott, Emmett Jay. *Scott's Official History of the American Negro in the World War*. Washington, D.C.: Homewood Press, 1919.

Seidel, Michael. *Ted Williams: A Baseball Life*. Lincoln: University of Nebraska Press, 2003.

Seymour, Harold, Dorothy Z. Seymour, and Jane Mills. *Baseball: The People's Game*. New York: Oxford University Press, 1991.

Shampoe, Clay, and Thomas R. Garrett. *Baseball in Norfolk, Virginia*. Charleston, SC: Arcadia Publishing, 2003.

———. *Baseball in Portsmouth, Virginia*. Charleston, SC: Arcadia Publishing, 2004.

Smith, Claire. "Belated Tribute to Baseball's Negro Leagues." *New York Times*, August 13, 1991.

Spink, J. G. Taylor, "Looping the Loop." *The Sporting News*, August 20, 1947.

Stanley, D. L. "Women in Negro Baseball League." *Atlanta Inquirer*, April 28, 2001.

St. Peter Claver Catholic Church. *St. Peter Claver Diamond Jubilee, 1892–1967*. Saint Paul: St. Peter Claver Church, 1967.

Stone, Toni. Interview with Bill Kruissink. March 27, 1996. National Baseball Hall of Fame and Museum, Inc., Cooperstown, NY.

Stone, Toni. Interview with Jean Hastings Ardell. April 1992. Ardell private archive.

Stone, Toni. Interview with Kyle McNary. September 1993. McNary private archive.

Stone, Toni. Interview with Larry Lester. January 3, 1991. Lester private archive.

Stone, Toni. Interview with Miki Turner. August 1992 Turner private archive.

"A Stop in Kansas City." *Kansas City Star*, April 15, 1997.

Street, Gabby. "It's Still Baseball." *American Legion Monthly*, No. 70, April 1932, n.p.

Strouse, Karla Farmer. "The Story of Toni Stone: When Baseball Began to Be Truly the National Pastime." *Baseball/Literature/Culture Essays, 1995–2001*. Peter Carino, ed. Jefferson, NC: McFarland & Company, 2003.

Swaine, Rick. *The Black Stars Who Made Baseball Whole: The Jackie Robinson Generation in the Major Leagues, 1947–1959*. Jefferson, NC: McFarland & Company, 2005.

Swank, William G., and James D. Smith III. "This Was Paradise: Voices of the Pacific Coast League Padres: 1936–1958." (Interview with Pete Coscarart.) *Journal of San Diego History*, Volume 41, no. 1, Winter 1995.

Sweeney, William Allison. *History of the American Negro in the Great World War*. Project Gutenberg ebook, 2005.

Taylor, David. *African Americans in Saint Paul*. Saint Paul: Saint Paul Historical Society Press, 2002.

Thomas, Ron. "Baseball's 'Intruder' Loved Game." *San Francisco Chronicle*, August 23, 1991.

———. "Baseball Pioneer Looks Back: Woman Played in Negro Leagues." *San Francisco Chronicle*, August 23, 1991.

———. "She Made It a League of Her Own." *Emerge*, May 1986.

Thornley, Stew. "Pay Days." *Ramsay County History*, Vol. 23, no. 1, 1988.

Trouppe, Quincy. *20 Years Too Soon: Prelude to Major League Integrated Baseball*. St. Louis: Missouri Historical Society Press, 1977.

Turner, Miki. "And Still She Rose." *Oakland Tribune*, August 28, 1992.

Tye, Larry. *Satchel: The Life and Times of an American Legend*. New York: Random House, 2009.

Tygiel, Jules. *Baseball's Great Experiment: Jackie Robinson and His Legacy.* New York: Oxford University Press, 1997.

Vail, James F. *The Road to Cooperstown: A Critical History of Baseball's Hall of Fame Selection Process.* Jefferson, NC: McFarland & Company, 2001.

Vascellaro, Charlie. *Hank Aaron: A Biography.* Santa Barbara, CA: Greenwood Press, 2005.

Voices of Rondo: Oral Histories of Saint Paul's Historic Black Community as Told to Kateleen Jill Hope Cavett of Hand in Hand Productions. Minneapolis: Syren Book Company, 2005.

Ward, Alan. "On Second Thought." *Oakland Tribune,* May 25, 1953.

Weaver, Mike. "Female Player Was a Minority of One." *San Jose Mercury News,* August 11, 1991.

White, Joseph. "Female Pitcher in Negro Leagues Enjoyed String 'Em Out." *Seattle Times,* May 10, 1998.

Williams, Donnie, and Wayne Greenhaw. *The Thunder of Angels: The Montgomery Bus Boycott and the People Who Broke the Back of Jim Crow.* Chicago: Lawrence Hill/Chicago Review Press, 2005.

Williams, Geraldine M. "Minnesota St. Paul." *Chicago Defender,* December 18, 1937.

Williams, Joe. "Please, Kiddies, Mr. Street Could Catch, Too." n.p., n.d. Gabby Street file. National Baseball Hall of Fame and Museum, Inc., Cooperstown, NY.

Wilson, Austin. "Black Pioneer Hangs to Threads of Hope." *Vicksburg Sunday Post,* August 7, 1977.

Withers, Ernest C. Essay by Daniel Wolfe. Edited by Anthony Decaneas. *Negro League Baseball.* New York: Harry N. Abrams, 2005.

Wittich, Porter. n.p., n.d. Gabby Street file. National Baseball Hall of Fame and Museum, Inc., Cooperstown, NY.

Woolard, Holly. "It's Etched in Stone—She's a Women's Hall of Famer." *Marin Independent Journal*, October 3, 1993.

Young, Doc. "Toss 'Em Out: Should Girls Play Ball; No, Says Doc." *Chicago Defender*, August 28, 1954.

Index